D1565726

EUCHARIST AND THE POETIC IMAGINATION IN EARLY MODERN ENGLAND

The Reformation changed for ever how the sacrament of the eucharist was understood. This study of six canonical early modern lyric poets traces the literary afterlife of what was one of the greatest doctrinal shifts in English history. Sophie Read argues that the move from a literal to a figurative understanding of the phrase 'this is my body' exerted a powerful imaginative pull on successive generations. To illustrate this, she examines in detail the work of Southwell, Donne, Herbert, Crashaw, Vaughan and Milton, who between them represent a broad range of doctrinal and confessional positions, from the Jesuit Southwell to Milton's heterodox Puritanism. Individually, each chapter examines how eucharistic ideas are expressed through a particular rhetorical trope; together, they illuminate the continued importance of the eucharist's transformation well into the seventeenth century – not simply as a matter of doctrine, but as a rhetorical and poetic mode.

SOPHIE READ is a University Lecturer in English and Fellow of Christ's College, Cambridge.

IDEAS IN CONTEXT 104

Eucharist and the Poetic Imagination in Early Modern England

IDEAS IN CONTEXT

Edited by David Armitage, Richard Bourke, Jennifer Pitts
and John Robertson

The books in this series will discuss the emergence of intellectual traditions and of related new disciplines. The procedures, aims and vocabularies that were generated will be set in the context of the alternatives available within the contemporary frameworks of ideas and institutions. Through detailed studies of the evolution of such traditions, and their modification by different audiences, it is hoped that a new picture will form of the development of ideas in their concrete contexts. By this means, artificial distinctions between the history of philosophy, of the various sciences, of society and politics, and of literature may be seen to dissolve.

The series is published with the support of the Exxon Foundation.

A list of books in the series will be found at the end of the volume.

EUCHARIST AND THE POETIC IMAGINATION IN EARLY MODERN ENGLAND

SOPHIE READ

CAMBRIDGE
UNIVERSITY PRESS

CAMBRIDGE UNIVERSITY PRESS
Cambridge, New York, Melbourne, Madrid, Cape Town,
Singapore, São Paulo, Delhi, Mexico City

Cambridge University Press
The Edinburgh Building, Cambridge CB2 8RU, UK

Published in the United States of America by Cambridge University Press, New York

www.cambridge.org
Information on this title: www.cambridge.org/9781107032736

First published 2013

Printed and bound in the United Kingdom by MPG Books Group

A catalogue record for this publication is available from the British Library

ISBN 978-1-107-03273-6 Hardback

Contents

Illustrations

Acknowledgements

Working on a book for many years naturally results in the incurring of many debts of various kinds. They deserve far greater acknowledgement than I can give here, but I would like nonetheless to record some specific thanks along with a more general sense of gratitude and good fortune. This project started life as a doctoral thesis, and so I owe a great deal to Jessica Martin; she was, throughout, a generous and exacting supervisor, and I benefited greatly from her scholarship and judgement. I was lucky to have advice and encouragement at this time from Colin Burrow, Simon Jarvis and Peter McCullough; Brian Cummings and Raphael Lyne examined the thesis, made invaluable suggesestions for rethinking and revision, and have remained important and supportive presences ever since.

The next stage of the project was overseen with exemplary tact by the book's first editor, Richard Fisher; I owe much to his experience, and to the patience and generosity of the board of Ideas in Context, in particular Quentin Skinner. Elizabeth Friend-Smith, who took over when Richard Fisher was translated to higher things, has been a model of efficiency and helpfulness, as have Elizabeth Spicer, Caroline Mowatt, Carol Fellingham Webb and Mary Dalton. I should record, too, my gratitude to Cambridge University Press's anonymous readers, whose objections, corrections and suggestions – delivered with varying degrees of stern benevolence – have been invaluable. They, and the book's other readers, have saved me from grave error and embarrassment; the flaws and faults that remain are of course my own.

For the past few years I have been teaching very happily at Christ's, and I would like to thank the Master and Fellows, particularly my close colleagues – Gavin Alexander, Helen Thaventhiran and Daniel Wakelin; Susan Bayly, David Reynolds and Caroline Vout – for making the college such a warm environment to work in, and for granting me a term's leave in which to make revisions on the book manuscript. More recently, my colleages at the English Faculty in Cambridge have offered help, advice and generous support; I should thank Helen Cooper and John Kerrigan specifically in this regard.

My debts of friendship are legion. Alison Davidson, my inspirational sixth-form English teacher, deserves special thanks for some foundational early encouragement. For their support and their society, I'd like to thank those who have taught, studied and worked with me: Ned Allen, Sara Crangle, Sarah Haggarty, Sam Ladkin, Leo Mellor, Ian Patterson, William Poole, Henry Power and Zoë Svendsen have each been more important than such a list implies. My good friends Mel Bach, Joanna Cook, Katherine Harloe, Tom Lee, Polly McMichael and Rose Taylor have offered continual encouragement, as well as endless diversion and happy times. I must record particular debts of gratitude to Rebecca Barr, Rowan Boyson, Michael Bywater, Louise Joy, Jane Partner and Neil Pattison for all of the above, for more material help of the reading and proof-reading kinds, and for the correspondence, conversation and friendship that has meant so much to me over the past few years. For his quiet good humour and loving helpfulness, I owe my husband, Jonathan Morgan, far more than I can say.

Finally, I would like to express my love, thanks and obligation to my parents, David Read and Priscilla Read, for their generous support, without which this project would never have been finished; also to my wonderful sisters, Emily Read and Olivia Read, for their affection and forbearance, and the pleasure and instruction of their company. It is to my family that this, my first book, is dedicted.

Note on the Text

With the exceptions of Southwell, where I have used a variety of early and contemporary editions, and Milton, where I have quoted from the twelve-book *Paradise Lost* (1674), I have preferred the standard Clarendon Press editions of authors' works. I have retained original spelling and punctuation, though I have modernised the <i/j> and <v/u> diagraphs in quotations from both early printed books and more recent editions where old conventions were retained.

Introduction

The eighty-odd years which this study spans, from the poems Robert Southwell wrote before his martyrdom in 1595 to the publication in 1674 of the twelve-book edition of Milton's *Paradise Lost*, were an eventful period in English history. To tell the story of the times is, to a great extent, to rehearse the fortunes of its system of organised religion: following the Reformation, theological concerns dominated the political arena whether as provocation or as pretext, and they had their impact, too, on the imaginative writing of the time. At the beginning of the seventeenth century, the nascent Protestant Church was a broad one; as it continued to evolve, its doctrinal battle lines became more clearly and more militantly drawn. Powerful personalities hardened divergent views on liturgy and worship into irreconcilable differences, and the struggle for ascendancy accelerated the country's trajectory of civil war, regicide and Restoration. Though it would be a simplification to claim that questions of religion were the only forces at work in these complicated events, they did prove incendiary at crucial moments, and certain kinds of political outlook did tend to go hand-in-hand with certain kinds of religious views: a supporter of Charles I's monarchy, for example, was more likely to incline towards the ceremonial and sacramental worship advocated by his controversial archbishop, William Laud, than the spare and stripped-down services favoured by the Puritan (or 'godly') faction at court.[1]

---

[1] The question of terminology is not the least difficult here. The old opposition of 'Anglican' and 'Puritan' has recently been challenged on the grounds of pejorative intent ('Puritan' was introduced as a term of abuse) and anachronism ('Anglican' was not coined until the nineteenth century). I nevertheless use the term 'Anglican' in this book – with some caution – to describe the system of beliefs of the churches of England and Wales in the late sixteenth and early seventeenth century. These beliefs are distinct both from the old Catholicism and from the hard-line Calvinism of continental reformers, and can be thought of as being expressed in Cranmer's Prayer Book and the Thirty-Nine

The sacrament of the eucharist, whose complex literary legacy is the subject of this book, came to be the ideological ground for contention at the centre of these differences: its symbolism and the mode of its celebration proved as divisive in the 1630s and 1640s as they had a century before, when the new Protestant outlook was gaining ground. As the Mass, this ritual of sacrifice, thanksgiving and remembrance had lain at the heart of the Catholic religion officially professed by the English people until the 1550s; the liturgical reforms proposed by continental theologians in the first part of the sixteenth century, and fitfully instituted by Thomas Cranmer in the Prayer Books of Edward VI's reign, compelled a fundamental reinterpretation of its meaning. The question on which confessional position came to be measured was whether or not Christ was really – that is, substantially, corporeally – present in the Host: and if so, to whom? And if not, then how? The implications of what might seem something of a metaphysical wrangle, remote from the concerns of most ordinary worshippers, were on the contrary both immediate and far-reaching: what was at stake was the salvation of their souls, and, slightly more circuitously, the government of their state.

The six writers considered in this study naturally had, whether clergymen or laity, an intimate interest in the question; but for them it has a professional as well as a personal relevance. Patrick Collinson describes the historiographical challenges of the era they were heir to in suggestive terms: 'The Reformation was awash with words. The historian who tries to catch its essence finds his net breaking under the weight of words.'[2] He intends by this both the sheer volume of print generated by contemporary debate – Luther's collected works alone, for example, run to more than a hundred volumes[3] – and, perhaps of more consequence for the literary critic than the historian, the colossal load borne by individual words. Interpretation, of the words of Scripture, phrases in the liturgy, scholastic terminology, became crucial; where a literal sense was no longer compatible

Articles of 1571. The convenience of the term in this case outweighs the disadvantage of its anachronism. I also retain 'Puritan' on similar grounds, and as having a wider currency than the alternative term 'godly', to describe those who were opposed to practices of worship that did not have an explicit scriptural warrant. See *The Oxford Dictionary of the Christian Church*, ed. by F. L. Cross and E. A. Livingstone, 3rd edn (Oxford University Press, 1997), pp. 64–7, 1351, and the discussions in Peter Lake, *Anglicans and Puritans? Presbyterianism and English Conformist Thought from Whitgift to Hooker* (London: Allen and Unwin, 1988) and Brian Spinks, *Sacraments, Ceremonies and the Stuart Divines: Sacramental Theology and Liturgy in England and Scotland, 1603–1662* (Aldershot: Ashgate, 2002), pp. xii–xiii.

[2] Patrick Collinson, *The Reformation* (London: Weidenfeld and Nicolson, 2003), p. 27.

[3] *D. Martin Luthers Werke*, 104 vols. (Weimar: Hermann Böhlau, 1883–1999). The English translation (*Luther's Works*, ed. Jaroslav Pelikan *et al.* (St Louis, MO: Concordia; Philadelphia: Fortress)) runs to 55 volumes.

with orthodox doctrine, it could be cast instead as a figurative one. There is no more powerful or significant example of this than the words spoken by Christ at the Last Supper and subsequently adopted as the words of institution: *Hoc est enim corpus meum* ('This is my body'). What happens to the phrase when uttered by someone other than Christ, though a pressing liturgical question, becomes in some ways secondary to what precisely Christ meant when he said it. This moment had long been cited to support the contention that Christ was indeed present in some way in the eucharistic Host, and that the Mass was therefore an iterative act of sacrifice; in the sixteenth century, however, the words underwent a rhetorical redescription that allowed their retention in a reformed communion service: one that rejected both the notion of bodily presence, and the idea of sacrifice. Christ had spoken truly, but the truth of his words was now to be understood only as a metaphorical truth: 'is' means no longer 'is', but 'signifies'.[4]

The ramifications of finding this fissure in what we might want to think of as one of the most securely literal words, the present tense of 'to be', are far-reaching indeed, and have of late proved of central interest to critics of Renaissance literature; Judith Anderson calls this 'Zwingli's seminal insight into the metaphoricity inherent in the verb of being', and recognises that it heralded a linguistic and conceptual reformation every bit as significant as the doctrinal one by which it was determined:

> The eucharistic debates of the earlier half (roughly) of the sixteenth century constitute an epistemological watershed between the earlier age and the one to come. Alone, they hardly cause this overdetermined cultural crisis, but even aside from their contribution to its content, they critically organize and crucially express it.[5]

The eucharist, then, becomes the location of a profound imaginative shift: the process of working out how this rite signifies under the new dispensation in fact forges new ways of understanding signification itself, as well as serving more immediately practical liturgical purposes. 'Be they heresies, abuses, manipulations, extensions or extrapolations,' Miri Rubin explains, 'different eucharistic utterances were testing the language, exposing its capacities, filling its spaces and spelling out its possibilities.'[6] The generation that inherited this legacy of epistemological contention and verbal *legerdemain*

---

[4] These words, spoken by Christ to his disciples at the Last Supper, are related four times in the Bible (Matthew 26:26, Mark 14:22, Luke 22:19, 1 Corinthians 11:24); they appear also in the communion liturgy of the *Book of Common Prayer* ('Take, eate, this is my bodye'). See below, pp. 19–30.

[5] Judith H. Anderson, *Translating Investments: Metaphor and the Dynamic of Cultural Change in Tudor–Stuart England* (New York: Fordham University Press, 2005), pp. 44, 48.

[6] Miri Rubin, *Corpus Christi: the Eucharist in Late Medieval Culture* (Cambridge University Press, 1991), p. 288.

inevitably exploited its literary as well as its devotional possibilities; how one informs the other (how, that is, the particularities of faith can influence the process of composition at a structural level, and be shaped in their turn by the rhetorical frameworks through which they are expressed) is the subject of what follows.

This enquiry takes its co-ordinates from a number of critical discourses: religion in Renaissance literature has never been an entirely neglected subject, and some of the most important frameworks for debate were established decades ago. Louis Martz's seminal 1954 work *The Poetry of Meditation*, which argued for the influence of Catholic devotional practice on seventeenth-century English poetry, was answered in 1979 by Barbara Lewalksi's *Protestant Poetics*: Lewalski maintained against Martz's view that the crucial imaginative basis of this writing was 'contemporary, English and Protestant'.[7] In some sense, each subsequent contribution has situated itself between these poles, and the prospect of final resolution seems distant, if not actually undesirable; gradations of belief do not always submit to precise confessional categorisation, something also witnessed in the exchanges of church and constitutional historians over related questions in a cognate disciplinary realm.[8] The new historicist critics, influential to the point of dominance over the past twenty years, tested their methodologies and refined their concerns against this background of lively dispute in both historical and literary studies of the period. In the first sentence of what amounts to a disciplinary manifesto, *Practicing New Historicism*, Catherine Gallagher and Stephen Greenblatt offer a disarming apologia for ill-assorted interests: 'This book is probably more in need of an introduction than most: two authors, two chapters on anecdotes, two on eucharistic doctrine in the late Middle Ages and the Renaissance, and two on nineteenth-century materialism.'[9] The list turns out not to be as haphazard as it is made to sound: its central term, at least, has remained central for critics, if sometimes in problematic ways. Problematic, because the new historicist focus is both primarily secular and – in effect if not in intention – interested in the material, theoretical and cultural contexts of literature at the expense of its aesthetic properties; thinking about the way Renaissance writers think about the eucharist has proved difficult without a precise and nuanced

---

[7] Louis Martz, *The Poetry of Meditation: a Study in English Religious Literature of the Seventeenth Century*, 2nd edn (New Haven: Yale University Press, 1962); Barbara Lewalski, *Protestant Poetics and the Seventeenth-Century Religious Lyric* (Princeton University Press, 1979), p. 5.

[8] See p. 1, n. 1, above.

[9] Catherine Gallagher and Stephen Greenblatt, *Practicing New Historicism*, 2nd edn (University of Chicago Press, 2001), p. 1.

consideration of contemporary theological and rhetorical viewpoints, as Sarah Beckwith's critique of Greenblatt's methods has started to show.[10]

More recently, there have been several important works that have sought to redress this imbalance, and to match a historicist rigour with profound aesthetic engagement; Brian Cummings's *The Literary Culture of the Reformation: Grammar and Grace* is exemplary and influential in the depth of its historical and doctrinal learning, and the sensitivity with which that learning is brought to bear on literary concerns. Studies by Robert Whalen, Judith Anderson, Timothy Rosendale, Regina Schwartz and Frances Cruickshank, among others, have in various productive ways followed this lead, and most have made the eucharist central to their accounts of poetic sensibility (Donne and Herbert feature prominently in their accounts, as they do here).[11] This rise of interest testifies to a growing sense that early modern disputes over the theology of the eucharist and its expression in doctrine and liturgy were a way of testing the nature of language as well as the nature of belief; critics have started to look to theologians as well as to rhetoricians for contemporary theories of figuration, which are then used to illuminate the imaginative writing of the period. This is not to overlook the importance of the critical discourse around rhetoric itself, as a discipline and an art, which has undergone a parallel advance over the past few decades; since the efforts at rehabilitation in the work of Richard A. Lanham, Terence Cave, Brian Vickers and Debora Shuger in the 1970s and 1980s, a number of critics – usually writing about either pedagogic history or individual authors – have offered valuable perspectives on rhetoric as a creative and dynamic process, and, latterly, as related in fundamental ways to processes of cognition.[12]

---

[10] Sarah Beckwith, 'Stephen Greenblatt's *Hamlet* and the Forms of Oblivion', *Journal of Medieval and Early Modern Studies*, 33 (2003), 261–80. Beckwith points out the shortcomings of Greenblatt's account of 'eucharistic anxiety' in the play by means of a detailed exploration of 'the ritual and liturgical settings' he ignores (273).

[11] Brian Cummings, *The Literary Culture of the Reformation: Grammar and Grace* (Oxford University Press, 2002); Robert Whalen, *The Poetry of Immanence: Sacrament in Donne and Herbert* (University of Toronto Press, 2002); Anderson, *Translating Investments* (2005); Timothy Rosendale, *Liturgy and Literature in the Making of Protestant England* (Cambridge University Press, 2007); Regina Schwartz, *Sacramental Poetics at the Dawn of Secularism: When God Left the World* (Stanford University Press, 2008); Frances Cruickshank, *Verse and Poetics in George Herbert and John Donne* (Farnham: Ashgate, 2010).

[12] Richard A. Lanham, *The Motives of Eloquence: Literary Rhetoric in the Renaissance* (New Haven: Yale University Press, 1976); Terence Cave, *The Cornucopian Text: Problems of Writing in the French Renaissance* (Oxford: Clarendon Press, 1979); Brian Vickers, *In Defence of Rhetoric* (Oxford: Clarendon Press, 1988); Debora Shuger, *Sacred Rhetoric: the Christian Grand Style in the English Renaissance* (Princeton University Press, 1988). See also Russ McDonald, *Shakespeare and the Arts of Language* (Oxford University Press, 2001), and Peter Mack, *Elizabethan Rhetoric: Theory and Practice*

The current study seeks to unite elements of these two methodologies by giving theological enquiry a firm rhetorical focus: aspects of eucharistic theology are described by and themselves in turn describe a number of different figures and tropes, and so each of the chapters that follows is organised around the appearance of one such device in the work of a single writer where it has particular expressive significance. There are limitations as well as opportunities in such a structuring principle: poets and their poems cannot always be so neatly categorised, and in these cases I have preferred rather to deviate periodically from its parameters than to restrict the scope of the discussion. It is my hope, however, that the shape of this book (in particular this foregrounding of technical rhetorical terminology) describes a conviction that patterns of thought and belief are found naturally reproduced in patterns of figuration, which they anchor and animate; 'It seemethe verie conforme, to reason,' as one contemporary writer puts it, himself using a eucharistic metaphor by way of illustration, 'that poetrie and divinitie shouldbe matched together, as soule and bodie, bodie and garment, substance enwrapped with hir accidents.'[13] Or in Yeshayahu Shen's more prosaic formulation, 'basic cognitive principles underlie the use of figurative language in poetic discourse'.[14]

Rhetoric, as a tool for determining meaning, and as a system for establishing cognitive frameworks, is of incalculable polemical and poetical importance – as will become evident below, starting with the discussion of Cranmer's defences of his Prayer Book. This importance has not always been acknowledged. The suspicion influentially articulated by Plato (of rhetoric's propensity for 'insincerity, mere display, artifice, or ornament without substance'[15]), combined with a reluctance to engage with a quantity of elaborate and arcane terminology,[16] has led in subsequent centuries to the marginalisation of rhetoric as a pointlessly convoluted and hopelessly outdated system. Truly understood, however, the art is a dynamic instrument of composition and analysis, interested in codification only insofar as that

---

(Cambridge University Press, 2002). One of the most significant of the recent studies appeared too late to be given here the consideration it deserves: Raphael Lyne, *Shakespeare, Rhetoric and Cognition* (Cambridge University Press, 2011).

[13] F.W., quoted in Alison Shell, *Catholicism, Controversy and the English Literary Imagination, 1558–1660* (Cambridge University Press, 1999), p. 61.

[14] Yeshayahu Shen, 'Cognitive Constraints on Verbal Creativity: the Use of Figurative Language in Poetic Discourse', in Elena Semino and Jonathan Culpeper (eds.), *Cognitive Stylistics: Language and Cognition in Text Analysis* (Amsterdam, 2002), pp. 211–30 (p. 214).

[15] Vickers, *Defence*, p. viii.

[16] '[W]hile we may be impressed with the technical acumen which can applaud a "pretty epanorthosis"', Neil Rhodes, for example, observes, 'it is more difficult for us to feel the same kind of enthusiasm for such verbal effects' (*The Power of Eloquence and English Renaissance Literature* (London: Harvester Wheatsheaf, 1992), p. vii.

endeavour might aid the study of the emotional and intellectual processes that were constituted in writing and speech. Both Renaissance rhetoricians and the classical forebears from whom their accounts are derived intuitively recognise that language is a faculty not separate and apart, but one intimately involved with other conceptual and cognitive frameworks; 'metaphor, metonymy, metalepsis, and others', Raphael Lyne explains, 'may be treated not only as ways of conveying the results of complex thought, but also as maps of the way complex thought might actually happen'.[17] 'Take not a figure and make of it a plaine speech,' was Lancelot Andrewes's profound advice on Christmas Day in 1616; 'Seeke not to be saved by *Synecdoche*.'[18] Poetic expression is not aberrant or ornamental – the translation of something literal and anterior into different, more difficult terms – but a representation of ordinary structures of thought.

The foundational premise of this study is that particularities of belief can be made manifest in the verbal texture of a poem, and that rhetorical and theological planes of understanding are linked by a common mental framework. This is based on the notion that a sort of dual mapping is taking place: the shape of a liturgical cadence or a theological belief might be instantiated in a mind by custom or by force of attraction, and then reproduced by that mind in the rhetorical structures of a poem. A trope or figure does not simply express a thought or belief that has already been had, and which is reducible to some literal paraphrase, but *constitutes* it – has in itself a form of cognitive content. There is an important caveat: the poetry considered here is not, and could not aspire to be, 'eucharistic' in any direct or literal sense; literature is not liturgy. Which is not to suggest any kind of defeat or pretence, a poetic equivalent of pasteboard chalice and paper mitre: neither is liturgy literature. It is in fact the very analogical distance across which they must strain that generates, in poems interested in eucharistic operations, their devotional energy and their imaginative force.

One last question remains to be addressed before this introduction can move to the lengthy business of establishing the historical, theological and literary foundations for the argument that follows. Why 'eucharist and the *poetic* imagination'? Prose has at least an equal claim when thinking about rhetoric in this period, and there are significant genres (the sermon, the pamphlet) and indeed individual works that deserve attention in this regard; almost all of the authors represented here, with the exception perhaps of

[17] Lyne, *Shakespeare, Rhetoric and Cognition*, p. 9.
[18] Andrewes, *XCVI Sermons by the Right Honorable and Reverend Father in God, Lancelot Andrewes, Late Lord Bishop of Winchester* (London, 1629), p. 106.

Crashaw, produced notable prose writings which are mentioned only in passing. Part of the point of this argument, however, is to suggest that poetry had a particular status in the devotional economy of early modern England, as a mode both elevated (Milton describes writing in prose as 'hav[ing] the use, as I may account it, but of my left hand'[19]) and productive of considerable anxiety: Herbert's struggles with the form he thought of himself as rescuing from 'stews and brothels' into the service of the church are only the best known.[20] Cranmer chose to frame the vernacular liturgy in prose, thus rupturing the previously 'unselfconscious relationship between metrical form and lay devotion': poetry comes to be a thing apart, importantly connected to devotional practice through the example of the Psalms (themselves described by Sidney as 'a divine poem'), but still at a crucial distance from ordinary modes of worship.[21] The poets who form the basis of this study reserve a concentrated imaginative power for their writing in verse; the eucharist provides both subject and model for the cognitive connections and rhetorical transformations that characterise one of the most inventive periods in English poetry.

HISTORY OF A CONTROVERSY: RHETORICAL REFORMATIONS

To understand the circumstances which made the first half of the seventeenth century a period of such productive theological and linguistic instability, it is necessary go back some way to the origins of the differences then being played out. The literature on the impact of the Reformation is immense and contested, and this introductory summary is by no means designed as a comprehensive account: it seeks only to draw out some of the events and circumstances that establish the framework for this argument, at times perhaps in an elliptical or lopsided fashion. The decision, for example, to start this relation a hundred years before most of the works considered in subsequent chapters were written, and in a different country, is rather convenient than anything else: on the one hand, a little beforehand, and on the other, a little late, because any search for origins must always lead to the origins of those origins. But something of extraordinary and lasting

---

[19] John Milton, *The Reason of Church-Government* (London, 1641), p. 37.
[20] George Herbert, *Works*, ed. by F. E. Hutchinson (Oxford: Clarendon Press, 1941), p. 176.
[21] Ramie Targoff, *Common Prayer: the Language of Devotion in Early Modern England* (University of Chicago Press, 2001), p. 65; and see pp. 57–84 for an account of the place of rhyme in the liturgy; Sir Philip Sidney, *Sidney's 'Defence of Poesy' and Selected Renaissance Literary Criticism*, ed. by Gavin Alexander (London: Penguin, 2004), p. 7.

significance did happen in the continental Europe of the early sixteenth century. When Martin Luther, an Augustinian monk from Erfurt in Germany, expressed his dissatisfaction with the Catholic Church's practice of selling indulgences (pieces of paper that purported to guarantee time off Purgatory, then being assiduously peddled to finance the ambitious building projects of Pope Leo X), he acted as the catalyst for a series of events which would revolutionise the religious and cultural life of a continent. Luther's sense of the impossible burden of God's righteous wrath, combined with his anger at the corruptions and inadequacies of the church as he saw it, led him to formulate through careful exposition of his text an alternative understanding of the teachings of Scripture. His ideas, in embryonic form, were first made public in 1517 in a letter to Archbishop Albrecht of Brandenburg, and were most famously promulgated in the ninety-five theses he hammered to the church door in Wittenberg later that same year. In the decades that followed, adopted and developed by theologians and liturgists across Europe, the arguments that had led to Luther's excommunication from the Catholic Church became the basis for the new Protestant religion.[22]

At the same time, so closely related that they have become all but historiographically indistinguishable (inspired as they were by the same impulses, and enabled by the same technologies), there began a cross-continental movement whose cultural impact would be hard to overestimate: the translation of Scripture, hitherto inaccessible to the vast majority of the population of Europe, into the vernacular. Using Erasmus's Greek New Testament (the *Novum Instrumentum*, first published in Basel in 1516 and heavily revised and republished thereafter), in 1522 Luther produced a German translation of the Bible.[23] Tyndale's English New Testament followed in 1526, and though he was to be burnt for his book, its influence on the language and literature of subsequent generations of his countrymen is incalculable; 'The Englishing of theology', Brian Cummings observes, 'left its traces on English as well as on theology.'[24] This is a precise and

---

[22] See Diarmaid MacCulloch, *Reformation: Europe's House Divided, 1490–1700* (London: Penguin, 2003), pp. 115–57, from which this brief account is derived.

[23] Luther's was not the first translation into the vernacular; Derek Wilson points out that, in 1522, 'Vernacular bibles had existed in Germany for more than half a century and no less than eighteen versions were in existence' (*Out of the Storm: the Life and Legacy of Martin Luther* (London: Hutchinson, 2007), p. 182). It was, however, by far the most significant, due both to its mastery of the language in which it was composed – High German – and to its dissemination through the relatively new culture of print.

[24] Cummings, *Literary Culture*, p. 264. The scholars who prepared the 1611 Authorised Version of the Bible, perhaps the most influential work in (and on) the English language, made considerable use of Tyndale's earlier translation.

economical assertion of a vital truth about the Reformation: there is, in this period, an absolute interdependence between theological belief and the form of words in which it is expressed, most particularly if it is a native tongue that must be made to twist around them. The war of interpretative control is waged not just in the translation or exegesis of scriptural texts, but in the scholarly apparatus of a language: the vernacular grammars, the handbooks of rhetoric and style that are written to help the reader to a right understanding of literary (and so therefore of biblical) tropes. Janet Martin Soskice points out that 'if one's focus of interest is religious language' – as it certainly was for the reformers, though in a slightly different sense from the one she primarily intends – 'figures of speech are the vessels of insight and the vehicles of cognition'.[25] Recognising this, a significant number of early Protestant writers produced treatises on rhetoric and cognate disciplines, such important thinkers as Melanchthon and Zwingli among them; in addition, much of the most sophisticated and profound writing on the nature of language and figuration in this period is to be found not in handbooks of poetry, but in expositions of doctrine. To employ grammar and rhetoric as polemical tools was politic: there is a clear advantage in suggesting that the long-accepted views being challenged are nothing more than the mistaken interpretation of a scriptural text, and these kinds of argumentative strategies characterised, for instance, the doctrinal disputes of Erasmus (who remained Catholic despite some reformist tendencies) and Luther; 'In the absence of consensus on established meanings in Scripture, and in the interests of minimizing or avoiding violence, both parties availed themselves of the resources provided by rhetoric.'[26]

For these reasons, many of the first writings on rhetoric to be produced in the English vernacular were guides to the tropes of the Bible, or used scriptural texts to furnish their examples. Thomas Swynnerton's *The Tropes and Figures of Scripture* (c.1537) is one such work; the theological agenda of this evangelical Protestant preacher – 'one of the very earliest Englishmen "to embrace the light of the Gospel"', according to his modern editor – is fairly clear. 'Metonymia', Swynnerton declares, 'is when we gyve that power and vertue, to the Sacramentes, whiche properly belongeth to the thinges signified by them.'[27] Swynnerton's treatise was not published during his lifetime; other contemporary vernacular rhetorics that did make

[25] Janet Martin Soskice, *Metaphor and Religious Language* (Oxford: Clarendon Press, 1985), p. 54.
[26] Thomas M. Conley, *Rhetoric in the European Tradition* (University of Chicago Press, 1990), p. 111.
[27] Thomas Swynnerton, *A Reformation Rhetoric: Thomas Swynnerton's The Tropes and Figures of Scripture*, ed. by Richard Rex (Cambridge: Renaissance Texts from Manuscript, 1999), pp. 8, 135. This argument is made in Calvin's *Institutio Religionis Christianae* (hereafter *Institutes*): 'I say that the expression which is

it into print were perhaps less barefaced in their proselytising, but are nonetheless obviously influenced by Protestant ideology. The earliest such work is *The Arte or Crafte of Rhetoryke* (1530) by Leonard Cox, a slight volume treating only the art of invention, which slips in some scriptural allusions among its classical examples.[28] Thomas Wilson published *The Arte of Rhetorique* in 1553; this work demonstrates what it would like to be taken for casual Protestantism in, for example, its definition of 'Intellection', or synecdoche: 'All Cambridge sorowed for the deathe of Bucer,' Wilson writes, 'meaninge the most parte. All Englande rejoyseth that pilgrimage is banished, and Idolatrye for ever abolished: and yet all England is not glad, but the most parte.'[29] More significant still because of its wider currency is Henry Peacham's *Garden of Eloquence*, published in 1577 and in an enlarged second edition in 1593; Peacham was a minister of the church, and has frequent recourse to the Bible to illustrate the great range of tropes and figures he marshals. As with Swynnerton, this can sometimes work the other way round; there are subtle doctrinal implications in some of the examples Peacham gives for 'Metaphor': 'Psalme 34. Taste and see how gracious the Lord is, for, trye how gracious the Lord is. Hebrues 2. And have tasted of thy heavenly giftes, for, have hadde knowledge of thy heavenly gyftes.'[30] Readers are encouraged to discard the corporeal surface of such scriptural expressions in favour of an immanent spiritual sense; the doctrinal agenda is clear.

This close connection between rhetorical theory and a reformed theological outlook persists throughout the sixteenth and seventeenth centuries, partly as a result of the influence of the *Book of Common Prayer* and its animating principles of figuration (explored in detail below). Protestant

---

uniformly used in Scripture, when the sacred mysteries are treated of, is metonymical' (Jean Calvin, *Institutes of the Christian Religion* (1559), trans. by Henry Beveridge (Grand Rapids, MI: Eerdmans, 1989), IV. xvii. 20 (pt. II, p. 573)). Given that the first, shorter, edition of the *Institutes* was published in Basel in 1536, Swynnerton would have had to be very quick off the mark indeed for Calvin to be a direct source, if Rex's dating of his manuscript is accurate.

[28] Cox relied heavily on Philipp Melanchthon's *Institutiones Rhetoricae* (1521) – the *Arte* is largely a translation of Book I – as did many of his successors: 'Virtually every rhetoric produced in England from 1530 to the end of the century shows marks of [Melanchthon's] influence' (Conley, *Rhetoric in the European Tradition*, p. 135).

[29] Thomas Wilson, *The Arte of Rhetorique* (London, 1553). Martin Bucer was a continental reformer who came to England at Cranmer's invitation and was instrumental in his revision of the Prayer Book (see p. 26 below); Lee A. Sonnino remarks on Wilson's 'quaint examples' (*A Handbook to Sixteenth-Century Rhetoric* (London: Routledge and Kegan Paul, 1968), p. 240). According to Susan Doran and Jonathan Woolfson, the 'Protestant sentiment' in this work led to Wilson's imprisonment and torture by the Inquisition in Italy during his exile from the Marian regime; see their entry for 'Wilson, Thomas (1523/4–1581)', in *DNB* online.

[30] Henry Peacham, *The Garden of Eloquence* (London, 1577), p. [7]. For an account of the tensions between the sacred and the secular in this work, see Cummings, *Literary Culture*, pp. 275–7.

tenets are emphasised under the cover of pedagogical instruction, as, for example, in the instructive orations of the *Booke Called the Foundacion of Rhetoricke* (1563) by Richard Rainolde, or Dudley Fenner's *Artes of Logike and Rethoricke* (1584). Both men are ordained and both profess reformist views; Fenner is a committed Puritan (or 'godly') thinker and, as might be expected, he also puts the words of institution firmly under the heading of 'chaunge of name or Metonimie'.[31] In the following century, scriptural rhetorics include John Barton's *The Art of Rhetorick Concisely and Compleatly Handled, Exemplified out of Holy Writ* (1634), John Prideaux's *Sacred Eloquence* (1659) and John Smith's *Mysterie of Rhetorique Unveil'd* (1665). Prideaux, Bishop of Worcester from 1641 to his death in 1650 (his book was published posthumously), was a more ambivalent figure politically than some of his predecessors, but his views on Christ's eucharistic presence are never in doubt. '[W]hat more frequent in the Old and New Testament, then Sacramentall metonymies?', he asks; 'In which metonymi-call sense, the words of institution of the Lords Supper must be understood . . .; except we would make a prodigie of the blessed Supper, appointed to set at variance, not in unitie to fix believers.'[32] This tactic did not, of course, go unnoticed by those who adhered to more traditional forms of belief; the Jesuit John Radford firmly refutes reformed rhetoric along with doctrine in his *Briefe and Plaine Discourse* (1605): 'they knewe no such figure, as the sacramentaries have devised', he says of the Church Fathers: 'they never could tell of *Synecdoche* or *Metonymia*, they knewe sacramentall, and not rhetoricall figures, mysticall, & not poeticall, holy and not prophane'.[33]

If rhetoric can be a way of arguing in this period, then it can also be a mode of argument, and this presents some difficulties for the scholar of early modern eucharistic controversy; a great deal of confusion stems from rhetorical habits of expression, and from the conflict of interpretation over certain key words. A common feature of sixteenth-century polemic is the distortion or exaggeration of the adversary's position, which means that it is impossible to gain an accurate picture of contemporary Catholic practice and belief from hostile reformist commentary, or even, in fact, an accurate picture of how those hostile reformers themselves actually

---

[31] Dudley Fenner, *The Artes of Logike and Rethorike . . ., for the . . . Resolution or Opening of Certayne Partes of Scripture* (Middleburg, 1584), p. [20].

[32] John Prideaux, *Sacred Eloquence: Or, the Art of Rhetorick, as it is Layd Down in Scripture* (London, 1659), pp. 10–11; and see A. J. Hegarty, 'Prideaux, John (1578–1650)', in *DNB* online.

[33] John Radford, *A Directorie Teaching the Way to the Truth in a Brief and Plaine Discourse Against the Heresies of this Time* ([England], 1605), p. 217.

understood contemporary Catholic practice and belief. Words used to describe Christ's presence in the eucharist – 'real', 'true', 'natural' – are alarmingly subject to semantic shift, according to who is using them and to what ends. In addition, Francis Clark identifies a need to distinguish between Protestant objections to points of doctrine, on the one hand (for example, a belief in Purgatory), and to 'practical abuses', on the other (in this case, the corresponding sale of indulgences): 'The relevant question to ask about them [objectionable practices] is whether they were the abuse of what was good and true or the exploitation of what was false and evil.'[34] In this instance, as with the mode of Christ's presence in the eucharist, there is a real and fundamental difference of belief which is paradoxically in danger of being obfuscated through being overstated. Just as it was in the reformers' interests to stress their own figurative interpretation of words of Scripture, so it served them to caricature the Catholic view of presence as reductively carnal and intellectually unsophisticated: as logically and rhetorically unsound. Cranmer's *Defence* is typical in this respect:

They say, that in the sacrament, the corporall membres of Christe be not distaunt in place, one from another, but that wheresoever the head is, there be the feete, and wheresoever the armes be, there be the legges, so that in every parte of the bread & wyne, is altogither, whole head, whole feete, whole fleshe, whole bloud, whole hearte, whole lunges, whole brest, whole backe, and altogither whole, confused, and mixte withoute distinction or diversitie. O what a foolishe and an abhominable invencion is this, to make of the moste pure and perfect body of Christe, suche a confuse and monstruous body?[35]

It is impossible to tell from such *reductiones ad absurdum* whether or not the polemicist thinks he is giving an accurate statement of his opponents' beliefs; the power of this argument is not in plain reason, but in trope and figure: hyperbole and alliteration, syllogistic parison, cumulative anaphora. 'Thomas Cranmer was not a great theologian,' Peter Newman Brooks observes;[36] he was, however, a great rhetorician, and the crucial difference between his reformed position on sacramental presence and the traditional belief in transubstantiation he parodies here is one of signification. Cranmer insists on the iconicity of the elements; he restores to symbols, whether verbal or physical, their power to represent.

---

[34] Francis Clark, *Eucharistic Sacrifice and the Reformation*, 2nd edn (Oxford: Blackwell, 1967), p. 72.
[35] Thomas Cranmer, *A Defence of the True and Catholike Doctrine of the Sacrament* (London, 1550), p. 47.
[36] Peter Newman Brooks, *Thomas Cranmer's Doctrine of the Eucharist: an Essay in Historical Development*, 2nd edn (London: Macmillan, 1992), p. 55.

EUCHARISTIC FIGURATION: LUTHER, ZWINGLI, CALVIN

From the dawn of the Reformation, then, theological and rhetorical understandings developed alongside one another in a kind of conceptual symbiosis, with far-reaching implications for each. Swynnerton's early rhetorical
explanations seek to establish a figurative interpretation of certain passages
of Scripture, and to claim furthermore that any other interpretation is
simply mistaken, a failure to read right. Fifty years later, Fenner does the
same thing; 'So Christ sayde: This is my bodie, that is, a signe or sacrament
of my bodie' is an example of 'Metonimie', just as it is for Prideaux, writing
in the 1640s.[37] This shared act of reading shows these men as direct, if
distant, inheritors of Luther's thought: behind it lies the embrace of
Protestant teaching on the efficacy of the sacraments, and behind that an
acceptance of the Protestant position on grace. For the most significant and
contentious challenge Luther made to orthodox Catholic doctrine when he
issued his theses in 1517 was over the question of *how* humankind might be
saved: he came to believe that grace was something freely given by God,
absolutely outwith the power of sinful humankind either to merit through
inherent virtue or to earn by good works. Faith alone could ensure salvation,
and only God could grant the gift of faith.[38] This doctrine, known as the
doctrine of justification, was not an entirely original one, or even that much
of a significant departure from mainstream theological thought; Luther was,
after all, greatly influenced by Augustine's teaching on the subject. The
novelty came both in the way the doctrine was restated, and in the particular
political conjunction that gave it such force at this time. To point out its
convenience for secular leaders looking to shake off the yoke of a powerful
church (for the doctrine in many ways represented a challenge to institutional authority) is to risk a dangerous oversimplification of an extremely
complex situation, but their receptiveness to the idea undoubtedly con-
tributed to its influence, and to the passionate and protracted disputes over
its validity. Whatever the reasons, Luther's promulgation of the doctrine of
justification had a huge impact on early sixteenth-century Europe, largely –
as these definitions of 'metonymia' and 'metonimie' demonstrate, in their

---

[37] Fenner, *Artes of Logike and Rethorike*, p. [20].
[38] This is the matter stated, as ever, in its most basic terms, and is therefore inevitably rather reductive;
there is not room here to explicate the subtleties of the doctrine of predestination, or to attempt to cut
the Gordian knot of contemporary controversy over its operation. One of its most vexed implications
was the existence of a justified 'elect', destined for salvation and unable to fall from this state of grace.
For a comprehensive account, see Alister E. McGrath, *Iustitia Dei: a History of the Christian Doctrine
of Justification*, 2 vols. (Cambridge University Press, 1986).

own small way – because of its inevitable consequences for the central rite of Catholic Christianity: the Mass.[39]

Following the logic of Luther's argument, the ceremony must cease to be an act efficacious in itself, and become a symbol, not a vessel, of that grace already given. Christ's single, historical sacrifice on the cross is sufficient to expiate for human sin for all time, and does not need to be reiterated; if the priest is believed to be offering the sacrifice again, as would be the case if Christ were really present on the altar, this would both derogate from the sufficiency of the crucifixion, and imply that human effort might have a place in the economy of salvation. This would stand in direct contradiction to the rejection of the system of 'works' which was one of Luther's chief tenets of belief; as Clark explains of the continental reformers' emphasis on the doctrine of justification, 'it was this inner logic of their position that made their rejection of the Catholic doctrine of Eucharistic sacrifice inevitable and unambiguous'.[40] It had another corollary: minimising the function and importance of the sacrament in this way necessarily diminished the role of the priesthood; Christ is not materially present and so cannot be offered by a minister of the church, whose power is therefore commensurately less. A receptionist doctrine, which transfers the focus from the sacrament to the elect communicant and his or her relationship to Christ, reduces the work of the priest in consecration by an order of magnitude. Max Weber is succinct in outlining the huge ramifications of such a line of thought: 'Every consistent doctrine of predestined grace inevitably implied a radical and ultimate devaluation of all magical, sacramental and institutional distributions of grace.'[41] The devaluation in this case was exacerbated by Luther's rejection of the old understanding, on a model derived from the works of Aristotle, of the mode of Christ's presence in the eucharist. This theory divided categories of being into 'substance' and 'accidents', and held that the substance of the Host, its essence, was changed by the words of

---

[39] 'The liturgy lay at the heart of medieval religion, and the Mass lay at the heart of the liturgy' (Eamon Duffy, *The Stripping of the Altars: Traditional Religion in England, c.1400–c.1580* (New Haven: Yale University Press, 1992), p. 91).

[40] Clark, *Eucharistic Sacrifice*, p. 130; he is quite clear that 'Luther's rejection of the sacrifice was bound up with his doctrine of justification' (p. 106).

[41] Max Weber, *The Sociology of Religion*, trans. Ephraim Fischoff (London: Methuen, 1965), p. 203. Weber goes on to add: 'By far the strongest such devaluation of magical and institutional grace occurred in Puritanism.' Keith Thomas confirms this view: 'Protestantism thus presented itself as a deliberate attempt to take the magical elements out of religion, to eliminate the idea that the rituals of the Church had about them a mechanical efficacy, and to abandon the effort to endow physical objects with supernatural qualities by special formulae of consecration and exorcism' (*Religion and the Decline of Magic* (London: Weidenfeld and Nicolson, 1971; repr. Harmondsworth: Penguin, 1991), p. 87.)

consecration into the body of Christ, while the accidents (external irrele-vancies such as appearance, smell, taste and so on) remained the same. This process, known as 'transubstantiation', was described thus by Aquinas in the thirteenth century: 'We have under this sacrament . . . not only the flesh, but the whole body of Christ, that is, the bones and nerves and all the rest.'[42] It was re-expressed in the 1562 decree of the Council of Trent on the sacrifice of the Mass: 'Christ himself is contained' in the Mass, and 'his body and blood are offered to the Father under the appearances of bread and wine'.[43] Luther argued that the rational analysis offered by Aristotelian categories was inappropriate to the mystery of the sacrament, which should instead be apprehended and accepted purely as a matter of faith. This teaching was a 'time-bomb', and it 'soon blew apart any unity in Protestantism'.[44]

For Luther did not, in fact, follow through his own argument on sacramental grace, maintaining consistently that there was some sort of physical presence in the eucharist. He developed a doctrine, later known as 'consubstantiation', which held that the whole substance of the body and blood are simultaneously present in the consecrated elements with the whole substance of the bread and wine. The theory of ubiquity on which this depends (Christ is everywhere, so there is no reason he should not be in the Host) proved to offer too diffuse a comfort to exert a lasting attraction even for his closest followers.[45] The logical extension of Luther's original principles was left to Huldrych Zwingli and John Calvin, two of the most influential of the continental reformers. Their respective positions on the scriptural evidence for Christ's corporeal presence in the Host (how literally to take the words 'this is my body', in short) are summarised by Dom Gregory Dix in his monumental work on the history of the liturgy: 'Luther insisted that [Scripture] must mean what it plainly said,' he writes. 'Zwingli and Calvin replied that if it were to be accepted in this sense it must overthrow the whole protestant conception of the sacraments and with that the cardinal doctrine of justification by faith alone.'[46] Zwingli's stance was the more extreme: he saw the eucharist as simply an act of

[42] Thomas Aquinas, *Summa Theologiae* (London: Blackfriars, 1964–80), 3a.76.1.
[43] Quoted in Clark, *Eucharistic Sacrifice*, p. 94. The Council of Trent was the Counter-Reformation ecumenical council of the Church of Rome. Clark points out that Catholic theology in the post-Lutheran period was characterised by a desire to close ranks and to re-express traditional doctrine, rather than to innovate; this is not to imply, however, that the doctrine of transubstantiation had been a constant in Catholic thought. For a full account of its development in medieval times, see Rubin, *Corpus Christi*.
[44] MacCulloch, *Reformation*, p. 130.   [45] See Clark, *Eucharistic Sacrifice*, pp. 160–1.
[46] Dom Gregory Dix, *The Shape of the Liturgy* (London: A. and C. Black, 1945; repr. 1993), p. 634.

remembrance, a way to imagine though not to participate in or to reiterate Christ's passion, which was in itself an entirely sufficient redemptive sacrifice. It was in order to support this view that he proposed his revolution in reading: 'The whole difficulty lies not in the pronoun "This" but . . . the verb "is". For this word is often used in Holy Scripture in the sense of "signifies",' Zwingli writes; 'To eat sacramentally can be nothing else but to eat the sign or figure.'[47] The inescapable corollary of Luther's thinking on grace was, for Zwingli, a sacrament that was a sign, and only a sign: his insistence on this interpretation (a position known as 'memorialism') caused a deep rift in the Protestant Church almost from its inception. A colloquy was held at Marburg in 1526, attended by reformers including Luther, Melanchthon and Zwingli, in order to reach a consensus on this and other points of doctrine; though a form of words was found to which all subscribed, it was little more than 'a studied exercise in ambiguity'.[48]

Calvin, though he might be thought of as being close in some ways to Zwingli's position – they are in agreement, for example, in their opposition to Luther's belief that bread and wine become body and blood in an objective sense – stops ingeniously short of denying Christ's presence in the eucharist. 'There is no ground to object that the expression is figurative, and gives the sign the name of the thing signified,' he asserts in the *Institutes*; 'we duly infer from the exhibition of the symbol that the thing itself is exhibited. For unless we would charge God with deceit, we will never presume to say that he holds forth an empty symbol.'[49] This influential teaching occupies a conceptual middle ground in early Protestant thought, between Luther's sense of Christ's real presence in the eucharist, on the one hand, and on the other, Zwingli's insistence that this presence is only figurative. It combines a clear rejection of the notion that consecration can transform the eucharistic elements into body and blood with an equally clear assertion that the body and blood are indeed in some way received by the elect believer: 'in the mystery of the Supper, by the symbols of bread and wine, Christ, his body and blood, are truly exhibited to us'.[50] Precisely how this happens is not susceptible of conception, much less of explanation: 'though the mind is more powerful in thought than the tongue in expression', Calvin writes, 'it too is overcome by the magnitude of the subject'.[51] Calvin negotiates the paradox of a theory of predestination coexistent with

[47] Huldrych Zwingli, *On True and False Religion* (1525), quoted in Darwell Stone, *A History of the Doctrine of the Holy Eucharist*, 2 vols. (London: Longmans, 1909), II. 40.

[48] Brooks, *Cranmer's Doctrine of the Eucharist*, p. 61. See also MacCulloch, *Reformation*, pp. 172–4.

[49] Calvin, *Institutes*, IV. xvii. 10 (pt. II, p. 564).   [50] Calvin, *Institutes*, IV. xvii. 10 (pt. II, p. 564).

[51] Calvin, *Institutes*, IV. xvii. 10 (pt. II, p. 561).

the eucharist as an instrument of grace by making divine presence in the Host mysterious and contingent on the faith of the communicant: only the elect receive Christ's substance in the eucharist, because to eat God means life, and the unregenerate cannot be saved.

This brief summary has necessarily flattened out many of the subtleties of an intricate and profound debate, but the point nonetheless emerges that there were, in sixteenth-century theological thought, four broad positions on the nature of Christ's presence in the eucharist to which it was possible to subscribe. On a spectrum moving from the most to the least corporeal, or from the literal to the literary, these are: the traditional Catholic view of transubstantiation; Lutheran consubstantiation, also known as a belief in the 'real presence'; Calvinist focus on Christ's spiritual presence in the eucharist; and Zwinglian memorialism, which rested on a purely figurative interpretation of Christ's words at the Last Supper. What is notable in all of these formulations, though perhaps most marked in the three Protestant ones, is their shared terminology and subsequent reliance on the need for right interpretation of language that is, as all concede, on some level figurative. Different ways of understanding the mode of Christ's presence in the eucharist are founded on different ways of reading, and on competing symbolic economies. This also of course works the other way around: the exponents of each position are compelled to exploit varying degrees of distance between sign and referent; in effect, to evolve theories of rhetoric that will justify their theological stances. Though he resisted its full logical implications, therefore, one of Luther's most significant contributions to Renaissance culture was to make eucharistic doctrine as much a rhetorical as a theological matter. Having early on rejected the notion and the name of transubstantiation, Luther sought an alternative way to explain the mode of Christ's presence in the Host; what he came up with was something he called *Fleischbrot* ('fleshbread'), a sort of composite substance that avoids the problematic dynamic of one physical reality supplanting another. Brian Gerrish describes what such a theory involves in these terms: 'The words "This is my body" are therefore not an instance of symbolism but of synecdoche, naming the part for the whole, since what Christ offered his disciples at the Last Supper was his body *with* the bread.'[52] Even a Lutheran belief in a corporeal presence, that is, involves a figurative understanding of the words of institution: there is a necessary gap between what is said and

---

[52] B. A. Gerrish, *Grace and Gratitude: the Eucharistic Theology of John Calvin* (Edinburgh: T. and T. Clark, 1993), p. 165.

how it should be taken, and the interpretative tool is a rhetorical device – synecdoche.

When Calvin came to elucidate the same difficulty, he too took advantage of the opportunity presented by saying one thing and meaning something slightly different; on the surface, nothing could be clearer than his assertion of eucharistic presence: 'I willingly admit any thing which helps to express the true and substantial communication of the body and blood of the Lord.'[53] As Dix points out, though, his stance is not as straightforward as it sounds. 'There is a presence of Christ at the eucharist – [Calvin] does not hesitate to call it a "Real Presence".' But, Dix cautions, 'such traditional language must not mislead us as to his real meaning'.[54] Calvin turns old terminology to new ends, redeploying Catholic phrases to describe reformed ideas; it is not just the words of Scripture that undergo a rhetorical realignment, but those words customarily used to explain and amplify its meaning. His theology works on the principle of maintaining volatile concepts in tension: the fissures are there, between sign and reality, but he seeks to contain them with a linguistic ambiguity that reflects a genuine theological position. That position is distinction without separation; just as the two natures of Christ, the divine and the human, are perfect, entire and indivisible, so are the eucharistic bread and body: the substance that holds them in a state of mystical suspension is faith. 'It was', MacCulloch writes, 'the perfect model to be used by this theologian so consciously striving for a Catholic balance.'[55] As continental reformed thought on sacramental presence developed in the first half of the sixteenth century, then, it sophisticated the verbal and interpretive technologies that were needed to sustain it. It is one of the central contentions of this book that the rhetorical opportunities thus provided were to have a profound impact on English poetry for at least the next hundred years; the chief vehicle through which this influence was conveyed, the liturgy of the Protestant Church newly established under the Tudors, is the subject of the next section.

TYPES OF AMBIGUITY: *THE BOOK OF COMMON PRAYER*, 1549–1559

If a judicious ambiguity was useful for Calvin in establishing the Protestant formularies of worship in Geneva, it was to prove even more so for Cranmer in his attempts to produce a liturgy for the English church that would be a

---

[53] Calvin, *Institutes*, IV. xvii. 19 (pt. II, p. 571).   [54] Dix, *The Shape of the Liturgy*, p. 633.
[55] MacCulloch, *Reformation*, p. 250.

reasonable exposition of the reformed theology he embraced, whilst still preserving enough of a connection with the old rites to be acceptable to the more traditionally minded among his fellow clergy (and indeed the laity on whom it was to be imposed). *The Book of Common Prayer*, a monumental liturgical achievement, was both more and less successful than its author could have foreseen. When Cranmer died in 1556, executed for heresy during Mary Tudor's brief Catholic reign, the two versions of the Prayer Book he had instituted had been used for a little over three years; reintroduced by Elizabeth I in 1559, it was to endure, with one short but significant interlude, as the liturgy of what would be known as the Anglican Church in England and abroad for the next four centuries. (This extraordinary longevity would perhaps have gratified Cranmer, though he might have been surprised to learn of the diversity of doctrinal belief his orders of service in practice engendered and allowed.) There can be no doubt that the impact of the *Book of Common Prayer* on the intellectual lives of the members of the church, among whom are numbered the six writers in this study, was very considerable: as applied doctrine, a rite rehearsed and sung across parishes throughout the period and beyond, it had more impact on the formulation of belief than even the most power-fully argued treatise could hope to achieve. This influence was felt not just in borrowed words, structures and cadences, though they abound, but in the ideas about language and rhetoric enshrined in the expression of its theology. Inspired by the theological and rhetorical methodologies of the continental reformers, restricted by the political circumstances of Edward VI's reign, Cranmer produced a liturgy of deeply productive ambiguity which was to be of defining importance for imaginative writing in the Renaissance.[56]

The subject of Cranmer's influences and his innovations in constructing this work is a complex one, to say nothing of the history of its reception, and of its revisions over the subsequent century; no short survey can hope to be comprehensive, and so the account that follows attempts simply to give a general overview and to make a few connected points about what could be described as the literary repercussions of the circumstances of the Prayer Book's composition, in particular the eucharistic theology set forth in its

---

[56] This is, surprisingly, a relatively unexamined area, though two recent studies have taken the influence of the *Book of Common Prayer* on literature as their subject: Targoff, *Common Prayer*; Rosendale, *Liturgy and Literature*. The latter is particularly useful in drawing out the implications of Prayer Book worship for imaginative writing: 'What ultimately emerges from the Reformed understandings of the Eucharist, and from the theologically ambivalent formulations of the Prayerbook, is a figurative, interpretive, *readerly* conception of the sacrament' (p. 107).

Order for Holy Communion.[57] One of the first difficulties consists in understanding precisely what the text, in each of its versions, hopes to achieve: liturgy provides a template and direction for active worship, and though it is a practical and communicable expression of theological doctrine, it is in itself neither treatise nor article of faith. The rite exists as a structure separable, that is, from the beliefs of those who composed it: it stands as independent and eminently interpretable. Judith Maltby makes an important point about the ways in which Cranmer's words could act: 'the Prayer Book', she reminds us, 'is first and foremost "liturgy"; that is "work", intended not so much to be read in a passive sense, but to be used, performed, experienced'.[58] This means that calibrating Cranmer's personal theology of sacramental grace, though a crucial endeavour, is of only so much help in construing the services of communion even in the versions of the Prayer Book he oversaw (1549 and 1552); the political circumstances in which he was operating, as well as his own inclination to find devotional formulas that could unite an emergent Protestant faction with fully as wide a shading of belief as that found on the continent, made for a work whose governing characteristic was a careful ambivalence.[59] (It is notable that the version that must be thought of as approaching most closely to Cranmer's own doctrinal position, the revised Prayer Book of 1552, was also the shortest-lived; Rosendale remarks that it is the only version 'that, abortively, staked itself on clarity rather than ambiguity'.[60]) That so much of the Prayer Book is adapted or translated from traditional sources presents an additional interpretative crux. Above all, Cranmer was skilled in linguistic salvage: in borrowing the communal, authoritative (but not authored) voice that came with those old forms, but investing them with new meaning. MacCulloch notes 'Cranmer's extraordinarily omnivorous pursuit of a good phrase which could be captured from the enemy and put to godly use': the frame

---

[57] There are a number of studies that offer much fuller explorations of various aspects of these questions; for an account of the development of Cranmer's thought, see Brooks, *Cranmer's Doctrine of the Eucharist*; for the composition and early reception of the *Book of Common Prayer*, see Diarmaid MacCulloch, *Thomas Cranmer* (New Haven: Yale University Press, 1996), pp. 351–409, 504–13, *et passim*; for its place in a wider liturgical context, see G. J. Cuming, *A History of Anglican Liturgy*, 2nd edn (Basingstoke: Macmillan, 1982); for a parallel-text collation of the changes between successive versions, see F. E. Brightman, *The English Rite: Being a Synopsis of the Sources and Revisions of the Book of Common Prayer*, 2 vols. (London: Rivingtons, 1915). Brian Cummings's introduction to *The Book of Common Prayer: the Texts of 1549, 1559, and 1662* (Oxford University Press, 2011) offers a concise and helpful overview of its history and use.

[58] Judith Maltby, *Prayer Book and People in Elizabethan and Early Stuart England* (Oxford: Clarendon Press, 1998), p. 3.

[59] As Clark observes, 'At that critical stage, vagueness and ambiguity were preferable to a clarity which might disrupt the forces of the Reformation' (*Eucharistic Sacrifice*, p. 167).

[60] Rosendale, *Liturgy and Literature*, p. 89.

of the traditional devotions stayed the same, but their words underwent the kind of radical reinterpretation that is familiar from the strategies of thinkers like Zwingli, whose magical formulation 'is = signifies' opened up such rhetorical possibilities for the reformers.[61]

Thomas Cranmer's eucharistic theology evolved gradually over the latter part of Henry VIII's reign; the king, though anxious for doctrinal reform for political reasons, remained liturgically conservative, and it was not until the accession of his son that real innovations could be made in the forms of worship. There is some speculation over when precisely Cranmer, influenced by his chaplain Nicholas Ridley, crossed 'the great theological divide between real and spiritual eucharistic presence' – from a Lutheran belief, that is, to something closer to a Zwinglian memorialism – though some time around 1546 seems likely.[62] In any case, by the time Edward VI came to the throne in February 1547 Cranmer's thinking had matured; the reformers were in the ascendant at court, and plans for a reformed English liturgy seemed likely at last to come to fruition. Cranmer's vernacular liturgy, *The booke of the common praier and administracion of the Sacramentes and other rites and ceremonies of the Churche*, officially superseded the collection of old Latin rites that had hitherto been in use on Whitsunday, 9 June 1549. It is in many ways a puzzling work: a carefully but-half-reformed interim measure, always intended to be replaced with increasingly more progressive forms of worship; a patchwork of various sources translated from various languages, probably composed at various times; a masterfully equivocal exercise in practical theology that is also one of the most resonant and powerful prose compositions in the language. Though clearly reformist in intention, its verbal structures were braced between the old beliefs and the new, just about susceptible of either interpretation. Nowhere was this more evident – or more important, given its central place in distinguishing doctrinal difference – than in the order for celebration of communion; 'Cranmer's Canon', as Brooks recognises, 'cleverly concealed revolution behind the conservative forms of hallowed usage'.[63]

The 1549 service announces a deceptive ecumenism in its title: 'The Supper of the Lorde and the Holy Communion, commonly called the Masse'; it follows the shape of the Sarum Missal (a widely used Latin

---

[61] MacCulloch, *Thomas Cranmer*, p. 417. Brightman's careful scholarship at the start of the last century uncovered the extent of Cranmer's liturgical borrowing; see *English Rite, passim*.

[62] MacCulloch, *Thomas Cranmer*, p. 355. Brooks favours 1546 (see *Cranmer's Doctrine of the Eucharist*, p. 36), though MacCulloch finds definitive evidence of the transformation only in the next year. He also rejects Brooks's terminology of a change from a belief in 'real' to 'true' presence.

[63] Brooks, *Cranmer's Doctrine of the Eucharist*, p. 75.

order originating in Salisbury), and incorporates material from Cranmer's own 'Order of the Communion', an English insert in the ceremony composed the previous year as a reformist place-holder.[64] As might be expected, both the text (words to be spoken by minister, or congregation) and the rubric (instructions for preparation and reception of the sacrament) tend towards undermining the idea of any real presence in the Host, whether this is understood in a Catholic or a Lutheran sense. The celebrant makes it clear in his first exhortation that 'the moste comfortable Sacrament of the body and bloud of Christ' is to be accepted 'in the *remembraunce* of his moste fruitfull and glorious Passyon'; that these substances are there 'to feede upon *spiritually*' (my italics).[65] In the canon, which comprises a prayer for 'the whole state of Christes church', the act of consecration and the words of institution ('Take, eate, this is my bodye which is geven for you'), things are left a little more open:

with thy holy spirite and worde, vouchsafe to bl✚esse and sanc✚tifie these thy gyftes, and creatures of bread and wyne, that they maie be unto us the bodye and bloude of thy moste derely beloved sonne Jesus Christe.[66]

Timothy Rosendale points out the subtlety of this phrasing: 'the trans-formational consecration is made into a metaphorical one as transubstan-tiation is replaced by trope'.[67] Despite its figurative intent, though, there are aspects here that are patient of a more traditional interpretation. Most striking are the twin black crosses, which interrupt the priest's words with an intimation of ineffability; these extra-linguistic signs mark the moment of consecration as something apart, a divine intervention in the text. In the more thoroughly reformed Prayer Book of 1552, they are gone.

The first *Book of Common Prayer* had a discomfiting reception. It was not radical enough for some (the firebrand bishop John Hooper called it 'very defective and of doubtful construction, and in some respects indeed man-ifestly impious'), and it met with an unwelcome if sardonic approbation from others. Stephen Gardiner was a deeply conservative bishop and an old adversary of Cranmer's; his claim that 'touching the truth of the very presence of Christ's most precious body and blood in the Sacrament, there was much spoken in that book as might be desired' was, in the circumstances, double-edged to say the least.[68] Gardiner's is a cleverly exploitative response to a liturgy whose efforts to temporise between the conservatives on one hand and the ultra-radicals on the other had left it

---

[64] MacCulloch, *Thomas Cranmer*, pp. 384–5.   [65] Cranmer, *Book of Common Prayer* (1549), p. 24.
[66] Cranmer, *Book of Common Prayer* (1549), p. 30.   [67] Rosendale, *Liturgy and Literature*, p. 212.
[68] Quoted in Brooks, *Cranmer's Doctrine of the Eucharist*, p. 139.

fraught with ambiguity, and vulnerable to such wilful misinterpretation. He was a lawyer by training, and he had a precise and elegant style of argumentation; it is not at all clear that Cranmer came off better in the pamphlet battle that followed the publication of the new liturgy. His two contributions to the conversation, however, the *Defence* of 1550 and the *Answer*, published in the following year, are the fullest and most explicit expressions of his mature eucharistic theology; what emerges very clearly from both is Cranmer's absolute commitment to the idea of figurative language.[69] Again and again he asserts that the words of institution cannot be understood literally, and accuses those who do so of a disastrous lack of literary sophistication: 'as for this saying of Christ, this is my body, it is a figurative speach, called *Metonymia*, when one thing is called by the name of another', he writes in the *Defence*; and again, in the *Answer*: 'the bread after consecration is not called Christ his body, bycause it is so in deed, for then it were no figurative speach, as all the old authors say it is'.[70] Gardiner approves the Prayer Book but questions the explanation of its eucharistic theology offered in Cranmer's *Defence* because he perceives a gap between them that can be exploited to polemical ends; this is a valuable opportunity for Gardiner, but it does not come from anything so simple as a mistake on Cranmer's part. The two men, rather, are of a fundamentally different cast of mind: they exemplify alternative rhetorical outlooks, and their theological divergences are involved, whether as symptom or cause, in interpretative differences in thinking about language. For Cranmer, there is no necessary literal level to which figurative expression can be reduced. 'I doe as plainly speake as I can,' he says with evident sincerity, 'that Christes body and bloud, be geven to us in deede, yet not corporally, and carnally, but spiritually, and effectually.'[71]

Cranmer's investment in the possibilities of figuration is thorough-going and far-reaching. Rejecting the doctrine of real presence redirects the focus from priest and Host to communicant and word, from objective meaning to subjective interpretation. As the previous quotation suggests ('in deed'), it does not diminish the power of that word. In this dynamic, the linguistic transcends the corporal – has, in fact, no need of it: 'it is the nature of al sacramentes to be figures', Cranmer writes, in a near equation of spiritual

---

[69] Cranmer, *Defence*; Cranmer, *An Aunswere . . . Unto a Craftie and Sophisticall Cavillation* (London, 1551). Gardiner's response to the first, which was refuted in the second, was the *Explication and Assertion of the True Catholique Fayth*, privately printed – probably at Rouen – in 1550. For a fuller account of the controversy see MacCulloch, *Thomas Cranmer*, pp. 485–92.
[70] Cranmer, *Defence*, p. 58; *Aunswere*, p. 189.   [71] Cranmer, *Aunswere*, p. 34.

with rhetorical efficacy.[72] As the exchanges with Gardiner demonstrate, doctrinal necessity led Cranmer to crystallise a method of reading that centrally distinguished between word and referent, and so allowed him to use traditional frames and phrases (in the liturgy and elsewhere), but to mean something different by them. His trust in this method's power and transparency made him impatient of what he regarded as ignorant misinterpretation (Cranmer complains of how those 'not used to reade olde auncient authors, nor acquanted with theyr phrase and manner of speech … dyd carpe and reprehend, for lacke of good understanding');[73] such frustrations did not, however, prevent him from exercising the considerable creative licence implied by this mode of interpretation in his own writing. 'Cranmer mocks a literalism baffled by metalepsis and metonymy,' Anderson explains; 'at the same time, his examples attest to the figurality even of ordinary language.'[74] It is significant that the realist rhetoric of the revised Prayer Book liturgy is matched by some unrepentantly immediate and affective passages in Cranmer's polemical works:

the eatyng and drinkyng of this sacramentall breade and wyne, is as it were a shewyng of Christ before our eies, a smellyng of hym with our noses, a feelyng and gropyng of hym with our handes, and an eatyng, chawyng, digestyng and feedyng upon hym to our spirituall strength and perfection.[75]

'As it were.'[76] And again:

with our fayth wee see Christ crucified with our spirituall eyes, and eat his flesh, thrust thorow with a speare, and drinke his blowd springing out of his side with our spirituall mouthes of our fayth.[77]

To those who did not share Cranmer's faith in figuration, the modifying phrases which insist on a metaphorical reading here ('with our fayth', 'spirituall'), even doubled up as they are, might seem a flimsy protection against the vivid corporeality of his imagery.

Gardiner's pseudo-approbation of the 1549 *Book of Common Prayer* was not the only factor influencing its revision, but it is notable that none of the aspects singled out for praise by the truculent bishop survived; not

---

[72] Cranmer, *Defence*, p. 72.   [73] Cranmer, *Aunswere*, p. 236.

[74] Anderson, *Translating Investments*, p. 46.   [75] Cranmer, *Defence*, p. 11.

[76] For the significance of this formula in Cranmer's prose, see Joe Moshenska's illuminating work: '"A Sensible Feeling, Touching and Groping": Metaphor and Sensory Experience in the English Reformation', in *The Passions and Subjectivity in Early Modern Culture*, ed. by Brian Cummings and Freya Sierhuis (forthcoming).

[77] Cranmer, *Aunswere*, p. 340. Brooks quotes this moment, observing: 'It is surprising what realist language Cranmer can use' (*Cranmer's Eucharistic Doctrine*, p. 102).

surprisingly, it was the communion service that underwent the greatest alteration. Cranmer probably anyway planned to revolutionise the liturgy in stages, according to his own inclinations and in correspondence with other Protestant thinkers; soon after its first publication, for example, he asked for a critique from the Strasbourg reformer Martin Bucer, then (at Cranmer's invitation) Professor of Divinity in Cambridge.[78] The subtle-minded suggestions of the resulting *Censura* (1551) seem to have been as influential as Gardiner's dry mock, if the movement towards memorialism is anything to go by. Bucer's eucharistic theology was close to that of Zwingli, but with 'finer shadings'; 'there is a figure in the words of the Lord', he believed, 'because more is understood than is said'.[79] His own liturgical reforms exploited the kind of figural ambiguity that Cranmer found so intellectually congenial; it was fitting, then, that his untimely death in exile in the fens should be remembered in Wilson's instance of synecdoche.[80]

Whether intended from the start, or framed in response to hostile or friendly comment, the changes made to the Order for Holy Communion in 1552 transform the nature of the ceremony by banishing its equivocations. There are revisions, major and minor, to its structure and to the wording of both prayers and rubric, all of which tend to the elimination of any residual opportunity to hold to a real presence doctrine; 'a whole series of changes', Cuming remarks, 'aimed at removing any suspicion of transubstantiation'.[81] The word 'Masse' is dropped from the title; 'altar' is replaced by 'table' or 'Lord's table'; the reordering of prayers and priestly action ruptures the old integrity of the Canon, and removes the moment which might have allowed for a secret adoration of the sacrament: now, communion happens immediately after the elements are consecrated, with no oblation or prayer in between.[82] There are signs that the body of Christ had vanished even in the smallest and most practical of details. At the end of the ceremony, as at its start, the rubric makes clear that what was offered is just bread; should there be any left over, 'the Curate shal have it to hys owne use'.[83] Whereas in 1549 the Host was administered directly into the mouths of the congregation, lest the efficacious fragment be spirited away and employed in some nefarious

[78] See MacCulloch, *Thomas Cranmer*, pp. 505–8. Clark remarks that the two men 'were kindred spirits in their desire to reconcile the rival parties in Protestantism and in their skill in devising formulas to which as many as possible could subscribe' (*Eucharistic Sacrifice*, p. 122).
[79] Brooks, *Cranmer's Doctrine of the Eucharist*, p. 64; Letter by Bucer (1533), quoted in Stone, *History of the Eucharist*, II. 45.
[80] See p. 11 above.   [81] Cuming, *History of Anglican Liturgy*, p. 106.
[82] For a full list of the changes, see Brightman, *English Rite*, pp. cl–clv.
[83] Thomas Cranmer, *The First and Second Prayer Books of Edward VI*, ed. by E. C. Ratcliff (London: Everyman, 1910; repr. 1999), p. 392.

purpose, now the minister gives it 'to the people in their handes kneling', to pocket if they feel like it.[84] And if they still kneel, it is through ordinary respect, and not superstitious belief that they prostrate themselves before a present divinity, as the notorious 'black rubric' appended at the last minute to the 1552 Prayer Book explains:

> it is not ment thereby, that any adoracion is doone, or oughte to be doone, wyther unto the Sacramentall bread or wyne there bodily receyved, or unto anye reall and essencial presence there beeyng of Christ's naturall fleshe and bloude . . . And as concernynge the naturall body and blood of our saviour Christ, they are in heaven and not here.[85]

What symbolism is left is carefully controlled; as Cummings observes, this is a liturgy 'undeniably more verbal and less visual'.[86]

The verbal aspects too, are, thoroughly revised. The words of invocation and consecration lose their permissive ambiguity along with their black crosses: blessing and sanctifying are gone, as is the reference to 'thy holy spirite and worde'; communicants may be 'partakers of his most blessed body and bloud', but what they receive is 'thy creatures of bread and wyne'. Rosendale summarizes the effect of this change: 'The ambiguous metaphoricity of the 1549 formula is refracted and reoriented here in what Dix notes amounts to a formula of non-consecration.'[87] This movement continues in the moment of communion. As the Host is administered, the words spoken by the officiant turn the emphasis very firmly from an idea of intrinsic efficacy in the elements to the devotional and intellectual work required of the recipient. In 1549:

> The body of our Lorde Jesus Christe whiche was geven for thee, preserve thy bodye and soule unto everlasting lyfe.

In 1552:

> Take and eate this, in remembraunce that Christ dyed for thee, and feede on him in thy hearte by faythe, with thankesgeving.[88]

What is given here is thanks to God, not Christ to the people. The language of this second formulation recalls Cranmer's explanations in his dispute with Gardiner; 'feede on him in thy hearte by faythe' is a liturgical rendering of the polemical 'eat his flesh, thrust thorow with a speare, and drinke his bloud springing out of his side with our spirituall mouthes of our fayth'. Both are clearly invested in an idea of belligerent figuration, predicated on

---

[84] Cranmer, *First and Second Prayer Books*, pp. 230, 389.   [85] *First and Second Prayer Books*, p. 393.
[86] *The Book of Common Prayer*, ed. Cummings, p. xxxiii.
[87] Rosendale, *Liturgy and Literature*, p. 98; citing Dix, *Shape of the Liturgy*, p. 664.
[88] Cranmer, *Book of Common Prayer* (1549), ed. Cummings, p. 34; *First and Second Prayer Books*, p. 389.

the responsibility of the hearer or recipient to read right. There is no room in this revised liturgy for another form of belief, no loophole or lifeline left for doctrinal conservatives like Gardiner; England at last had a vernacular liturgy that was thoroughly and unequivocally reformed.

Not, however, for long. Cranmer's revised *Book of Common Prayer* came into effect on All Saints' Day 1552; on 6 July 1553 King Edward VI, always sickly, died, and after a brief and doomed scramble for a Protestant accession, his Catholic sister Mary took the throne. One of her first acts was to repeal the Prayer Book, and to reinstate the Latin Mass; it is at this point that Cranmer's authorial involvement with the English liturgy ends. After a trial for heresy and a repudiation of his reformed beliefs, he was burned at the stake in 1556; on the last day of his life he dramatically reverted once more to the Protestant faith, and held the hand that had signed his recantation steady in the flames.[89] Cranmer did not live to see the order change, once again, on Mary's death just two years later; how he would have regarded the lightly revised vernacular liturgy reinstituted by the new Protestant queen Elizabeth is therefore a matter for speculation. In any case, the work that was Cranmer's lasting legacy now takes on an existence independent of the theology of its chief author, obliquely and contestedly expressed as that was even in the two versions produced in his lifetime. Whatever they may have thought about it, the writers in this study – with the possible exception of Robert Southwell (who was, from the age of fifteen, educated on the continent) – all had a deep familiarity with a *Book of Common Prayer* written by Cranmer, but which did not necessarily reflect either his own beliefs or the agreed doctrine of the church in England.[90] This Prayer Book, the last revision for a hundred years, was instituted in 1559 with 'three minor but significant changes' from the 1552 version: fulminations against the Pope's 'detestable enormities' were removed from the Litany; the 'black rubric', which offered a pragmatic rationale for kneeling during communion, was dropped; a new formula for administration was devised by simply bolting the 1549 words on to those of 1552.[91] Collectively, these alterations move the liturgy away from

---

[89] MacCulloch, *Thomas Cranmer*, pp. 601–3.
[90] Dix sees a contradiction enshrined at the most fundamental level of the liturgy: 'It could not reasonably be maintained that Anglicanism as such has ever been Zwinglian in doctrine. But a great part of Anglican history is taken up with difficulties caused by the fact that the Anglican rite was framed with exquisite skill to express this doctrine which the Anglican Church had always repudiated, tacitly since 1559, explicitly since 1563' (*The Shape of the Liturgy*, p. 670).
[91] Bryan D. Spinks, *From the Lord and 'The Best Reformed Churches': a Study of the Eucharistic Liturgy in the English Puritan and Separatist Traditions, 1550–1633* (Oregon: Wipf and Stock, 1984), p. 21; Cranmer, *First and Second Prayer Books*, p. 362; *Book of Common Prayer*, ed. Cummings, p. 117.

what doctrinal stability it had achieved in 1552; the revisions of 1662, when the *Book of Common Prayer* returned from continental exile after its Interregnum absence, continued this conservative trend.[92] Ambiguity is resurgent, a belief in the real presence of Christ in the eucharist tolerated if not encouraged; the Prayer Book that would endure was once again an interpretatively permissive, complicatedly figurative text.

In some ways, the details of the distinction between what the Prayer Book says and what it means are almost irrelevant for the argument that follows: what is important is to recognise that the Anglican Church embodies in its doctrinal foundation a culture of fissure and flexibility when it comes to words and their significations, and that this could be seized on with devotional intent by the poets and writers who were members of that church. Because thinking about the nature of God must ultimately entail the nature of language, worship and writing, the respective practical expressions of these activities, are cognate: a rhetorical figure can describe, and describe the shape of, a theological belief. Cranmer's new Prayer Book establishes a framework for this dynamic both in its liberties with words and in the peculiar status it accords them: the vernacular liturgy, on the one hand, makes the word absolutely central to worship, and, on the other, it robs it of its power to effect itself, or to claim any but a figurative truth. The qualified literalism of the old Catholic rite has disappeared, and left in its place a world of rhetorical possibility: words cannot turn into things, or turn things into other things, but they can assert and even enact their ability so to do. Hyperbole can insist on Christ's presence in the Host; punning can perform it. However gradually, and whatever the subtleties of the situation at any given point, the Reformation acted as a lever to separate the sign from what it signified, to institute a distinction between symbol and reality; the literary history of the succeeding century is in many ways the record of how writers responded to what was at once a loss and an opportunity. '[I]t is hard to avoid the conclusion', Gerrish writes, 'that something portentous was making its appearance in Zwingli's explanation of the sacraments, and that poetry and art had as much cause for alarm as did divinity.'[93] Though he is absolutely right to identify the importance of

---

[92] The communion service in the Restoration Prayer Book was substantively the same as that of 1559, but with the rubric changed to make it even less radical in its stance on eucharistic presence; the left-over consecrated elements were no longer given to the curate's own use, for example, but he was directed 'immediately after the blessing, reverently [to] eat and drink the same' (Brightman, *English Rite*, II. 717). For a description of the changes, see Stone, *History of the Eucharist*, p. 321; for the fortunes of the Prayer Book during the Interregnum and on Charles II's accession, see Cuming, *History of Anglican Liturgy*, pp. 146–67.

[93] Gerrish, *Grace and Gratitude*, p. 167.

this cultural revolution, Gerrish misjudges its effect: what may have been cause for alarm for divinity was, on the contrary, cause for excitement for poetry and art; the central place that ritual had held in the religious life of the people was to be taken by words, and the creative possibilities that resulted from this monumental shift were limitless.

WRITING AFTER THE REFORMATION: 1559–1674

From its inception, the Protestant Church in England held within it the potential for – even an inevitability of – conflict over its theology of the eucharist. The rhetorical interest of this fact, its implication for a theory of signification, has been explored; its political consequences were also highly significant for the writers that inherited this masterfully equivocal liturgy, and who form the subject of this study. A doctrinally ambivalent communion service would inevitably have been a cause of tension in an ostensibly Calvinist institution, even were it not for the additional complication of the non-conformist views (both Catholic and, more significantly as the new century progressed, Puritan) that came swiftly to challenge its orthodoxy. At the end of the Elizabethan period, however, and throughout the reign of James I, on the surface the situation seemed, if fundamentally elastic, at least relatively stable. Prayer Book worship was increasingly established, and it attracted in Richard Hooker a forceful and eloquent defender; the monumental fifth book of his *Laws of Ecclesiastical Polity* (1597) discusses in great detail the devotional prescriptions of the *Book of Common Prayer* in the course of outlining what would come to be known as the Anglican 'via media', or middle way, between Puritanism and Catholicism. Hooker advocates the ambiguity he finds enshrined in Cranmer's liturgy, and condemns questions about the manner of Christ's presence in the communion service as 'enemies to pietie'. He also borrows the archbishop's vividly figurative mode of expressing himself: 'let curious and sharpe witted men beate their heades about what questions themselves will', he writes;

> the very letter of the word of Christ giveth plaine securitie that these misteries doe as nayles fasten us to his verie Crosse, that by them we draw out, as touching efficacie, force and vertue, even the bloud of his goared side, in the wounds of our redeemer we there dip our tongues, wee are died red both within and without.[94]

Hooker measures precisely the same rhetorical distance as Cranmer between corporeal vehicle and spiritual tenor; the 'nayles', for all their

---

[94] Richard Hooker, *Of the Lawes of Ecclesiasticall Politie: the Fift Booke* (London, 1597), p. 181.

startlingly bloody effect, are simply a powerful figure for the eucharistic 'misteries'. His, too, both doctrinally and stylistically, was an influential example.

For all its temperate idealism, the *Laws of Ecclesiastical Polity* comes out of a situation of some strain; a recent editor writes of Hooker's 'perception of the age as a perilous one, a time in which persistent and conflicting discontents with the 1559 settlement threatened the most basic social and spiritual values'.[95] A significant sector of the population was ideologically estranged from the common worship, whether from adherence to tenets of the old faith, or from a conviction that the reforms did not go deep or far enough. Elizabeth's government was ruthless in outlawing and punishing the defaulters. Jesuit renegades like Robert Southwell, the subject of the first chapter of this book, were supressed with an efficient savagery that may have suggested a certain anxiety on the part of those in power, but also demonstrated clearly the strength of Protestant authority. As a fervent Catholic and early exile from his country, Southwell stands at an oblique angle both to the institutional structures described here and to the literary tradition that continues to efface his influence; he represents, in the terms of this study, a rhetorical oddity that nonetheless provides a foundation for much of what follows. Southwell's *oeuvre* is an early attempt to forge a voice for devotional poetry in the vernacular; it picks up on a hint in Sir Philip Sidney's *Defence of Poesy* (*c.*1580) that instead of writing 'lyrical kind of songs and sonnets', poets would be better employed 'singing the praises of the immortal beauty, the immortal goodness of that God who giveth us hands to write and wits to conceive'.[96] Important as Southwell's poetry was in both missionary and devotional terms, however, the word was never so central to his imagination as the flesh – Christ's, as the transubstantiated elements he administered to England's recusant community, and his own, offered as imitation and response in his martyr's death. Southwell favoured the figure of paradox, and in one sense his position as a priest and writer was itself paradoxical: he believed, perhaps more firmly than any other writer considered here, in the sacramental efficacy of words, but not in the transference of that efficacy across the domain of liturgy to that of literature. The rhetorical opportunities presented by Cranmer's polemical insistence on the figurative nature of realist language proved intellectually uncongenial to the young Catholic.

---

[95] Richard Hooker, *Of the Laws of Ecclesiastical Polity*, ed. by Arthur Stephen McGrade (Cambridge University Press, 1989), p. xv.
[96] Sidney *'Defence of Poesy'*, pp. 48–9.

Twenty years after Southwell was hanged at Tyburn, the grounds of contention in English church politics had shifted decisively, and the most significant disagreements were no longer between Protestants and the now-routed Catholics. Two opposing factions had developed in the newly-established church: the first remained staunchly Calvinist on the subject of predestination, valuing its grace as conveyed by the preached word of God over any benefit that might be conferred by the eucharist; the second group, the Arminians, took a contrary stance, elevating the role of outward worship (public prayer, the administration of the sacraments) to the position of prime importance.[97] On the accession of Charles I, the Arminians rose into the ascendancy, led by the notorious figure of Archbishop William Laud. John Donne and George Herbert (who died within a few years of one another, in 1631 and 1633 respectively) were spared the escalating doctrinal and political tensions of the 1630s that culminated in the drastic upheaval of the established church and, ultimately, the executions of archbishop and king. While the precise causes of the civil war in England remain in dispute, it is generally allowed that the Arminian policies pursued by Laud with such inflexible rigour played a significant part in bringing matters to a crisis; his insistence on the importance of the external accoutrements of worship – the fabric of the church, its adornment and decoration, the splendour and positioning of altar and font – was viewed by the Puritan element with a suspicion bordering on hysteria. The rationale behind such an emphasis was the real point at issue: Christ's presence in the Host, and so in the church, demanded a setting of appropriate magnificence; it also posed a serious threat to the Calvinist doctrine of predestination, and therefore to the whole basis of the Protestant faith. 'Arminian rejection of the central Calvinist doctrines of assurance and perseverance', Peter Lake explains, 'opened the way to what the Godly regarded as a popish doubtfulness on the issue of personal salvation and an equally popish reliance on human

[97] See Nicholas Tyacke, *Anti-Calvinists: the Rise of English Arminianism, c.1590–1640* (Oxford: Clarendon Press, 1987). As a description of those who believed in this kind of sacramental ceremonialism, 'Arminian', after the Dutch theologian Jacobus Arminius, is a vexed term: historians who have challenged Tyacke's account of a harmonious Calvinist establishment undermined by the insensitive imposition of quasi-popish practices and rituals have also challenged the accuracy of his label. See, among others, Peter Lake, 'The Rise of Arminianism Reconsidered', *Past and Present*, 101 (1983), 34–54. The term 'anti-Calvinist' used in preference is, however, equally problematic, particularly for this study: it refers specifically to the main divisive issue, which was predestination, without necessarily taking account of Calvin's (admittedly contradictory) views on eucharistic presence, which were in fact closer to those of men like Lancelot Andrewes and Laud than those of their opponents. To avoid confusion, and because it has the advantage at least of being a contemporary term, I will use 'Arminian', with the usual caveats.

works to merit salvation.'[98] Among other pressing ideological and political concerns, England went to war over the question of real presence: the conflict was in one sense the legacy of the Prayer Book's ambiguity over the sacraments, itself an inevitable inheritance from the bifurcated theologies of the earliest continental reformers.

Donne and Herbert, though in rather different positions within its hierarchy, both developed their rich and intricate understandings of sacramental grace in a culture of broad conformity within a national church. The case of Donne, who converted from Catholicism and went on to be one of the most influential Protestant divines of his day, is evidently rather more complex, as I will go on to discuss in greater detail in Chapter 2 below: whatever the precise nature of his mature beliefs, however, he was at least able to hold them as part of an established institution. This is certainly not to suggest that the church he served was internally unified, or proof against attack from without; its liturgy and practice of worship had, though, the stability of a couple of generations' use, its bishops a relationship of mutual support with a monarch who enjoyed the confidence of the majority of his subjects. Unlike Herbert, Donne never found a convincing way to write about the eucharist in his devotional poetry. An older doctrinal apprehension keeps him, so passionately resourceful in other ways, 'strategic rather than euphoric' when thinking directly about this subject, though he often exploits the trope's doubling and splitting possibilities in his secular verse.[99] It was his younger friend, Herbert, who would prove to be the truest inheritor of the culture of permissive figuration instituted by Cranmer's Prayer Book, and shored up by Hooker's *Laws*; first as University Orator at Cambridge, and then as the incumbent of the living of Fugglestone-with-Bemerton in Wiltshire, he evolved a devotional poetics and a faceted theology of the eucharist alongside one another. The old controversy over the shades of Herbert's belief is at least partly a result of his reliance on a rhetoric which, to borrow Sidney's words again, 'never affirmeth';[100] he found the English church of the 1620s and 1630s a hospitable place to experiment with forms of expression that were inward and ambivalent enough to shape his experience of eucharistic grace.

For Richard Crashaw and Henry Vaughan, born respectively in 1612/13 and 1621, the situation was rather different. Charles I was an awkward and

---

[98] Peter Lake, 'Anti-popery: the Structure of a Prejudice', in *Conflict in Early Stuart England: Studies in Religion and Politics 1603–1642*, ed. by Richard Cust and Ann Hughes (Harlow: Longman, 1989), pp. 72–106 (p. 90).

[99] Cruickshank, *Verse and Poetics in George Herbert and John Donne*, p. 97.

[100] Sidney, '*Defence of Poesy*', p. 34.

aloof ruler, his hold on power less firm than his father's; the new king's position was fatally weakened by the high-handed dismissal of Parliament, just four years after his accession in 1625, which ushered in an eleven-year period of Personal Rule. During this time, Charles compounded the imposition of unpopular policies such as the annual levying of 'Ship Money' – a non-parliamentary levy which was widely condemned as unlawful and expedient – with religious beliefs that were perceived as suspiciously high church.[101] His attempt to impose an order of worship on Scotland that was Laudian in temper, if not actually authored by Laud, led directly to a crisis in relations between the two countries when it was violently rejected by Scottish worshippers. Known as the 1637 *Book of Common Prayer*, the rite used only the words of administration of 1549 (unleavened even by the receptionist formula of 1552), thus 'stressing that the sacramental elements were in some way the body and blood of Christ'; this retrograde step proved unacceptable to congregations north of the border, and the resulting riots led to the bishops' wars between England and Scotland which immediately preceded the English Civil War.[102] As ever, political and doctrinal concerns were closely allied: 'Dost thou say Mass at my lug?' was the cry of Protestant outrage said to have greeted the first performance of the 1637 liturgy in Edinburgh.[103]

Within England, too, the conflict took doctrinal lines, and the ascendant parliamentarians sought to impose their own order of worship on its congregations. John Morrill describes the fate of the religion Crashaw and Vaughan had grown up with: 'the old church was dismantled piecemeal between 1641 and 1646. Laudian innovations in doctrine, government, discipline and liturgy were overthrown, and ecclesiastical jurisdiction was emasculated.'[104] It was not just the recent changes in practice that came under attack. During this period, the *Book of Common Prayer* suffered its only real eclipse in England between 1559 and the mid-twentieth century: its use was prohibited by Parliament on the same day as its bill of attainder against Archbishop Laud.[105] Cranmer's Prayer Book was replaced by the

---

[101] See L. J. Reeve, *Charles I and the Road to Personal Rule* (Cambridge University Press, 1989), pp. 212–13 *et passim*.

[102] Spinks, *Sacraments, Ceremonies and the Stuart Divines*, p. 96; see pp. 69–112 for a full discussion of the abortive 1637 Prayer Book.

[103] *The Writings of Thomas Carlyle: Historical Essays*, ed. by Chris R. Vanden Bossche (Berkeley: University of California Press, 2002), p. 637.

[104] John Morrill, 'The Church in England, 1642–1649', in *Reactions to the English Civil War, 1642–1649*, ed. by Morrill (Basingstoke: Macmillan, 1982), pp. 89–114 (p. 92).

[105] As Rosendale points out; 'indicating', he goes on to explain, 'the high and related priority of both actions' (*Liturgy and Literature*, p. 6).

Directory of Public Worship (1645), a much simpler liturgy with no set forms; these were felt to inhibit spontaneity, and so to be injurious to the operation of the spirit. The result was a much slimmer volume, running to only forty pages as against the 1559 Prayer Book's three hundred and twenty-four. The order for the 'Celebration of Communion, or the Sacrament of the Lord's Supper', for example, gives only hints and suggestions in place of the long prayers formerly demanded of the officiant:

The Elements being now sanctified by the Word and Prayer, The Minister, being at the Table, is to take the Bread in his hand, and say, in these expressions (or other the like used by Christ, or his Apostle upon this occasion:)
   According to the holy Institution, command, and example of our blessed Saviour Jesus Christ, I take this Bread, and having given thanks, I break it, and give it unto you (There the Minister, who is also himself to communicate, is to break the Bread, and give it to the Communicants:) *Take ye, eat ye, This is the Body of Christ which is broken for you, Do this in remembrance of him.*[106]

The effect was to dispense with the idea of 'common' prayer altogether; as a counter-proclamation issued by the king claimed, 'it will break that uniformitie which hitherto hath been held in Gods service'.[107] Although it is possible to overstate the centrality of the eucharist as a structural feature of ordinary parishioners' lives (most attended communion only about once a year), it is clear that there was some imaginative attachment to the service whose celebration now, in some areas, 'dwindled away almost to nothing'.[108]

Certainly both Crashaw and Vaughan were deeply committed to the old order, and regarded its defeat by Puritan forces with dismay; their poetic responses to the spiritual disenfranchisement represented by the change, and the consequent reformulations of their beliefs about the eucharist, are discussed in Chapters 4 and 5. That the poetry of each was shaped by these events and their implications for worship is not in doubt. Crashaw, removed from his fellowship at Peterhouse, left for the continent in 1644 and converted to Catholicism – a move that critics have traditionally seen anticipated in the opulent and excitable poetry he was writing even while still in England. Vaughan had no living to lose (though his brother did, and lost it); he remained firmly Anglican, and expressed his tenacity and his dispossession in the two volumes of *Silex Scintillans* (1650 and 1655) which

[106] *A Directory for Publique Worship of God thoughout the Three Kingdoms of England, Scotland, and Ireland* (London, 1645), p. 25.
[107] *His Majesties Proclamation, Concerning the Book of Common-prayer, and the Directory for Publike Worship . . . With some Observations Thereupon* (Oxford [London], 1645), p. [2].
[108] Arnold Hunt, 'The Lord's Supper in Early Modern England', *Past and Present*, 161 (1998), 39–83 (82).

constitute his major poetic achievement, though he was to live for another forty years after writing them. For both men, the republican Interregnum, with its hostile anti-Laudian policies, constituted an absence which compounded a deeper absence. The loss of the rites and ceremonies of their church was a blow, but underlying both Crashaw's move to Catholicism and Vaughan's nostalgic adherence to Anglicanism was a longing for a more securely sacramental mode of worship: an assurance of grace, and of Christ's presence in the world. What Crashaw found in the Church of Rome, Vaughan sought in the devotional writings of his predecessors: Cranmer's Prayer Book, the Bible, Herbert's *Temple*.[109] Cummings remarks on 'a royalist habit of collecting antiquarian prayer books as precious relics during the Interregnum',[110] and this is what Vaughan does in spirit, if not in fact. He, more than Crashaw, creates a poetics of compensation: 'The relationship Vaughan wants his readers to have with his text', John Wall observes, 'is one of finding in it a common meeting ground in a shared experience of loss.'[111] The idea of eucharistic presence becomes in *Silex Scintillans* something more gentle and diffuse, and also more distant, than the fleshly confrontations that populate Crashaw's verse; both men, though, are driven by an increasingly hopeless desire to find a mode of rhetorical incarnation that will supply the liturgical deficiency, and the doctrinal lacuna that underlies it.

The last writer in this study, John Milton, offers a complicated contrast to the writers considered in earlier chapters. As a committed – if doctrinally idiosyncratic – Puritan, and a staunch republican, Milton occupies an ideological position quite opposed to that of his younger contemporaries; he is a fair distance as well, of course, from the beliefs that characterise the writings of Southwell, Donne and even Herbert. The overthrow of the established church that so dismayed Crashaw and Vaughan was for Milton a cause of great satisfaction; it is its re-establishment at the restoration of Charles II in 1660, a bitter defeat for the old anti-monarchist, that prompts the sense of disillusion and dispossession felt in his late works. Milton was 'radically antiliturgical' throughout his career, and he was vehemently opposed to the set forms of the *Book of Common Prayer*.[112] The executed Charles I is contemptuously excoriated in the *Eikonoclastes* for borrowing a

---

[109] Vaughan's reliance on these sources, a marked feature of his work, is discussed briefly in Chapter 4, pp. 154–8, below.

[110] *Book of Common Prayer*, ed. Cummings, p. xiv.

[111] John N. Wall, *Transformations of the Word: Spenser, Herbert, Vaughan* (Athens, GA: University of Georgia Press, 1988), pp. 281–2.

[112] Rosendale, *Literature and Liturgy*, p. 181.

prayer from Sidney's *Arcadia* ('a Prayer stol'n word for word from the mouth of a Heathen fiction praying to a heathen God'); this reliance on the words of others is held up as an act of spiritual and intellectual poverty: 'he who wants a prayer to beseech God in his necessitie', Milton sniffs, ''tis unexpressible how poor he is'.[113] Milton's response to the reinstitution of the Prayer Book in 1662 can be imagined; he was not a regular church-goer in the last years of his life. Achsah Guibbory describes Milton's poetic response to the altered political situation in terms oddly reminiscent of Wall's vision of the recusant Vaughan: 'As encoded histories of idolatry that spoke to the situation of Restoration England,' she writes, 'Milton's poetry also constituted a site for true worship in an England polluted by idolatrous forms.'[114] This may be so: though Milton's aesthetic of absence is clearly different from the younger poet's, proceeding from quite contrary causes and finding an entirely individual expression, *Paradise Lost* is nonetheless a work, as the title asserts, that responds to some profound consciousness of loss. The final chapter of this book investigates this loss in terms of Milton's thinking about the eucharist, and seeks to demonstrate that the poem both has a perhaps surprising continuity with the devotional literature of the preceding century, and is its consummation. A preoccupation with the absent body of Christ and its refiguration in words characterises the post-Reformation writings of Southwell, Donne, Herbert, Crashaw and Vaughan; despite his polemical vituperation of the idea, it finds an echo and an answer in the great post-Restoration achievement of Milton's *Paradise Lost*.

EUCHARIST TROPED

This study follows the literary afterlife of a shift in orthodoxy and its concomitant polemical discourses that transformed the sacrament of the eucharist from a vessel of grace into its symbol. What had previously been understood literally – the words Christ spoke at the Last Supper, and which became the words of institution – Cranmer invested with a rhetorical force; when a prosecutor at his trial objected that Christ would not use misleading figures in his last testament, the former archbishop replied, 'Yes, he may use them well enough. You know not what tropes are.'[115] The implication of

---

[113] Milton, *Eikonoklastes*, 2nd edn (London, 1650), pp. 11, 15.
[114] Achsah Guibbory, *Ceremony and Community from Herbert to Milton: Literature, Religion and Conflict in Seventeenth-Century England* (Cambridge University Press, 1998), p. 189.
[115] Cranmer to Oglethorpe; quoted in Anderson, *Translating Investments*, p. 52.

this shift for lyric poetry is the subject of what follows; the six authors considered here span the early modern period, and represent between them a variety of doctrinal and confessional positions, from Jesuit to Puritan. The book is based on the idea that particularities of belief can be made manifest in the verbal texture of a literary work: that there is an analogy between the rhetorical and theological planes of understanding, and that their relation can be traced quite precisely. The most characteristic figures or tropes in a body of devotional poetry in this period are often used to express a conception of the mechanics of the eucharistic transformation, even when that is not the explicit point on which a poem meditates. Because the incarnation (word made flesh) and its liturgical re-enactment (bread made body) are fundamentally concerned with the power and possibilities of language, they exert a compelling imaginative pull. Protestant sacramentalism privileges the figurative, and the eucharist acts as a model for rhetorical expression: 'The eucharist is the perfect combination of divine and human, a sacred movement encompassing the real, imaginary and symbolic. It is an identification from the body toward language and return.'[116] Each chapter of this study therefore takes as its subject the eucharist, and associated notions of real presence and transubstantiation, as they are expressed by or refracted through a rhetorical trope that is particularly significant in a writer's *oeuvre*: paradox in Southwell; punning in Donne; *metanoia* in Herbert; metonymy in Crashaw; synecdoche in Vaughan; and, lastly, metaphor in Milton.

The case studies that comprise this book illuminate and develop a central thesis about the continued importance of the transformative dynamic of the eucharist for poets and writers well into the seventeenth century, as a matter of literary and rhetorical, and not just doctrinal, concern. This way of confronting the texts unites the two most marked trends in recent criticism: the historical approach, which reads a sermon or a poem exclusively for what it might say about a contemporary political or theological situation, and the more technical rhetorical approach, which interests itself in particular occurrences of a figure or trope regardless of context. One thing this book does not attempt, however, is a revisionist reassessment of its subjects' confessional stances; it does not seek to surprise Catholic sentiments in Protestant mouths, or vice versa: rather it notices the surprising diversity of contemporary orthodoxy, and the

---

[116] Kathleen O'Grady, 'The Pun or the Eucharist?: Eco and Kristeva on the Consummate Model for the Metaphoric Process', *Literature and Theology*, 11 (1997), 93–115 (105).

possibilities of ambiguous expression allowed by the post-Reformation literary climate. Though this way of reading does offer at times an insight into an unexpected perspective, its primary interest is not in doctrine or in the calibration of belief, but in the pressure brought to bear on the world of the imagination and the language of poetry by the eucharistic controversies of the seventeenth century.

CHAPTER I

Southwell and paradox

Robert Southwell, Jesuit priest, martyr and poet, occupies a curious place in the genealogy of the devotional lyric in English. He is an early practitioner, and this accident alone sets him apart: Southwell's choice of career prevented him from surviving into the seventeenth century, where most studies of the subject find their focus, as well as determining much of the material and method of his work. Compared with figures like Donne, Herbert and even Crashaw, he is not much read, but in some ways his position can be seen as both central and influential; the defence of sacred verse and its valorisation over its secular counterpart that prefaces his first collection is framed in strikingly familiar terms. 'Poetes by abusing their talent', it opens, 'and making the follies and feyninges of love the customary subject of theire base endeavors, have so discredited this facultye that a Poett a lover and a lyer, are by many reckened but three wordes of one significacon.' So far so reminiscent of Sidney, Aristotle, Plato. After invoking the Psalms as a scriptural precedent, another manoeuvre since become proverbial, Southwell goes on to offer his own efforts as a humble corrective to the decadent modern practice of amorous verse: 'because the best course to lett them see the error of their works is to weave a newe Webb in theire own loome; I have heere laied a few course thridds together to invite some skillfuller Wittes to goe forward in the same or to beginne some fyner peece wherein it maye be seene, how well Verse and Vertue suite together.'[1] The spirit of this manifesto is reproduced in practically all its particulars in, for instance, George Herbert's verses of worldly repudiation; 'The Forerunners' adopts its shape, too: 'beautie and beauteous words should go together'. From his earliest preserved verses, those printed in Walton's *Lives*, Herbert favours this Southwellian trope: 'Doth Poetry | Wear *Venus*

---

[1] Robert Southwell, in *Collected Poems*, ed. by Peter Davidson and Anne Sweeney (Manchester: Carcanet, 2007), p. 1. Subsequent references to the poems will be to this edition, and will be given as line numbers in the text.

Livery? only serve her turn? | Why are not *Sonnets* made of thee?'[2] Herbert makes no explicit reference to his predecessor in this appeal to God, unless the 'whole showls of *Martyrs*' who burn with heavenly love and earthly fire in the sonnet's opening lines can be understood as such, and that would be unusually ecumenically minded. Not mentioning him is not the only disservice Herbert does Southwell; the later poet comes to take what might be regarded as Southwell's place in subsequent accounts as the fount and origin of devotional verse in English. Here is Henry Vaughan in the preface to *Silex Scintillans*, another piece which both recalls and effaces Southwell: 'The first, that with any effectual success attempted a *diversion* of this foul and overflowing *stream*,' as he describes the parlous state of contemporary poetry, 'was the blessed man, Mr *George Herbert.*'[3]

The absence of Robert Southwell from the official history, as Alison Shell has demonstrated, cannot simply be put down to the fact that his works were not read by contemporaries; though his influence, she acknowledges, is 'much more discernible from internal than external evidence', more than a dozen editions of *Saint Peters Complaynte* appeared between 1595 and 1640, the vast majority from mainstream Protestant presses.[4] This absence has to do, rather, with the circumstances of his life and death, and with a particular quality of his verse; the two are, as he meant them to be, inseparable: I will consider this question at greater length below. Southwell's place at the start of this study is merited regardless of his influence or importance for contemporary poetics, however, though a convincing case could be made for both; the apostolic Catholicism that ensured both his martyrdom and his literary marginalisation also produced writing shot through with and shaped by a powerful commitment to a living sacramentalism that is distinct in surprisingly subtle ways from anything that comes after. Southwell's investment in a eucharistic dynamic is everywhere evident, but almost always as subject more than as method; as a priest with the power of transubstantiation quite literally at his fingertips, its poetic replication became less a matter of intellectual commitment than pragmatic pastoral necessity. His writing at times falters rhetorically because it privileges a Catholic literalism that was not available for seventeenth-century successors of any denomination; the complex set of interrelated substitutions that is such an important trope for

---

[2] Herbert, *Works*, pp. 176–7, 206.
[3] Henry Vaughan, *The Works of Henry Vaughan*, ed. by L. C. Martin, 2nd edn (Oxford: Clarendon, 1957), p. 391.
[4] Shell, *Catholicism, Controversy and the English Literary Imagination*, pp. 59, 61.

Southwell, book for body and words for wounds, is fulfilled finally beyond the text. This is because he was able to inhabit his own metaphor with unmatched immediacy and conviction: for him, its terms were realised in being reversed. His books stood in for his body in his mission as a recusant priest, ministering to the recusant community he could not physically reach; in martyrdom, the final act of his apostolate, that body was instead to stand in for his books, and the figurative was to give way to the literal. The message of faith and resistance Southwell imagined being inscribed by his punishment always took precedence over anything he himself could write, and his poetry is ultimately inhibited by this impulse to locate meaning outside the text.

Southwell understands martyrdom as the highest sacrament, the moment in which inward conviction is embodied in an outward and visible sign; it is an act of devotion and imitation, and a formative paradox that finds ultimate glory in horrible suffering. His creative powers were turned to this end from his early maturity. Verbal artistry in his work is always secondary to its imagined consummation, the figure that foreshadows the truth; because of the press of circumstances, however, and the way in which he would come to be read, Southwell's writing exhibits the first tremors of a rhetoricised sacramentalism that was to define the devotional poetry of the next generation. This study seeks neither to assimilate Southwell easily into this tradition by minimising the significance of his confessional position, nor to use his Catholicism to situate him outside the current of contemporary poetics and at a distance from its development. His work cannot be read apart from a consideration of his Jesuit apostolate, but neither its inspiration nor its interest was confined to recusant circles. If sacramental poetry is understood as an attempt to make present what is absent, then in an important sense this is what Southwell, whose works were intended for the solace and instruction of a disenfranchised congregation, was writing; but the absence he seeks to supply is not terminal as it is for later writers, and he has in mind another way to witness and enact Christ's presence on earth.

PARADOX, ANONYMITY AND THE JESUIT AESTHETIC

Some of what Southwell wrote is not very good. Though his exact contemporaries include Spenser, Sidney and Shakespeare, much of his verse sounds awkward in this company. Its plain rhythms, stark paradoxes and lucid chimes lack the flexibility and artistry of the verse-forms that evolved in the last decades of the sixteenth century, and recall instead the earnest sonneteers of Tottel's *Miscellany*. 'I dye alive' exhibits a kind of dutifully revised Petrarchanism, blunt and stagey:

> I live but such a life as ever dyes
> I dye but such a death, as never endes
> My death to end my dying life denyes
> And life my living death no whitt amends.   (ll. 5–8)

The reader is not, nor is she expected to be, surprised by such venerable reversals, though they have their own charm; the insistent impression is that Southwell cares more about the fact of the paradox than its reflex expression, or that his thoughts are focused slightly to one side of what he is writing. Various explanations have been put forward for this stylistic anachronism, this rhetorical naiveté. At fifteen Southwell was sent to be educated abroad, first at Douai and then at Rome; he did not return to England until he was a man of nearly thirty, when he began his mission and the writing in English that was an essential part of it. Scholars have speculated that Southwell may in the interim have forgotten his native language, or perhaps preserved intact the aesthetic standards of his youth, unaware that in his absence things had moved on.[5] In his astute study of the poet, F. W. Brownlow offers a more convincing, politically inflected version of this argument, reading Southwell's method as a mark of defiant doctrinal nostalgia: 'the new Renaissance English style was too closely associated with either a Protestant or a paganizing humanism for a recusant writer to adopt it, especially a Jesuit poet', Brownlow writes; 'one concludes that the Recusants' refusals evidently covered literature as well as churchgoing'.[6]

Southwell's style certainly reflects deeply held beliefs both in its rhetorical particularities and in its characteristic modes of expression. Paradox is found remarkably frequently in prose as well as poetry: it is the dominant figure in his work, and it features not just in the form of the verbal reversals he was almost automatically drawn to (which are not, it should be added, seen at their best in the predictable gaucheries of 'I dye alive'), but at a profound conceptual level as a cognitive framework within which to make sense of his political, cultural and theological situation. Sadia Abbas, in her persuasive account of this figure's operation in Southwell's work, defends him from the charge of lazily relying on an outmoded rhetorical trick by pointing out its

---

[5] See, for example, Pierre Janelle, *Robert Southwell, the Writer: a Study in Religious Inspiration* (London: Sheed and Ward, 1935), p. 32; Janelle cites a contemporary account which remembers that Southwell 'applied himself with much diligence to the study of his native tongue, which he had already nearly forgotten, because he had left England very young'.

[6] F. W. Brownlow, *Robert Southwell* (New York: Twayne, 1996), pp. 80, 85.

contemporary force: 'Southwell's fondness for paradox, which has also incurred the charge of *preciosité*, derives in part from the paradoxes, uncertainties, and confusions rife in English national and religious history at the time. The content motivates and earns the form.'[7] For this recusant priest in Elizabeth's reign, a figure which offered the possibility of radical reinterpretation proved compellingly seductive: what seems like power is weakness, subjection, strength; the imprisoned man is free and an agonising death on the gallows is a triumphant birth into eternal life. Brownlow calls this 'the martyr's looking-glass world in which things are their opposites', but for Southwell this way of thinking had become completely instinctive.[8] Paradox is twice at the heart of the Christian religion: in the incarnation of Christ, where base flesh and divine spirit are impossibly fused; and in his crucifixion, an experience of shame and suffering which is also, and *consequently*, the moment of greatest glory and exaltation. These are the patterns Southwell's mind traces in his rhetoric, and the mighty inversions they promise are imagined as monumental historical realities as well as instantiated very intimately in the flesh.

Gary Kuchar recognises the political ends to which these patterns may be put: 'Armed with the paradoxes of incarnationalist theology,' he writes, 'Southwell made of disempowerment a strangely empowering and socially disruptive stance.'[9] He may be thinking here of the great prose works, the *Epistle of Comfort* or *An Humble Supplication*; precisely this dynamic is also at work, however, in 'The Nativity of Christe', a short lyric that embodies the essence of Southwell's poetic. It progresses from a simple devotional meditation on the incarnation to a passionate asseveration of martyrdom, through the relentless logic of paradox. 'Behould the father is his daughters sonne,' it begins, 'The bird that built the nest is hatched therein' (ll. 1–2). The familiar contradictions of the incarnation are used to guarantee the real presence of Christ in the eucharist – a comparable defeat of human logic, riddlingly expressed: 'This gift doth here the giver given bestowe' (l. 15). The Host is a gift, Southwell concludes, that gives its recipient to God, and he determines to respond in kind; incarnation underwrites transubstantiation, which now impels martyrdom: 'God is my gift, himself he freely gave me | Gods gift am I and none but God shall have me'

---

[7] Sadia Abbas, 'Polemic and Paradox in Robert Southwell's Lyric Poems', *Criticism: a Quarterly for Literature and the Arts*, 45 (2003), 453–82 (458).

[8] Brownlow, *Robert Southwell*, p. 30.

[9] Gary Kuchar, *Divine Subjection: the Rhetoric of Sacramental Devotion in Early Modern England* (Pittsburgh: Duquesne University Press, 2005), p. 91.

(ll. 17–18). Paradox here, as elsewhere, is used to generate and underwrite a political position.[10]

Another feature of Southwell's writing that might be regarded as paradoxical, and which makes it seem unfamiliar in the lyrical context in which it is usually read, is its calculated submergence of the self. Even when the message has clear personal application, as when he offers himself as sacrifice in 'The Nativity of Christe', the poet uses a typological mode as a technique of deflection. The most intensely internal moments look not into the known individual but into an alternative scriptural reality: Southwell writes with passionate insight, but never about any human experience that is not an empathic, imaginative living through the history and ritual of the church. By conjuring biblical narrative in a way that is often perceptive and visually precise, Southwell seeks to bring before a readership deprived of the imagery and affect of traditional religion a verbal alternative for devotional contemplation. He ventriloquises the Virgin Mary, Mary Magdalene and of course St Peter, in the long poem *Saint Peters Complaynte* on which his seventeenth-century reputation chiefly rested; he describes with sympathetic acuity Joseph's discomfiture on discovering his virgin wife's pregnancy. The 'wakefull spie of jelious minde' wars with a conviction of her innocence, and 'Josephs Amazement' explores this miserable impasse without offering a resolution. 'She is a friend to love a foe to lothe,' is Joseph's final thought; 'And in suspence I hange betwene them bothe' (ll. 83–84). It is for the reader to supply the happy ending from scriptural knowledge, and to understand, too, that Joseph's difficulty in getting to grips with the idea of incarnation is reasonable, but that human fallibility requires the correction of faith. The poet has by the end withdrawn his own voice completely: in the absence of overtly directive writing, the lesson is to be learned by active critical reading that notices and interprets gaps and silences as well as what is actually there in the text; it is a subtle method of instruction. Scott Pilarz characterizes this as 'a kind of sacramental or ritual anonymity', as if Southwell were diminishing his own influence in order to emphasise the more significant divine presence in his work.[11] The result is a poetics of absence and immediacy that aspires to be the conduit for an apprehension of divine grace: that seeks to replicate, in other words, the function of the remote or incarcerated priest.

---

[10] This is a major point of Abbas's argument: 'Paradox frequently turns into polemic in Southwell's poems' ('Polemic and Paradox', 460).

[11] Scott Pilarz, *Robert Southwell and the Mission of Literature, 1561–1595: Writing Reconciliation* (Aldershot: Ashgate, 2003), p. 224.

Southwell is the least egotistical of poets, privileging imitation over invention, translation and commonplace over artistic originality; polemical self-effacement is the defining feature of his verse, and his prose, too, is drawn to the dissolution of the subject. The letter to Sir Robert Cecil, sent from prison two years before he died, was the last thing Southwell wrote; it splits under the twin pressures of civil brutality and the prospect of salvation, unsure whether to sue for mercy or death. He incriminates himself with an ingenuous optimism, confessing what tortures had failed to elicit, his status as a Jesuit priest, but trying to take refuge in old arguments of benignity and legitimacy: 'I have here sent you a sharp sword, yet as I suppose, well sheathed – I mean that which you conceive as a capital crime with that which I esteem a reasonable excuse.'[12] Eight months spent in the hands of the pursuivant Richard Topcliffe (an 'atrocious psychopath' in Geoffrey Hill's formulation) has unsettled the customary neat integration of paradox, and threatens the disciplined self-suppression of earlier works; by the end, though, Southwell resolves the conflict of his position by submitting to the loving violence of his faith and tricking himself into asking with elegant indirectness for execution: 'If I have been too coarse in the tenor of my compliments,' he writes as he draws to the end of this difficult letter, 'I need allege no more but that by this time the reader knoweth that the writer was no courtier.'[13] Southwell sues politely for the advancement of his own death; he succeeds, once more, in losing himself in the moment of self-assertion which this letter marks.[14]

Writing inspired by such an ethos feels exponentially more distant to a modern reader than Herbert's or Donne's, for all its simplicity; a greater effort of sympathy is required to understand the motives and appreciate the function of a work when personality is so far secondary to principle, and literary considerations are subsidiary to doctrinal ones. Southwell's writing is half of a project that was designed to end in martyrdom; it takes on multiple significations throughout his life and after his death, as a substitute for divine service or for the body of the priest – sometimes in surprisingly literal ways – and as memorial and relic. That project was, of course, a missionary one; since he entered the Society of Jesus in Rome in 1578,

[12] Robert Southwell, 'Letter to Sir Robert Cecil' (1593), in *Two Letters and Short Rules of a Good Life*, ed. by Nancy Pollard Brown (Charlottesville, VA: Folger Shakespeare Library, 1973), p. 83.
[13] Geoffrey Hill, 'The Absolute Reasonableness of Robert Southwell', in Hill, *The Lords of Limit: Essays on Literature and Ideas* (Oxford: Clarendon Press, 1984), pp. 19–37 (p. 22); 'Letter to Cecil', p. 85.
[14] Ronald J. Corthell describes this as 'a piece of courtship which uncannily aspires to transcendence of courtship, since the "advantage" it foresees is martyrdom' ('"The Secrecy of Man": Recusant Discourse and the Elizabethan Subject', *English Literary Renaissance*, 19 (1989), 272–90 (284)).

Southwell had been intent on returning to his native country to minister and proselytise to the dispossessed and discontented: this he was permitted to do in 1586. His six years at liberty in England were spent keeping recusant Catholics strong in the old faith and winning others to the cause; that his mission would end, almost inevitably, in the punishment of a traitor's death was more of a draw than a deterrent.

SOUTHWELL'S LITERARY APOSTOLATE

Because of the dangers involved in ministering to a recusant population in Elizabeth's England, very few priests came over from the continent, and fewer still survived the government's fearful vigilance for any length of time. Southwell's notional constituency, those who kept to the old faith, was numerous and widely dispersed. Writing had always been central to the Jesuit mission, even constitutive of it: priests far from their fellows were encouraged to correspond regularly, despite the obvious difficulties, in order to preserve a record of their work and to sustain morale in a situation often precarious and isolated. The written accounts of the lives and saintly deaths of others in the order took on a totemic significance; they were 'copied, circulated and retained by the recusants', Anne Dillon has found, 'and many ... became devotional texts of the Jesuit community'.[15] To extend this emphasis on the power of the written word into other aspects of his apostolate was for Southwell no great leap, and his verse as well as his prose must be understood as profoundly inspired and determined by his calling. This is not literature in a pure sense, if there is such a thing, but work that dramatises a spiritual state or evokes a sacramental presence: that teaches, counsels, consoles, demands devotional reading. As Robert Carballo notes, 'there can be no doubt that his literary work was an integral part of his Jesuit mission as much as it was the fruit of his Jesuit spirituality'.[16] Anne Sweeney, too, sees vocation and artistic production as mutually interdependent, and points out moreover an operational affinity: 'A connection between the function of rhetoric and pastoral practice', she writes, 'fixes Southwell's English poetic agenda clearly and completely to his Jesuit ministry.'[17] It is

---

[15] Anne Dillon, *The Construction of Martyrdom in the English Catholic Community, 1535–1603* (Aldershot: Ashgate, 2002), p. 77. She goes on to observe that 'The Jesuits Southwell, Weston, Garnet and others were careful collectors of such accounts'; Southwell had himself, while still in Rome, written one of these narratives, of the martyrdom of Christopher Baylis and Nicholas Horner (p. 84).

[16] Robert Carballo, 'The Incarnation as Paradox and Conceit in Robert Southwell's Poetry', *American Benedictine Review*, 43 (1992), 223–32 (225).

[17] Anne Sweeney, *Robert Southwell: Snow in Arcadia: Redrawing the English Lyric Landscape, 1586–1595* (Manchester University Press, 2006), p. 52.

the most elevated of pragmatic undertakings. The difficulty of ministering individually to each member of England's recusant community is to an extent overcome by offering the written word as a substitute for divine service; instead of sacrament or sermon administered in person by the priest, poems or devotional tracts circulate as surrogates. To be found in possession of such a document, of course, was to risk being prosecuted for treason, but these associated dangers simply compounded the significance of the work.

Southwell's writings construct a virtual church in an England where no other is possible; the arguments he makes, polemic or poetic, are his most effective means of pursuing his ministry, and there is a commensurate weight and urgency to his rhetoric. One of Southwell's most influential works, both itself derivative and much imitated, is *Mary Magdalens Funerall Teares* (1591); this extended prose meditation on the grief of the penitent Magdalen at the discovery of Christ's empty grave is vivid and empathic, a dramatisation of internal anguish in the form of various imagined exchanges that allow multiple first-person perspectives. The work is patient, richly varied in its shifts of tone and cadence, but with an unflinching concentration on its subject; the biblical narrative from which it is ultimately derived, John 20:1–18, is ornamented alternately with moments of surprising literal-mindedness and a numinous mysticism. Mary Magdalen's attractiveness as a figure of conversion and as a type of constancy and perseverance is clear, and Southwell's dedication makes explicit the topicality of this steadfast sinner-saint in a Counter-Reformation context. '[A]mong other glorious examples of this Saints life, I have made choise of her Funeral Tears, in which as shee most uttered the great vehemency of her fervent love to Christ, so hath she given therein largest scope to dilate uppon the same,' he writes to Dorothy Arundel, to whom the work was addressed: 'a theame pleasing I hope unto your self, and fittest for this time'.[18] Southwell's representation of the scene of Mary's distress in the garden, and its relief as a resurrected Christ appears to her, is almost forensic in its detailed evocations. He expounds with relentless grace the logic of every impulse of emotion, the obsessive circularity of every thought: his promise to dilate upon the theme is no idle one. 'Thou art . . . wholly inherited by the bloudy tragedy of thy slaughtred Lord,' the narrator tells Mary, and it is a preoccupation he shares (p. 27); this is a picture of the utter distraction of love bereaved, intended to be felt with allegorical force.

The climactic moment of the piece is Christ's appearance to Mary after her anguished hours of longing and searching for his body. This is not a

---

[18] Robert Southwell, 'Epistle Dedicatorie', *Mary Magdalens Funerall Teares* (London, 1591), unpaginated. Subsequent references will be to this edition and will be given as page numbers in the text.

drama of fulfilment, however, but a complex recalibration of expectation; first, Mary does not recognise the risen Christ, despite the sensuous asceticism of her fixation on his physical body in the preceding passages. It is only when the figure she takes for a gardener speaks her name that she realises who he is, and she acknowledges him with a single word, *Rabboni*, or 'Master': for all the verbal proliferation of the preceding pages, confronted with the object of her desire she is unable to speak.

Love would have spoken, but feare enforced silence. Hope frameth the words, but doubt melteth them in the passage: and when her inward conceits strived to come out, her voice trembled, her tongue faltered, her breath failed. (p. 59)

Southwell characteristically slows the narrative down to explore each instant with anatomising interest, switching tenses for immediacy and listening even for the vibration of a stillborn sound in her throat. Mary has finished with verbal utterance, though, and seeks expression through action in throwing herself at Christ's feet: 'She staied not for any more words, being now made blessed with the word himselfe' (p. 60). This turns out, though, to be a misreading. In one of the most curious turns of the biblical narrative, the restored Christ withdraws from Mary, saying 'Do not touch me.' Southwell makes this a powerfully didactic moment: Mary does not understand the form in which Christ is made present to her, and by disdaining words she has deprived herself of the Word. It is a salutary lesson for the sixteenth-century recusant, and this imposed movement from the literal to the figurative is explained by Christ himself:

It is now necessary to weane thee from the comfort of my externall presence, that thou mayst learn to lodge mee in the secretes of thy heart, and teach thy thoughts to supply the offices of outward senses. (p. 63)

'Through this transition from letter to spirit, from body to word,' Kuchar comments, 'we are presented with the devotional and rhetorical forms that produce the ideally pious recusant subject.'[19] Historical circumstance has necessitated a change in outward worship, and Southwell uses Mary Magdalen to figure the model response. As she has lost Christ's body from his tomb, so English Catholics have lost his real presence in the outlawed Mass; they must, as Mary does, find an alternative way to understand and experience divine proximity.

In *Mary Magdalens Funerall Teares* Southwell offers both instructions for the transposition and a text to compensate the lack; 'it may be', as the

---

[19] Kuchar, *Divine Subjection*, p. 61.

narrator speculates, 'thy inward presence supplieth thine outward absence' (p. 12). This is a meditation that stands self-consciously in for the service whose origins as a substitute for another kind of physical presence it describes. Imagery of food and eating runs through the piece, much of it explicitly eucharistic: 'Jesus is mine,' Mary asserts, 'sith on his bodie I feede' (p. 31). The physical privation of her vigil is entirely consonant with its spiritual deprivations, and one is made to figure the other: 'shee hath not what to eate, nor wherewith to foster her famished soule', the narrator reminds Christ, 'unlesse thou by discovering thy selfe, doest minister unto her the bread of thy body, & feede her with the foode, that hath in it all taste of sweetnesse' (p. 55). Southwell here describes a state familiar to English Catholics; though there is feeling and even emotional intimacy in the portrayal, his own voice is, as ever, lost in its ritual distance and stylistic abundance. But this is not simply a work to console and to inspire sacra-mental meditation; the contemporary situation is too urgent not to make itself felt. There is flint at the heart of this piece, and its message, familiar from Southwell's more explicitly polemical tracts, is one of no compromise. A delicately encoded warning reminds readers of the dangers of outward conformity; an imitation Mass, that is, a bloodless Protestant communion, is to be rejected at all hazards. *Mary Magdalens Funerall Teares* insists on the difference between a legitimate experience of Christ's presence (even if that must be clandestine or conjured imaginatively) and an illegitimate one; to the grieving Mary, even the angels who come to comfort her by the graveside are contemptible counterfeits of the real thing. '[T]hey were to thee', the narrator observes, 'like the glistering sparkes of a broken Diamond, and like pictures of dead and decaied beauties, signes, not salves of thy calamitie, memorials, not medicines of thy misfortune' (pp. 28–29). 'Signes, not salves'; 'memorials, not medicines'. Such is the cold comfort of a Reformation eucharist.

Southwell, though, must tread carefully here; his distinctions between the kind of mental work that is allowed and the kind that is not must be drawn with assurance, or else his priestless eucharist might end up resem-bling the institutional version it seeks to supplant. Throughout the piece there has been an emphasis on the constructions of memory, on the need to preserve imaginatively that which has been lost; at one point the narrator explains that it is only this impulse that stops Mary wishing for death: an 'unwillingnesse that his Image should die with her, whose likenesse love had limmed in her heart' (p. 5). The living memory is described as a 'relique', a sanctified object hidden in the closest of internal caskets. That Christ commands her to 'lodge mee in the secretes of thy heart' (p. 62) even after his resurrection turns this practice from a lesser form of communion into the ideal way of worshipping; recusants can carry with them an inalienable capacity to experience sacramental grace by remembering its operation, and a sensation of absence is paradoxically an assurance of presence. That secrecy here is presented in such a positive light is another polemical move. The Elizabethan state feared that which was hidden or concealed, the inner conviction of the inscrutable subject; traitors, as recusant priests and those who helped them were categorised, were punished by evisceration in a symbolic and theatrical exposure of secret inner spaces. Francis Barker makes the connection with contemporary dramatic modes: 'The discovery of the bleeding heart is the last act of both the tragedy of the blood and the terrible price of treason.'[20] The interpretative struggle around the martyr's last moments, to which I shall return, demonstrates a related unease: to impose judicial silence, as officials often did by interrupting the condemned man's speech, or as Southwell's gaolers accomplished over a longer period by refusing him ink and paper, was to compound a dangerous inwardness. Scrutineers couldn't let words pass because they were not confident of understanding hidden meanings or secret resonances (what has been called the 'hieroglyphics of the recusant poetic'): it is a recognised trope of Catholic martyrologies to claim that these meanings are anyway inscribed in the bodies and actions of the dying men, a triumphant reversal of the punitive intent of such expository butchery.[21]

BODY AS TEXT: IMITATION AND MARTYRDOM

Southwell always understood that his body would become a site of meaning in a way that was neither literal nor straightforwardly metaphorical, and this knowledge is of foundational importance for his literary work. Relatively early on in his training, he recognised and embraced the possibility that his life as a priest would end in martyrdom.[22] A seventeenth-century engraving, one of the few likenesses that exist (it is number 89 in a set of portraits of Jesuits), captures this sense of a life lived in anticipation of its end: Southwell looks with clasped hands and grave resignation out of the

---

[20] Francis Barker, *The Tremulous Private Body: Essays on Subjection* (London: Methuen, 1984), p. 90.

[21] Peter Davidson, 'Secret Southwell', paper given at the conference 'Robert Southwell: New Perspectives', St Edmund Hall, Oxford, 26 April 2008. Clifford Davidson comments that 'The power of his words during his years of freedom in England may also be attested by the fact that in order to silence his pen in prison he was apparently only once allowed writing materials' ('Robert Southwell: Lyric Poetry, the Restoration of Images, and Martyrdom', *Ben Jonson Journal*, 7 (2000), 157–86 (177)).

[22] 'From the time Southwell entered the Jesuit College in Douai, his life was a preparation for martyrdom, and his writing was part of that preparation' (Brownlow, *Robert Southwell*, pp. 23–4).

89

P.ROBERTVS SOVTHVELL, *Soc. Iesu*
Londini pro Cath.fide fuspensus et sec-
tus .3. mar. 1595.

Figure 1.1 Engraving of Robert Southwell.

frame, dagger already buried in his breast and rope knotted around his neck; an angel offers a heavenly crown. The iconography is conventional, but even so it is an uncanny match for Southwell's proto-martyrological imaginings. There is, however, something other than an insidious masochistic aesthetic in the welcome he extends to this fate. Literary frameworks are used to figure the tortures of the flesh: they become rewritings, allusive experiences connecting him with his church's past and, ultimately, with the broken body of Christ on which it is founded. '[L]et toil come,' he asks in the *Spiritual Exercises* written while he was still a young man at Rome; 'let come chains, imprisonment, torture, the cross of Peter and Andrew, the gridiron of Lawrence, the flayer of Bartholemew, the lions of Ignatius': his imagined tormentors cannot offer a stroke that will not recall and be sanctified by the memory of past martyrdoms. As this fantasy gathers pace and increases in intensity, the shadowy executioners of God's will disappear; the point is the pain, and he imagines it instantly and directly, with histrionic dignity:

by Thy wounds and the sufferings of Thy Saints, by thy merits and theirs, I most humbly beg that they [his agonies] may begin now at this very moment when I am writing, and last until the very end of my life. For thy sake allow me to be tortured, mutilated, scourged, slain and butchered. I refuse nothing.[23]

By the time Southwell comes to write *Mary Magdalens Funerall Teares*, there is greater rhetorical distance and more humility in the conceit, but the intellectual commitment to an emulative immolation has not changed; it has, if anything, focused itself with a more loving precision. Mary's thoughts of fitting herself to Christ's cross are brought up short by a realisation of unworthiness; it is a characteristically Southwellian paradox.

I would be nailed to the same crosse, with the same nailes, and in the same place: my heart should be wounded with his speare, my head with his thornes, my body with his whips: Finally I would taste al his tormentes, and tread all his embrued and bloudy steppes. But O ambitious thoughts, why gaze you upon so high a felicity? why think you of so glorious a death, that are privy to so infamous a life? (p. 16)

Thinking of the body as a text is certainly not new with Southwell; it is, indeed, enshrined etymologically in the very idea of martyrdom: the word comes from the Greek for 'witness', and was used in classical rhetoric to describe someone who could prove something by virtue of having seen or experienced it. By extension, as Susannah Brietz Monta points out in a significant new study, 'in religious discourse the word "martyr" has come to mean a person whose words, actions, and death offer authoritative testimony': even when judicially imposed, punishment and execution can have their meanings determined by, and in, their subject.[24] From this early etymological and cognitive connection, a whole host of complex and related

---

[23] Southwell, *Spiritual Exercises and Devotions*, trans. by P. E. Hallett and ed. by J.-M. de Buck (London: Sheed and Ward, 1931), pp. 103–4.

[24] Susannah Brietz Monta, *Martyrdom and Literature in Early Modern England* (Cambridge University Press, 2005), p. 4.

resonances arose, and by the sixteenth century martyrdom was constructed as an act inescapably literary, overwhelmingly artistic; at its heart was a fanatical redescription of an agonising and humiliating death as the greatest victory and best reward. It is there in Mary's imagining of Christ, 'his injuries turned to honours, the markes of his misery to ornaments of glory, and the depth of thy heavinesse to such a height of felicity' (p. 54). It is there, too, in almost the same terms, in Southwell's words to the imprisoned recusant aristocrat Philip Howard: 'Our teares shalbe turned into triumphe,' he writes to him in the cell in which he is to die, 'our disgrace into glorye, all our miseryes into perfect felicitye.'[25] This is a grim investment in the transformative power of rhetoric, and in the capacity of the silenced voice to fix its own significance. For as Dillon explains, the martyred body was a profoundly contested site, a hermeneutic battleground; even, she suggests, a figure that might frame meaning in its own right: 'Beyond the literal act of martyrdom, therefore, the martyr functions as a rhetorical device, a fecund lexicon through which the writers and image-makers from opposing doctrinal positions define their positions and mark out their differences across the religious divide.'[26] The body is a double-edged device, a paradox open in its eloquence to conflicting constructions: either the triumphant bastion of a steadfast faith, or the bloodied and mangled evidence of stubborn and culpable error.

Critics, at least since Pierre Janelle's pioneering study in 1935, have converged on the idea of describing Southwell's death as 'a work of art of supreme beauty'; Brownlow writes of Southwell's 'understanding of life lived as art, in his case the art of the imitation of Christ', and Sweeney believes that 'His martyrdom was in part an *artistic* act designed around his experience of the martyrdom of his friends and fellows, the poetry a prolepsis.'[27] All, to slightly different ends, read the narrative of his life as deliberately following a determined trajectory, awarding him artistic agency over the civil forces that tried and executed him. Their cue comes partly from Southwell's own writings: pre-imprisonment, necessarily. (Apart from that one letter to Cecil, uneasy and uneven, he wrote nothing for the last two and a half years of his life; of his views on the artistry of the tortured body following his own sadistic interrogation we therefore have no record.) The *Triumphs over Death*, composed relatively late on in Southwell's

---

[25] Southwell, *An epistle of comfort to the reverend priestes, & to the honorable, worshipful, & other of the laye sort restrayned in durance for the Catholicke fayth* (London, 1587), p. 113; hereafter *Epistle of Comfort*.
[26] Dillon, *Construction of Martyrdom*, p. 19.
[27] Janelle, *Robert Southwell*, pp. 286–7; Brownlow, *Robert Southwell*, p. 133; Sweeney, *Snow in Arcadia*, p. 277.

ministry to console Philip Howard for the loss of his sister, is characteristic in its attitude towards human life: 'thinke so curious workes ever safest in the artificers hand, who is likeliest to love them', he counsels, 'and best able to preserve them'.[28] Southwell's emphasis here is on God's role as artist ('artificer'), but the transition to thinking of the poet as his own author is not hard to make, particularly when contemporary constructions of judicial death also lie behind the association.

By the last decades of the sixteenth century, the process of execution for treason had evolved a distinct and ritualised rhetoric.[29] Government officers, the condemned man and the London crowds all recognised this framework and understood what was required of them; central to the drama was the identification of the priest on the scaffold with Christ on the cross. It is hard to overstate the importance of this link; it became a kind of art, and I will discuss the question of its specifically sacramental dimension below. There are, however, more immediate political and polemical aspects: to perform the identification convincingly was crucial in a period of such interpretative volatility. This was the moment at which contesting modes of figuration, and the faiths upon which they were predicated, looked to be vindicated; the closer the abject body came to Christ, the better for the cause. Dying well, and dying in accordance with this trope, is the most extreme rhetorical move there is, and Southwell's confident parallelisms demonstrate an absolute faith in its efficacy: 'As we are fellowes of his passions, so shall we be of his comforte, and if with him we dye, with him shall we live, and if we suffer his Crosse, we shall be partners of his Crowne.'[30]

It was an analogy inhabited by the victim and promulgated vigorously by his martyrologists, as hotly rejected by the Protestant state; accepted or denied, though, the symbolism was indisputably powerful. Southwell being jolted through the filthy streets on a bitter February morning; reaching Tyburn and wiping his face clean for a little dignity; silenced by the under-sheriff; allowed at last to speak: 'I ame brought hether to performe the laste acte of this misery . . .' To point out that this is self-consciously theatrical and profoundly mimetic is not to detract from its gravity or to forget that it was real breath choked out of Southwell's body that day; for the victim and

---

[28] Southwell, *The triumphs over death: or, A consolatorie epistle, for afflicted mindes, in the affects of dying friends* (London, 1595), p. 15; hereafter *Triumphs over Death*.
[29] 'Rules of style or decorum had developed or been imposed. Tropes, typologies and expectations – aesthetic, political or religious – were well known' (Pilarz, *Robert Southwell and the Mission of Literature*, p. 278).
[30] Southwell, *Epistle of Comfort*, p. 22.

those of his faith, though, each utterance or action, even the most involun-
tary, was fitted into a pattern and invested with religious significance.
Southwell's body was written with rope, axe and knife, and read by
spectators versed in the language of martyrdom: a bystander carefully
records that 'His holy harte leaped in the hangmanes hand.'[31] 'The initial
text of martyrdom was ... inscribed upon the body of the martyr'; thereafter, the graphic descriptions of death and dismemberment seek to rein-
terpret incisions meant to punish and humiliate as indications of sanctity
and accusations of barbarism; the evisceration designed to expose the
priest's helpless humanity instead achieves the full meaning of the text of
martyrdom under the inadvertent author's hands.[32] There is a political
impulse in establishing a trope wherein Protestant brutality accuses itself;
Catholic writers, Southwell among them, identified their very weakness and
vulnerability to judicial process as a sign of grace, and in doing so sought to
appropriate the power, and to assert the initiative, in the transaction
between Protestant law-maker and Catholic victim. But there is also a
powerful devotional imperative at work. Southwell becomes Christ-like in
the moment he enacts the imitative principles that govern his art: as he loses
himself, at last, in what was for him the supreme devotional and rhetorical
sign. The Passion is a moment at which body and text are completely
identified 'in an act of punishment and signification', in Barker's terms,
'from which all other meanings flow': Southwell's desire to offer his body as
a figure for the crucified Christ at the moment of death comes, as his critics
have seen, from a profoundly literary impulse. It is the consummation of the
martyrological aesthetic that dominates his work.[33]

As his books were designed to stand in for his body in ministering to the
recusant community of England, so was his body to stand in for his books in
this, his apostolate's 'last acte', and the logic of both substitutions is
sacramental. Indeed martyrdom is, for Southwell, the highest sacrament:
'So muche therefore as immitation in deede, is better then representation in
the figure, and desyre in the thoughte: So muche doth the baptisme of
blood, surpasse those of water and spirite,' he writes.[34] When Southwell
imagines the lessons of Christ's wounds in his own flesh, there is little
figurative distance in the conceit. It is in the *Epistle of Comfort*, surely among
the least comforting works of comfort ever composed, that Southwell gives

[31] The account of Southwell's death and these two quotations are from *A Brief Discourse of the Condemnation and Execution of Mr Robert Southwell*, quoted in Janelle, *Robert Southwell*, p. 88.
[32] Dillon, *Construction of Martyrdom*, p. 77.   [33] Barker, *Tremulous Private Body*, p. 24.
[34] Southwell, *Epistle of Comfort*, p. 142.

the idea its most relentless and explicit elucidation. He writes to the imprisoned Earl of Arundel to keep him steady in his Catholic faith, and to prepare him for the ingenious and agonising death of the convicted traitor. As it happened, Arundel escaped martyrdom by dying of his own accord; Southwell alone met the end he envisions for them both, and with the grace and resolution the *Epistle* urges. It is an uncompromising work, fanatically committed to a dynamic of transformation whose only end is death, and an agonising, humiliating death at that; there is nothing so degrading or distressing that it cannot undergo the paradoxical redescription that will exalt it into its opposite. Brownlow pities Arundel as 'the perfect embodiment of the Southwellian man, his comfort a sheet of paper assigning him to the absolute as rigorously in its own way as his judges' sentence'.[35] Throughout the work there is a profound preoccupation with writing the body, a preoccupation which vivifies some of its most arresting passages. Southwell invokes the past afflicted, and establishes an equation between word and flesh: 'we cal all auncient writers to witnesse, who by their bookes & many by their bloode, have before us laboured in the same quarell & confirmed the same faith'. He joins his witness to theirs, and asserts that the tortured body has an even greater power of meaning than the proselytising word: 'Our prisons preach, our punishmentes converte, our deade quarters and bones confounde youre heresye.'[36] The source text that must be transcribed into the body of the believer is, of course, the wounded Christ. His injuries, almost in grammatical declension, are to be written on Catholic flesh, and what seems a disgraceful death of harrowing torment is revised by its divine original into an experience of emulative glory. Southwell yearns for this translation with ecstatic violence; the pleas for torture, mutilation, scourging, death and dismemberment that sound through parts of the *Spiritual Exercises* are not muted here, are articulated, if anything, with fiercer study. St Paul is the figure to whose example Southwell turns as an ideal lector of Christ: he had 'no other reader but the *Crucifixe*, no other letters but his *Woundes*, no other commaes but his Lashes, no other full poyntes but his Nayles, no other booke but his *open syde*, and finallye no other lesson But ... to knowe Iesus Christe & him Crucified'.[37] This is the body as book in the most graphic terms, and the *Epistle* is a vivid demonstration of just how nearly Southwell's imagination touches his fearful exemplar.

---

[35] Brownlow, *Robert Southwell*, p. 34.   [36] Southwell, *Epistle of Comfort*, pp. 83, 197.
[37] Southwell, *Epistle of Comfort*, p. 29.

Perhaps the most frequently quoted passage of the *Epistle* is that in which Southwell compares the martyred body to a piece of 'torne or fretted velvet' whose 'ruptures, breaches & wounds' will on that account be the more gorgeously ornamented by the embroiderer: which, 'being wroughte over with curious knottes or flowers', will 'fare excel in shew the other whole partes of the velvet'.[38] It is not a new thought: the *Spiritual Exercises* have a passage in which Southwell rehearses this idea of the body as garment whose ugly wounds or jagged rents become its most valuable embellishment. 'If a prince should chance to tear a precious robe upon a nail', he reflects, 'the craftsman will repair it with such care and diligence that far from spoiling the appearance of the robe, the rent will even add to its beauty and value.'[39] In both of these imaginings, the embroiderer is God, but this conceit might stand for Southwell's own writing practice, his compulsion to transfigure bitter pain to exaltation through rhetorical re-description. Southwell is, for Hill, 'foresuffering his own agony, even as he rises above the fear and the violence'; he is also probing the limits of his own rhetoric.[40] Consider the strikingly similar terms in which Puttenham characterises that art, in a treatise published just two years after the *Epistle*: 'Figures and figurative speeches', he writes, 'be the flowers as it were and colours that a Poet setteth upon his language by arte, as the embroder doth his stone and perle, or passements of golde upon the stuffe of a Princely garment.'[41] In both his prose works and his poetry, Southwell performs this manoeuvre with cease-less conviction, embroidering over the martyred body with his words, and giving its wounds a voice to answer to the wounds of the crucified Christ. Here again is the absolute confidence in the power of rhetoric so character-istic of Southwell's writing and of the way he lived his life; physical act is equated with verbal utterance, and invested with the same potential for subversive or transformative meaning. Brian Oxley elucidates the funda-mental connection between devotion and rhetorical art: 'the "curious knots or flowers" of Renaissance rhetoric become a metaphor for the divine art which rewrites a mutilated, into a glorious body; a means of representing the transfigured reality, which is seen or imagined in meditation'.[42] Dying as he did, suffering as he knew he would the fate the *Epistle* foresuffers, was

---

[38] Southwell, *Epistle of Comfort*, p. 203.   [39] Southwell, *Spiritual Exercises*, p. 70.

[40] Hill, 'The Absolute Reasonableness of Robert Southwell', p. 28.

[41] George Puttenham, *The Arte of English Poesie*, ed. by Gladys Doidge Willcock and Alice Walker, 2nd edn (Cambridge University Press, 1970), p. 138. Anne Sweeney also notices this tropic coincidence (*Snow in Arcadia*, p. 275).

[42] Brian Oxley, 'The Relation between Robert Southwell's Neo-Latin and English Poetry', *Recusant History*, 17 (1985), 201–7 (206).

for Southwell the truth that guarantees the sign: the original that is imagined with such powerful prolepsis in his sacralised rhetoric.

TEXT AS BODY: WRITING, RELIC, SACRAMENT

After Southwell's death, the opportunities for substitutive signification presented by the writings he left increased in number and complexity; where his prose had been sermons, his poems services, manuscripts and printed books could now take on the status of relics. 'The poems, when offered by a priest, were almost sacraments in themselves,' Sweeney observes; 'offered by a martyr in the mould of Campion they were relics.'[43] Literal relics, those curious scaffold-side mementos still popular then throughout Europe, were preserved in the belief that martyrs were touched with divinity at the moment of their death, and that the miraculous effect was transferred to and lingered on in splashes of blood or fragments of flesh. Relics took many forms: those who gathered at the scaffold swabbed blood from the gallows and streets with their handkerchiefs, or secured little pieces of bone and hair.[44] Hill quotes a Victorian enumeration of the remains of one Thomas Bolliquer, or Bullaker, a Franciscan friar martyred some half a century after Southwell: 'a little piece of his heart, some pieces of his bones and flesh, his liver, his diaphragm, some of his praecordia, two fingers, some hair, four towels dipped in his blood, the straw on which he was laid to be embowelled, some papers greased with his fat . . .'[45]

This is an unusually inventive and generous hoard; often only a part of the martyr was preserved, and for symbolic reasons that become evident this was frequently the finger used in consecration. Southwell was not singular in his investment in the idea of martyrdom as sacrament: Dillon notes that the eucharist 'became a fundamental point of contention between Catholics and reformers throughout the period . . . and was a powerful influence in the construction of the Catholic martyr'; she remarks too on the martyrologies' 'emphasis on the Eucharistic elements of martyrdom'.[46] It is no surprise, then, to find stories such as that of Robert Sutton, who died the year before Southwell, and whose thumb and index finger ('which had mediated the power of transubstantiation') miraculously survived intact for a year after the body was exposed.[47] Or there was Edmund Geninges, martyred in 1591; the wonder here is not preservation but acquisition. A virgin following the

---

[43] Sweeney, *Snow in Arcadia*, p. 285.
[44] See Pilarz, *Robert Southwell and the Mission of Literature*, p. xiii.
[45] *The Rambler*, new series, 8 (1857), p. 114; quoted in Hill, 'The Absolute Reasonableness of Robert Southwell', p. 30.
[46] Dillon, *Construction of Martyrdom*, pp. 22, 107.   [47] Dillon, *Construction of Martyrdom*, p. 108.

body as it is brought from the place of execution manages to tug off his thumb without anyone noticing. 'Worried about being caught, she nonetheless touches Edmund's right thumb, the thumb anointed at his ordination, consecrated to touch the sacramental host.'[48] It seems Southwell's consecrating and consecrated finger also survived his death: it ended up in the possession of Lady Anne Dacres, the widow of Philip Howard, Earl of Arundel. Robert Beddow gives an account of its application: 'In later life, Lady Anne when unwell would "betake herself to Blessed Father Southwell's remedy" … It was eventually discovered that the "remedy" was making the sign of the cross over the swelling, with the finger of the martyr which had had such therapeutic success during his own lifetime.'[49]

To the early modern Catholic sensibility, there is nothing macabre or superstitious in this; the pieces of bone or embalmed flesh are powerful sacramental signifiers, repositories of a divine presence that finds many ways to make itself felt in the world. The flesh that had performed the act of transubstantiation, turning the Host into the body of Christ, is itself transubstantiated in the sacrament of martyrdom and invested with an enduring salvific influence; it is sanctified, not degraded, by the brutality to which it has been subject. Nonetheless, an alternative attitude was gradually starting to prevail. The Protestant martyrs of Mary's reign left no such remembrances, and Foxe, in his successive revisions of the *Actes and Monuments*, avoids for the most part, too, extravagant claims of miraculous signs or happenings at the point of death. In the rival faiths' struggle to assert their own claims to truth, credibility was becoming more important than inimitability, and opposing sides moved closer in matching one another's polemical tactics. The idea of a Protestant dismissal of relics and marvels is, however, in need of refinement: these things were instead reconceptualised, as, for example, in the story of Julius Palmer. His modest miracle was to call on God ('Jesu') when everyone thought he was already dead: an act that is wonderful, but does not produce an artefact miraculously preserved, and so is final – except in its retelling.[50] Words start to be thought of as relics, as there is a move away from the original, the material, the singular, towards the iterable witness. This may originate in Protestant scepticism, but it is adopted in recusant circles where the notion that

[48] Monta, *Martyrdom and Literature*, p. 72.
[49] Robert Beddow, 'The English Verse of Robert Southwell: a Critical Study of Southwell's English Lyrics within their Recusant Context', unpublished doctoral dissertation (Cambridge, 1987), p. 118. Beddow's source is C. A. Newdigate (ed.), *The Life of Lady Anne Dacres, Countess of Arundel* (*The Month*, London, March 1931).
[50] Monta, *Martyrdom and Literature*, pp. 57–9.

sanctity can lodge in a word as easily as in a shard of bone has obvious practical appeal; this goes some way to explaining the readiness with which Southwell's writings acquired the status of relics after his death. A seventeenth-century publisher, William Barrett, describes in his preface to a 1620 edition of the poems how he 'collected these dismembered parcels into one body'; he commends them to his (Protestant) dedicatee, Richard Sackville, Earl of Dorset, to be 'reanimated' by his reading.[51]

POETRY AND THE FAILURE OF SACRAMENTAL
SUBSTITUTION

That Southwell's books should be invested with sacramental significance as martyrological relics is a natural corollary of his style and choice of subject as well as the circumstances under which he was writing. Catholic conceptions of martyrdom were framed in sacramental terms: what happened in the eucharist was, after all, one of the chief grounds of the dispute with the Protestant authorities, and the main principle these men were dying to vindicate. Southwell anticipates his fellow Jesuit John Radford in rejecting a figurative Protestant understanding of presence: 'We must defend the Sacrament of the Altar', Southwell writes, 'agaynste *Berengarius* and the *Ichonomachie*, that made it but a figure of Christes bodye.'[52] Southwell's imaginative embrace of the conjunction in works which were written not to complement but to constitute his apostolate was profoundly influenced by his certainty that he would be a martyr, and his sacramental conception of that act. Critics have commented on Southwell's immediacy as a writer; since Louis Martz's influential treatment in *The Poetry of Meditation*, this has been ascribed to his practice of the Ignatian method of meditation, which privileges imagination and affect above theological knowledge or doctrinal understanding.[53] Cummings, though, has warned against looking to the meditative method as 'poetic elixir'; Southwell's work is often too active and indeed too demanding to sit happily in such a category, as Kuchar, too, recognises: 'By enacting as well as confessing sin', he writes, 'Southwell's poems possess a rhetorical dimension that is necessarily absent from both his and Ignatius' *Spiritual Exercises*.'[54] There are other ways to

---

[51] Robert Southwell, *St Peters complainte. Wth other workes of the author R:S* (London, 1620).
[52] Southwell, *Epistle of Comfort*, p. 84. See the introduction, p. 12, above.
[53] Martz, *The Poetry of Meditation*, pp. 179–210.
[54] Brian Cummings, 'Grammar and Grace: the Language of Theology in Works by Fulke Greville and Robert Southwell', unpublished doctoral dissertation (Cambridge, 1988), p. xxxi; Gary Kuchar, *The Poetry of Religious Sorrow in Early Modern England* (Cambridge University Press, 2008), p. 34.

understand these characteristics: 'Southwell's audaciousness', Shell believes, is 'largely a question of doing away with neo-platonic machinery and other transitional figures between human and divine; his poetry seeks an apprehension of God with which even a heavenly muse would interfere.'[55] I have discussed above the combination of immediacy and careful absence that distinguishes Southwell's poetic; it is not simply a vivid and empathic imagination of scriptural events, but one that conceptualises itself as usefully sacramental. The verse occupies a position at once central and nebulous in the complex of related tropes that allows an equation between book and body – word and flesh – in terms of both function and symbolic resonance. Whether the poems are understood as standing in for the living body of the priest (as metonyms for divine service) or the dead body of the martyr (as efficacious relics), the governing figure and frame is fundamentally eucharistic.

'Christs bloody sweate', one of Southwell's finest achievements, is a poem in which this economy of exchange can be seen explicitly at work. It turns on an urgent concern to identify Christ's real body with Christ's body in the eucharist, and it ends in anticipating a shared sacrifice: the poet's participation in the Mass will be a participation in the martyrdom. The scriptural moment which Southwell remembers is itself an anticipation: in the gospel of Luke, Christ suffers in the garden the night before he is crucified. 'And being in an agony he prayed more earnestly: and his sweat was as it were great drops of blood falling down to the ground' (Luke 20:44). The blood thus shed, unprovoked, is interpreted as a triumphant assertion of agency over the authorities who will later force blood from Christ's body in punitive fulfilment of this type; the episode has a clear interest for someone with Southwell's concern for retaining interpretative control over a body subject to judicial process. Despite what might be thought of as a compelling personal context, however, the poem is profoundly figurative. Its opening lines take the form of a series of vivid and insistent scriptural analogies for the crucifixion, capable of being read down as well as across:

Fatt soyle,	full springe,	sweete olive,	grape of blisse
That yeldes,	that streames,	that powres,	that dost distil
Untild,	undrawne,	unstampde,	untouchd of presse
Deare fruit,	cleare brooks,	fayre oyle,	sweete wine at will (ll. 1–4)

This conceit upsets chronological progression in favour of the typological logic in which the poem is invested; it is a rhetorical enactment of Southwell's desire to establish a network of equivalences, and his belief that Christ's

[55] Shell, *Catholicism, Controversy and the English Literary Imagination*, p. 67.

sacrifice is not a historical event but a present and continuing reality. The second stanza pursues this method, imagining Christ fulfilling the traditional emblems of his Passion and Resurrection as if these were not ascribed after the event: 'How coulde he joyne a Phenix fyerye paynes | In faynting pelicans still bleeding vaynes' (ll. 11–12). The pelican, believed to feed its starving young with the blood from its breast, is the symbol of self-sacrifice; the phoenix, which rises anew from the ashes of its own immolation, that of rebirth. Here they are joined in a figure which questions their emblematic adequacy with a characteristically mystical paradox: the stream of pelican blood that should extinguish the phoenix's fire instead feeds its flames. The same sacramental image is at the heart of 'The burning babe', where floods of compassionate tears serve only to fuel the fires of love that burn the apparition of the Christ-child; in a final eucharistic sacrifice, in that Christmas Eve midnight Mass, he will 'melt into a bath to washe them' – that is, sinful humankind – 'in my bloode' (l. 14).

The third stanza of 'Christs bloody sweate' moves to another mode of oblique understanding, with a reference to the Old Testament story of Elijah. This comes in 1 Kings 18:38, and tells of how the prophet defeats his false rivals with an all-consuming fire that burns wood, stones, dust and water as well as the sacrificial offering. What catches Southwell's interest is its analogical potential: again, blood becomes the unnatural food of this blaze. 'Such fire is love that fedd with gory bloode | Doth burne no lesse then in the dryest woode' (ll. 17–18). 'Love is the fire', too, in 'The burning Babe' (l. 10): the poet imagines a blaze that purifies and refines, wherein he might join himself to the sacrificial figure of Christ. That this is a fantasy of martyrdom becomes explicit in the extraordinary last stanza of 'Christs bloody sweate', simultaneously abasement and exultation, which ends with a quietly brutal pun:

> O sacred Fire come shewe thy force on me
> That sacrifice to Christe I maye retorne
> If withered wood for fuell fittest bee
> If stones and dust yf flesh and blood will burne
> I withered am and stonye to all good.
> A sacke of dust a masse of flesh and bloode.   (ll. 19–23)

'This is no less than a prayer to be subsumed into figures,' Brownlow writes: 'to have one's body transformed into a text of typological correspondences.'[56] While it is true that the lines are profoundly rhetorical, figuration implies no palliation. Southwell does not flinch from the fate he

---

[56] Brownlow, *Robert Southwell*, p. 114.

contemplates, and for him its savagery guarantees its efficacy: the two are as intimately related as sign and signified, or maybe more so. The 'masse of flesh and blood' is both Christ's real presence in the eucharist and the sacramental sacrifice that must be its surety, the pulpy body of the martyr that will be tortured into premature decrepitude and then 'hanged and cutte downe alyve, his bowelles to be burned before his face, his head to be streeken of, his bodie to be quartered and disposed at her majesties pleasure'.[57] The pun here, and the paradox it embodies, is distinctively sacramental: it is itself transformative, and faith in its power to determine meaning reflects a mindset fixed on martyrdom.[58]

What interests Southwell, and allows him some of his most arresting effects, is a rhetorical process that seeks to find spiritual beauty in the ugly, the painful, the pitiful; to reveal the substance behind the improbable accident. This is a transubstantiation importantly analogous to, derived from and licensed by Southwell's priestly function as a celebrant of Mass, what Sweeney characterises as 'performance of the Eucharist in his text'.[59] 'The flight into Egipte' starts conventionally enough, with some atmospheric oppositions of light and dark designed to set the scene for Herod's bloody outrage on the lives of the innocents: 'Alas our day is forc'd to flye by nyghte,' it opens, before developing the conceit that the sun has hidden its face from such evil and left the soldiers' deeds in the dark (l. 1). The second stanza sees a characteristic inflation of the image: stars stain their beams in spilt blood, and are yoked symbolically together with the slaughtered children as Herod's spite extinguishes both: 'Their lives and lightes with bloody showres doth quenche' (l. 10). It is in the final stanza, though, that Southwell's gift for radical transfiguration is most vividly felt. He celebrates these first Christian martyrs, who died before they knew who they were dying for, and before He died himself:

> With open throates and silent mouthes you singe
> His praise whome age permits you not to name
> Your tunes are teares your instruments are swords
> Your dittie death and bloode in liew of wordes.   (ll. 15–18)

---

[57] These words are from the sentence passed on Southwell; quoted Janelle, *Robert Southwell*, p. 83.

[58] Oxley identifies this as an important stylistic trait: 'What seems to be original in Southwell's poetry', he writes, 'is the presence of embroidered and plain style together in tension, enacting, as it were, processes of transformation and trans-substantiation: the descent of God into a bloody mass, and the elevation of a bloody mass into a Sacred Mass' ('The Relation between Robert Southwell's Neo-Latin and English Poetry', 206–7).

[59] Sweeney, *Snow in Arcadia*, p. 236.

The image of gaping throats gorily hymning Christ, sounds of crying and stabbing providing a musical accompaniment, is macabre; instead of words, they offer blood, and once again Southwell establishes a sacramental equivalence between these two things. He has effected a transubstantiation hard to stomach; the shambles becomes a choir-stall, and that militant martyrs' slogan from the *Epistle of Comfort* – 'the baptism of blood surpasses that of water' – is uncomfortably realised.

Southwell's verse is at its most successfully sacramental when the approach is oblique, as in the poems discussed above; he chooses to confront the subject indirectly, too, in 'Sinnes heavie loade', and that is another work of considerable imaginative force. It argues through a series of parallels for the physical presence of Christ on earth, and posits an active, effectual faith that can demand and deserve such grace. The opening lines establish an intimate exchange by tripping the reader up over their pronouns: 'O lord my sinne doth overchardge thy breste'; 'flatt thou fallest with my faultes oppreste' (ll. 1, 3). The poem moves through a calibration of the weight of human sin, and its eucharistic elements are elegantly implicit: the idea that Christ 'seal[s] a peace with bleedinge kisse' (l. 28) plays on the notions of exchange so significant throughout, and glances on the equation of mouth and wound so dramatically deployed in 'The flight to Egipte'. If this conceit is reminiscent of some of Crashaw's lyrics, the final stanza would not be out of place in Herbert's *Temple*, with its pleas for correction and *metanoietic* movement:

> O prostrate Christ, erect my croked mynde
> Lord lett thy fall my flight from earth obtayne
> Or if I still in earth must needes be shrynde
> The lord on earth come fall yet once againe
> And ether yelde with me in earthe to lye
> Or els with thee to take me to the skye.   (ll. 37–42)

The point of this is Christ's physical presence, and its closeness; the poem reimagines the potential for divine immanence outside church ritual with confidence of spirit and a sureness of touch harder to find, perhaps surprisingly, in Southwell's most direct and extended work on the theme, 'Of the Blessed sacrament of the Aulter'. Here a strident and defensive emphasis on doctrinal detail threatens to stifle the more allusive or typological modes he usually favours, and the work of empathy and affect is restricted. For Beddow, the difficulty is clear: 'the Eucharist is described in terms which are wholly unmetaphorical', he writes; 'the point of the verse is that metaphor has given way to reality in the Mass, but what may be excellent

dogma makes for poor poetry.'[60] The prerogatives of Southwell's mission
have been privileged over concerns of artistry and style, and the poem's
literalism works against its literariness.

It is nonetheless a work crucial for understanding the relationship
between Southwell's poetry and his recusant apostolate: the first was a
facet of the second, and their close creative and imaginative association
suggests they need to be considered together. The eucharist is the trope on
which Southwell's conceptions of his writing and his life converge; poems
are designed as substitutes for divine service, transfigured into efficacious
relics after his death – an act executed in calculated imitation of Christ's
crucifixion and therefore sharing in its sacramental force. Southwell died to
bear witness to Christ's bodily presence in the eucharist, and he died
believing that he offered himself in a continuation of his priestly actions
in offering the transubstantiated host to his scattered and dispossessed
congregation, in accordance with the teachings of their church. The investment in paradox that determined the shape of much of Southwell's writing
also consigned him to the scaffold, and he lived what he wrote; in instruct-
ing Arundel of the recusants' imperative 'by yelding to subdue, by dyeing to
revive, by sheddinge bloode, and leesinge lyfe, to winne the goale of eternall
felicity', it is no rhetorical abstraction he has in mind.[61] 'On the Blessed
sacrament of the Aulter' opens with a distinction of utmost importance to
Southwell, the distinction on which the poem nobly wrecks itself: 'Tipes to
the tryth dymn glymses to the light | Performinge Deede presageing signes
did chase' (ll. 3–4). Words are type, shadow: deeds antitype, truth. This is an
unbridgeable disparity, and one that Southwell has been at pains to point
out throughout his career. '[N]o shadow should be more privileged then the
body,' the narrator admonishes Mary in the *Funerall Teares*; 'no figure in
more account then the figured truth' (p. 36);[62] and Peter, endlessly weeping
for his sins in his extended *Complaynt*, feels the inadequacy of a typological
comparison: 'His were but tipes, these are the figured thing' (l. 432). The
Epistle of Comfort, as always, expresses the idea in its most robust and
directed form. 'In the baptisme of water . . . the Passion of Christe worketh,
by a certayne figurative representation,' Southwell explains;

in the baptisme of bloode by perfecte imitation . . . So muche therefore as
immitation in deede, is better then representation in the figure, and desyre in the
thoughte: So muche doth the baptisme of blood, surpasse those of water and
spirite.

[60] Beddow, 'The English Verse of Robert Southwell', p. 149.
[61] Southwell, *Epistle of Comfort*, p. 135.   [62] Southwell, *Mary Magdalens Funerall Teares*, p. 36.

This I have quoted before. Its implications are not fully explored until twenty pages later, when a way of reading becomes a sentence of death: '[H]ow perfectly therfore doth Martyrs resemble theyr Captayne, seeinge these figures and types, that foreshewed him, maye also be aptely applied unto them?'[63] This is a completely literal understanding of sacramental action, which should hardly be surprising in someone of Southwell's confessional position; the only way of inhabiting, indeed embodying, the eucharistic trope is to be a martyr in the moment of death: to perform an 'immitation in deede'.

The insistent message of Southwell's writing is that it can never substitute for this suffering, though it may describe, anticipate and figure it; sometimes it abandons the attempt completely, and sounds straightforwardly like doctrine versified: 'Twelve did he feede twelve did their feeder eate,' 'On the Blessed sacrament of the Aulter' assures us; 'He made he dressed he gave he was their meate' (ll. 11–12). The strain of militant literalism that runs through both verse and prose also accounts for a contrary quality of abstraction bordering on automatism.[64] Southwell has his eye always on the 'figured thing', and that his types seem sometimes inappropriate or incoherent can be ascribed to his tendency to isolate a physical correlation without paying attention to its wider resonances or rhetorical effect; the passage on Elijah in 'Christs bloody sweate' flirts with this abstraction, as does the final stanza of 'The Nativity of Christe', where elaborate connections threaten to distract from the defence of transubstantiation they are designed to clinch:

> Man altered was by synn from man to best
> Bestes foode is haye haye is all mortall fleshe
> Now god is fleshe and lyes in maunger prest
> As haye the brutish synner to refreshe.
> O happy feilde wherein this foder grewe
> Whose taste doth us from beastes to men renewe.   (ll. 19–24, p. 7)

There is always a distance for Southwell between the revealed truth of Scripture and the project of his poetry, though it doesn't generate anything like the anxiety it will for Herbert; it is clear, too, where his emphasis lies: 'the articles of your fayth are no fables', he is sure: 'the words and contentes of the Scripture, no Poets fictions'.[65]

---

[63] Southwell, *Epistle of Comfort*, pp. 141, 161.
[64] This is recognised by Brownlow: 'Southwell's most intricate figurative structures often seem to come untethered from the reality they should stand for,' he writes, 'with the result that the poems can acquire an air of fantastic, ingenious abstraction' (*Robert Southwell*, p. 112).
[65] Southwell, *Epistle of Comfort*, p. 176.

Southwell's verse is set apart from that of his successors by more than just a few decades of literary advancement. Its characteristics of impersonality and fitful abstraction arise from a pioneering attempt to respond to a situation of liturgical deprivation by using poetry to figure sacramental presence; that the poet's attention is divided between type and truth accounts for the momentary failures as well as the powerful achievements of this work. The absence Southwell confronted was different in kind and quality from that experienced by the following century's generation of poets; it was politically contingent, geographically specific, and remediable by the celebration of a Mass in which he could still transubstantiate the bread of the Host into Christ's real body. For Southwell, poetry was never the principal point, and when a more extreme rhetorical gesture was required to confirm his faith, it was deeds and not words he chose. The most significant statement to emerge from Southwell's cell, and indeed his whole career as a writer, was himself: a body so forcefully pre-inscribed with its litany of imitation and protective paradox that no official process, however brutal, could overwrite what it said.

CHAPTER 2

Donne and punning

John Donne was born a decade after Southwell, and their early histories touch at curious points. Donne, too, was from a significant recusant family: he was related on his mother's side to the great Catholic martyr Sir Thomas More, and his uncle, Jasper Heywood, was for a time in the 1580s leader of the Jesuit mission in England. Donne was brought up Catholic, as Southwell was, and both travelled on the continent as young men, though Donne received his education in Oxford and the Inns of Court rather than at Catholic seminaries abroad. At some point in his early maturity, however, Donne took the step that was to ensure a sharp divergence in their stories: before the end of the sixteenth century, even perhaps around the time that Southwell was choking on a scaffold in Tyburn, he had converted to Protestantism. That this was a significant event, both biographically and psychologically, is generally agreed, but though there has been much speculation on when precisely the conversion took place, and what impulses or events may have prompted it, no critical consensus has been reached. Those details are not crucial to the interests of this study, though one circumstance does seem worth remarking: in 1593, Donne's younger brother Henry was arrested for sheltering William Harrington, a recusant priest. Harrington was hanged, and Henry Donne died in prison before he could be sentenced.[1]

Donne's public writings on Jesuits in general and their claims to religious martyrdom in particular display an energetic derision that comes, naturally enough, from an intimately empathic consideration of their motivation and beliefs. The *Pseudo-Martyr*, published in 1610 to recommend its author to James I, describes the imaginative influence of early conditioning: 'I have beene ever kept awake in a meditation of Martyrdome', Donne confesses, 'by being derived from such a stocke and race, as, I believe, no family . . . hath endured and suffered more in their persons and fortunes, for obeying

---

[1] See John Stubbs, *Donne: the Reformed Soul* (London: Penguin, 2006).

the Teachers of Roman Doctrine, then it hath done.'[2] Here, the glow of
family pride all but extinguishes the image of the little insomniac, up
contemplating horrors in the dark. In *Biathanatos*, his extended consideration of the ethics of suicide, Donne is more explicit about the habits of
mind framed in him as a boy, and more scornful of those he holds
responsible: 'I had my first breeding, and conversation with Men of a
supressed and afflicted Religion, accustomed to the despite of death, and
hungry of an imagin'd Martyrdom.'[3] As critics have thoroughly demonstrated, Donne's fascination with death, martyrdom, the dismemberment
or dissolution of the body and what happens thereafter stayed with him
throughout his life, and was a powerful spur to creativity in his poems and
sermons as well as in these early polemics. He is, though, eager to reformulate the connection that operated so powerfully for Southwell of physical
agony with religious rectitude, of suffering with salvation: the divine poems,
in particular, open up the possibility of an intellectual or emotional martyrdom that is a surer way to imitate Christ than public execution, or
succumbing to the pestilence of a prison cell. Donne moves away from
the literalism that is at the core of Southwell's sensibility, and he exploits all
the rhetorical opportunities such a breach offers.

   To open with a consideration of Donne's residual and transformative
interest in the idea of martyrdom is a somewhat oblique way to establish two
of the central premises of this chapter. The first is that a Catholic notion,
phrase or feeling in Donne's work does not demonstrate that his conversion
was an act of careerist expediency that left him either a closet Catholic or a
racked and treacherous apostate, as John Carey argues with some style and
vigour in his seminal *John Donne: Life, Mind and Art*.[4] The second, closely
related, is that his upbringing and the intellectual patterns which were then
instilled remain significant for Donne's writing in ways both explicit and
implicit, and at the level of structure as well as of subject: without the
implication, that is, that in exploring or responding to such ideas in his
poetry Donne reveals an unassimilated Catholic sensibility. His own formulation for expressing the cognitive imprint that might be taken and
carried from an early influence employs a monetary metaphor familiar
from his lyric poetry. A man who transfers from one religion to another,

---

[2] John Donne, *Selected Prose*, ed. by Helen Gardner and Timothy Healy (Oxford: Clarendon Press, 1967), p. 46.
[3] Donne, *Selected Prose*, p. 26.
[4] 'He was a martyr *manqué*', Carey writes, 'and had to live with a set of basic psychic configurations which had been oriented towards death by his educators' (*John Donne: Life, Mind and Art* (London: Faber, 1990), p. 213).

he wrote to his good friend Henry Goodyer, is like a coin that has had its features filed away to make way for a better likeness: 'You shall seldome see a Coyne, upon which the stamp were removed, though to imprint it better,' he says, 'but it looks awry and squint. And so, for the most part, do minds that have received divers impressions.'[5] Elsewhere, though, in a verse letter to a recent ordinand, he evinces more confidence in the efficacy of such a procedure; 'as new crowned Kings alter the face, but not the monies substance', he writes, his friend's new role simply changes 'Gods old Image by Creation | To Christs new stampe'.[6] In whichever light it is viewed, Donne's double stamp produced a tension that was profoundly productive, and his rhetorical advance from a writer like Southwell lies partly in the multiple perspectives he lets himself explore. An early recusant upbringing gave the younger poet, too, a fascination with martyrdom, sacrifice and imitation, but his conversion led him to trope them differently; he borrows the tricks of pun and paradox that Southwell used to seal his faith and fate, and turns them to other ends.

What follows is broadly shaped by an interest in the first of these rhetorical devices. Donne converted from Catholicism to Protestantism as a very young man and from licentiousness to piety as a slightly older one, and his writing is inevitably informed by memories, cultural and personal, of past states. Donne turns to the device of the pun (or, rather, to the variety of rhetorical figures now usually collectively dismissed as 'punning') as a way of holding divergent meanings in tension and expressing complex theological rethinkings. I use the term 'pun' for convenience, though it is not attested in this sense until a decade after Donne's *Songs and Sonets* was posthumously published: a Renaissance rhetorician would have preferred the words *syllepsis, antanaclasis, paronomasia* and so on to describe the doubling of sound or meaning comprehended in the modern term.[7] The pun, whether written or spoken, is a space where two things coexist, and its full potential is realised when both meanings are understood in being allowed to inflect one another: 'Two-faced, double-tongued,' Walter Redfern remarks; 'Janus and jackdaws are favourite analogies.'[8] The pun is a trope of

[5] Donne to Sir Henry Goodyer, [? April 1615], *Letters to Severall Persons of Honour* (1651), pp. 101–2.
[6] Donne, 'To Mr Tilman after he had taken orders', ll. 15–16, 17–18, in *The Divine Poems*, ed. by Helen Gardner (Oxford: Clarendon Press, 1952), p. 32. Future references to this edition will be given in the text as line numbers.
[7] [John Taylor], *Mercurius Aquaticus* (Oxford, 1643 [1644]), quoted in Catherine Bates, 'The Point of Puns', *Modern Philology*, 96 (1999), 421–38 (425–6 n.). For a more detailed account of the pun in this period, see Sophie Read, 'Puns: Serious Wordplay', in *Renaissance Figures of Speech*, ed. by Gavin Alexander and Katrin Ettenhuber (Cambridge University Press, 2007), pp. 81–94.
[8] Walter Redfern, *Puns* (Oxford: Blackwell, 1984), p. 13.

conversion, and as close a rhetorical enactment of sacramental operation as language can manage. This is more than simply a pleasing analogy; as suggested in the introduction to this study, the eucharistic controversy is crucially constructed along rhetorical lines, and history turns on the nature and degree of figuration understood in certain vital phrases. That the eucharist becomes essentially rhetorical like this, and rhetoric transformatively eucharistic, rather opens up literary possibilities than closes down theological ones. 'Writing is Donne's experience of making the word flesh,' Ramie Targoff believes, and punning is a particularly vivid way of treating words as if they are things: Donne's double-struck coin can serve as figure for the double-tongued pun, and for the stamped wafer of the Host that was both body and bread.[9]

THE SACRAMENTAL PUN

Inevitably, perhaps, given his interest in currency both material and linguistic, Donne found coins an attractive subject for punning. 'Women are all like Angels,' he writes in 'The Anagram'; 'the faire be | Like those which fell to worse'.[10] Beautiful women are Satan's legions, original brightness dimmed after the Fall; at the same time, exploiting the fact that 'angel' was, too, the name for a piece of common currency, their value is lowered by abundant circulation, and the faces of both are tarnished and deformed by passing through many hands. The ill-favoured woman celebrated by the poem, however, with her 'Anagram of a good face', represents a better investment: she is a 'soveraigne Plaister' for jealousy, as her lover need fear no infidelity (l. 37). Sovereign: the name for a coin is also a name for the king, and the coincidence facilitates an elegant compliment to Flavia's curative touch. The allusion here is to the King's Evil, and the coin presented to those scrofulous subjects fortunate enough to feel their monarch's hand was, of course, an angel; the argument is circular, and circulation and exchange are assured. The same pun on 'angel', so elaborated as to form its governing conceit, is found in another elegy, 'The Bracelet'. Here Donne mourns the loss of 'twelve righteous Angels' (l. 9) which must be melted down to form the replacement for a misplaced trinket belonging to his mistress; the anxiety is that his money will lose with its distinguishing

---

[9] Ramie Targoff, *John Donne: Body and Soul* (University of Chicago Press, 2008), p. 24.
[10] 'The Anagram', ll. 29–30, in John Donne, *The Elegies and the Songs and Sonnets*, ed. by Helen Gardner (Oxford: Clarendon Press, 1965), p. 21. Future references to this edition will be given in the text as line numbers.

marks its value, though the weight of the gold stay the same. As the fallen angels' goodness was transmuted to evil in the fires of Hell, he argues, so his coins will suffer a complete devaluation in the jeweller's furnace. In fact, they will be worse off than their heavenly namesakes: 'they are still bad Angels, mine are none | For forme gives being, and their forme is gone' (ll. 75–6). Matter cannot be separated from form, he asserts, and this is an implicit rejection of the doctrine of transubstantiation, which relies on a division between substance (matter) and accident (form). Robert Whalen is acute in reading Donne's preoccupation with the conceit of coining as sacramental in its emphasis on determining the value of a sign: 'the problem of monetary signification', he writes, is 'analogous to that of the sacramental sign's power to communicate its divine referent'.[11] Just like coins, though, words have their currency, and it is Donne's punning in these poems that carries their sacramental freight.

The consideration of Donne's doctrinal position on the sacraments, and in particular for the purposes of this discussion the sacrament of the eucharist, is not entirely straightforward. Unlike Southwell, or Herbert, or Crashaw, or Vaughan (Milton as usual is a slightly different case), Donne wrote no poem explicitly about the celebration of communion, no work that offers itself as a substitute for divine service; as Eleanor McNees points out, though, 'the divine poems are replete with eucharistic imagery', and many of the secular poems are too.[12] But he was also relatively unusual among early modern devotional poets in leaving a number of direct explorations of the nature of his understanding of the eucharist, in the form of sermons preached during his career as a Church of England divine. While in one way this makes things beautifully clear, the evidence of these works has not been accepted without question. The chronology of Donne's writing, complicated by his taste for manuscript circulation and dislike of the restrictive practice of dating ('in Letters', he writes, 'times and daies cannot have interest . . . because that which passes by them, is eternal and out of the measure of time'[13]), is hard to establish, but the sermons almost certainly postdate many if not all of his lyric poems. This means that the opinions they express may not be consistent with those Donne held as a younger man, before his ordination, whether because of mature reflection or artful

---

[11] Whalen, *Poetry of Immanence*, p. 36; see pp. 38–9 for Whalen's reading of 'The Anagram', and pp. 43–6 for his reading of 'The Bracelet'.

[12] Eleanor McNees, 'John Donne and the Anglican Doctrine of the Eucharist', *Texas Studies in Literature and Language*, 29 (1987), 94–114 (95).

[13] Donne to the Countess of Bedford, in *Letters* (p. 23). For Donne's practices of publication, see Arthur Marotti, *John Donne: Coterie Poet* (Madison: University of Wisconsin Press, 1986).

dissembling; R. V. Young, for example, expresses a suspicion that the sermons peddle an orthodox position in which their author did not necessarily believe: 'Donne must officially deny the Catholic doctrine of transubstantiation and its liturgical corollaries.'[14] Young nevertheless manages to find in passages he calls 'remarkably elusive and problematic', 'surprising', even 'extraordinary', a theology of the eucharist which amounts pretty much to that held by the Roman Church: 'difficult to reconcile with any of the formulations of the major continental Reformers', at any rate, 'or even the official doctrines of the Church of England'.[15] As Theresa DiPasquale warns, however, 'Donne was capable of combining Calvinist formulations and Catholic-sounding language,' and Malcolm Mackenzie Ross reached this insight fifty years earlier; 'despite deceptive Catholic surfaces of rhetoric', he writes of one passage on supererogation, '[it] is unmistakably Protestant at the core'.[16] To see the sermons as repositories of fact, whether straightforward or subterranean, risks overlooking their status as rhetorical constructs every bit as complex as the poems they have customarily been excavated to elucidate.

It is not the intention of this chapter to offer a revaluation or refinement of Donne's confessional position on the eucharist; the sermons explore, consistently and imaginatively, an outlook which is both orthodox and ecumenical. Donne resists too close an investigation into the manner of Christ's presence in the Host, advising his congregation that such scholastic speculations are unnecessary and may even be dangerous for their souls: 'wonder not at that, press not for that', he cautions; adopting a pugnacious stance on the mechanisms of grace may 'frustrate and disappoint thee of all that benefit'.[17] For himself, Donne steers an explicit course between Catholic transubstantiation and Zwinglian memorialism, which he characterises as opposing errors: 'there are other dissolutions of Jesus, when men will . . . mold him up in a wafer Cake, or a peece of bread', he writes; 'there are other annihilations of Jesus when Men will make him, and his Sacraments, to be nothing but bare signes' (*Sermons*, v: 135). Instead, Donne sees the eucharistic transformation as something which takes place

---

[14] R. V. Young, *Doctrine and Devotion in Seventeenth-Century Poetry: Studies in Donne, Herbert, Crashaw and Vaughan* (Cambridge University Press, 2000), p. 95.

[15] Young, *Doctrine and Devotion*, pp. 96, 97, 98.

[16] Theresa M. DiPasquale, *Literature and Sacrament: the Sacred and the Secular in John Donne* (Pittsburgh: Duquesne University Press, 1999), p. 10; Malcolm McKenzie Ross, *Poetry and Dogma: the Transfiguration of Eucharistic Symbols in Seventeenth Century English Poetry* (Rutgers University Press, 1954; repr. New York: Octagon, 1969), p. 167.

[17] Sermon, Christmas Day 1626: Donne, *The Sermons of John Donne*, ed. by George R. Potter and Evelyn Simpson, 10 vols. (Berkeley: University of California Press, 1953–62), vII. 290–1. Future references to this edition will be given in the text as *Sermons*, followed by volume and page numbers.

in the worthy recipient, who offers a kind of reciprocity in an imitation of Christ. There is a real change – he is always emphatically clear that the Host is more than a 'bare' sign – but this change is internal and spiritual rather than external and corporeal: 'There is the true Transubstantiation, that when I have received it worthily, it becomes my very soule; that is, My soule growes up into a better state, and habitude by it, and I have the more soule for it, the more sanctified, the more deified soule by that Sacrament' (*Sermons*, VII: 321). In this belief, Donne follows the logic of those reforming theologians for whom a trope might be substance as well as form; he expounds 'a securely orthodox Anglican stance toward the doctrine of Real Presence in the Eucharist'.[18] I will return to the implications of Donne's rhetorical masterstroke, his 'true Transubstantiation', below.

Donne is a crucial bridging figure in an argument for the eucharist as poetic trope: his life was a microcosm, which would have pleased him, of the external historical trajectory from the dormant sacramentalism of Southwell to the assimilated sacramental poetics of Herbert. The personal narrative of conversion from Catholic to Protestant is clearly significant in this, but equally important is a shift in literary culture brought about through the new pressures of an imperative to express reformed doctrine. For Southwell, the limits of rhetoric were clear, and the deficiency of the word might be supplied by the articulations of the flesh; Donne's imitation of Christ was not less ardent or efficacious for being purely verbal. This is not to suggest that any transition was seamless, untroubled or consistent: since Carey's astute characterisation of him as a pathologically inconstant thinker for whom volatility is a governing aesthetic, but who nonetheless displays a remarkable imaginative continuity, such a reading of Donne would seem injudicious. The rhetoric of sacramental, and specifically eucharistic, operation unloosed from its traditional doctrinal moorings is a powerful but unstable force in his work; thoughts about the manner and operation of presence are expressed in the letters and love lyrics as well as in – in fact more insistently than in – the sermons and devotional poetry. This perhaps is not surprising if they are considered 'fabrics of the same mind, controlled by similar imaginative needs', but it is an utterly different decorum from that adopted by a poet like Herbert.[19] Whalen calls the secular lyrics a 'startling record of the relevance of sacrament for the profane aspects of [Donne's] poetic experience', and it is here that a systematic consideration of Donne's sacramental poetics must begin.[20]

[18] McNees, 'Anglican Doctrine', 112.   [19] Carey, *John Donne*, p. 11.
[20] Whalen, *Poetry of Immanence*, p. xviii.

LOVE AND THE EUCHARIST

Many of Donne's love poems (with which this discussion will group the rhetorically cognate poems of friendship) are preoccupied with the twin problems of holding faith and manifesting presence in absence. While those addressed to an object of erotic or romantic desire often end in a position of doubt, his letters, both in prose and in verse, at times voice a remarkable confidence in their ability to transcend the distance separating friends. They effect a union of souls that Donne thinks of as specifically eucharistic: 'letters are friendships sacraments', he writes; '& wee should be in charyty to receaue at all tymes'.[21] Here in this early letter, and throughout those that survive, it is the text that mediates and makes possible a true communion of minds, and Donne takes great pleasure in imagining his words distilling an essence of personality that is released when the letter is read: his epistles are 'conveyances and deliverers of me to you', he tells Henry Goodyer.[22] In another letter to that friend, Donne makes the theological analogy explicit when he talks of 'my second religion, friendship'; he again plays on this idea by drawing a parallel between church ritual and letter-writing that is couched in specifically eucharistic terms.[23] 'It is a sacrifice', he writes:

> which though friends need not, friendship doth; which hath in it so much divinity, that as we must be ever equally disposed inwardly so to doe or suffer for it, so we must sepose some certain times for the outward service thereof, though it be but formall and testimoniall.[24]

The consistent rhetoric of sacramental operation is felt neither as ironic nor as disproportionate to its subject; Donne redeploys this theological framework with no sense of incongruity to express the ideal of communion represented by the transaction of text. 'In letters', Targoff writes, 'he felt he could create physical and spiritual modes of intimacy that would endure beyond the immediate moment': the real presence of the writer is guaranteed to transcend distance and even death by a folded paper which takes on transubstantiatory powers of reconstitution and embodiment.[25]

---

[21] Donne, from the Burley letters, printed in Evelyn M. Simpson, *A Study of the Prose Works of John Donne*, 2nd edn (Oxford: Clarendon Press, 1948), pp. 303–36 (p. 311). It is clear that Donne is thinking of the eucharist from his reference to the Prayer Book communion service: 'You that do truly and ernestly repente you of youre sinnes, and be in love and charitie with your neighbors . . .: Draw nere and take this holy Sacrament to your comfort' (Cranmer, *Book of Common Prayer* (1559), p. 133).
[22] Donne, *Letters*, p. 109.   [23] Donne, *Letters*, p. 85.   [24] Donne, *Letters*, p. 116.
[25] Targoff, *Body and Soul*, p. 27. See also Ronald J. Corthell, '"Friendship's Sacraments": John Donne's Familiar Letters', *Studies in Philology*, 78 (1981), 409–25.

In a verse letter to Sir Henry Wotton, Donne puts this intellectual communion above more bodily means of meeting and exchange: 'Sir, more then kisses, letters mingle Soules; | For thus friends absent speake' (ll. 1–2). While the homily that follows might at first seem rather too conventional to achieve the harmonious unity its opening lines promise, it is in fact, in the context of their correspondence, a graceful and intimate piece.[26] The act of writing here constitutes the ecstatic bond imagined as an ideal elsewhere in Donne's works; 'This ease controules | The tediousnesse of my life,' he writes (ll. 2–3), and the phrasing implicitly invites comparison with 'That abler soule' that 'Defects of loneliness controules' in 'The Extasie': the essences of the two lovers combined (ll. 43–4). It is the end of the poem to Wotton, however, that puts greatest weight on its words as vehicles of conveying the self. Donne compliments his friend by suggesting that all the guidance he has offered simply reflects back Wotton's own wisdom on to its source, and this reflexive manoeuvre does its best to 'mingle' the two men by confusing their roles of preceptor and pupil. The last lines offer an achievement of embodiment and accord in a triumphant pun on the writer's name:

> But if myself I'have wonne
> To know my rules, I have, and you have   DONNE:

This enacts the unity it describes by making one word bear two meanings. If he has understood his rules, which are of course Wotton's rules, then they have both finished (done): he has ownership of himself, and Wotton has ownership of him (DONNE). The rhyme fractures its twin, too: 'wonne' is also 'one', and again the two men share the space of a word. Here Donne's syllepsis manages to transcend the isolation of the individual in a way that is profoundly analogous to the spiritual effects of communion. This verse letter becomes a successful sacrament of friendship, sealed by what must be more than a phonetic coincidence to Donne.[27]

It doesn't always work. In a poem written to Thomas Woodward, the eucharistic model is used to express not confidence but anxiety as to how the epistle will be received, an inflection that brings it into line with some of the later love lyrics. There is, indeed, a Petrarchan air to this sonnet ('At once, from hence'), as Woodward is framed as the absent beloved from

---

[26] For a discussion of the background, see Ted-Larry Pebworth and Claude J. Summers, '"Thus Friends Absent Speake": the Exchange of Verse Letters between John Donne and Henry Wotton', *Modern Philology*, 81 (1984), 361–77.

[27] I will return to Donne's habit of punning on his own and his wife's names in my discussion of 'A Hymne to God the Father', pp. 92–4 below.

whom reassurance and affection is fretfully craved. This letter, Donne fears, might prove a substitute for the poet in a way that rather deprives him of the benefit of the connection than effectually embodies him to his friend; the dangers of mistaking the representative for what it represents, the sign for what it signifies, are clear:

> though I languish, prest with Melancholy,
> My verse, the strict Map of my misery,
> Shall live to see that, for whose want I dye.
> Therefore I envie them, and doe repent,
> That from unhappy mee, things happy'are sent;
> Yet as a Picture, or bare Sacrament
>   Accept these lines, and if in them there be
>   Merit of love, bestow that love on mee.   (ll. 7–14)

From desiring his words to be truly transubstantiatory, Donne jealously retreats to a position of Zwinglian memorialism, sending a 'bare Sacrament' whose purpose is to remind the recipient of its author and not to act as a devotional surrogate: to underline absence rather than constitute presence. The stance is precisely contrary to that adopted in the verses to Henry Wotton.[28] The discontented friend commits a doctrinal error in his failure of generosity; two, in fact, for having emptied the sacrament of its efficacy with one breath, he asks for its 'merit' to accrue to him with the next. As the liturgy makes clear, the sacrament of communion carries no merit in and of itself, but instead represents the grace of Christ's sacrifice.

The conjunction of emotional shortcoming with theological misapprehension is one Donne was to explore more seriously in the love lyrics, which present their own problems of unity in absence. Perhaps even more insistently than in his letters, the concerns of divided lovers are refracted through religious frameworks of possibility and understanding, as Donne returns again and again to the parallel between those seeking dissolution in each other's bodies and the yearning of the faithful for union with God. Sex is analogous to sacrament, and neither intimacy can offer assurance of the wished-for transfiguration of the flesh. The crisis of belief becomes a crisis of language, and Donne at times invokes formulations which sound truly Catholic in his search for an expression of embodied faith; erotic transactions become a way to work out the play between the power of the symbol

---

[28] As James S. Baumlin points out, this interpretation of sacramental operation 'empties the priest's – and poet's – language of being, restricting the words of Eucharistic celebration to a figural representation rather than a re-presenting or presencing of its transcendental subject' (*John Donne and the Rhetorics of Renaissance Discourse* (Columbia: University of Missouri Press, 1991), p. 168).

and the threatened vacancy of the written sign. Baumlin recognises in this strategy an appeal to an outmoded system of doctrine whose flaws under-write and ensure the failure of this mutually transformative love and the verse that tries to make it so: 'Naively, many of the *Songs and Sonets* cling to belief in a powerful, performative language,' he writes; 'naively, they hold fast to the hope of poetic presence, even as they admit the loss of Catholic sacramentalism.'[29] Eucharistic language is everywhere in these poems, though no coherent theological poetics emerges. Donne's finely calibrated understanding of the gradations of eucharistic belief allows him imaginative licence: a witty lover triumphs with a transubstantiatory argument in 'The Flea'; the faithless beloved who gifts her 'subtle wreath of haire' in 'The Funerall' exhibits a Zwinglian disdain for the truth of signs. If some poems strain for efficacy, others, just as the verse letters, recognise their words as the bare sacraments of a memorialist dispensation.

The first of these poems has a rich critical tradition explicating its sacramental context.[30] The syllogistic argument of 'The Flea' is that the insect which has bitten both the protagonist and his reluctant mistress has accomplished a sacramental union by mingling their blood in his body, 'these living walls of Jet' (l. 15). Her continued demurral is therefore futile, as this performative action has already consecrated a marriage; but when she kills the flea, sacrilegiously staining her nail with 'blood of innocence' (l. 20), the terms of the blandishment change from Catholic identification to Protestant separation of the sign and what it signifies, the sacrament from marriage to eucharist. The poem closes with a hermeneutic flourish: 'Just so much honor, when thou yeeld'st to mee | Will wast, as this flea's death tooke life from thee' (ll. 26–7). Part of the poem's charm is the sheer size of the hammer it takes to its erotic challenge: 'This flea is you and I' (l. 12) deliberately exerts the same splintering pressure on the present participle of the verb of being as the reformers did when they found it in the phrase 'This is my body.'[31] That Donne borrows eucharistic modes of meaning for what might be read as a libertine seduction lyric is not simply evidence of audacious *sprezzatura*; the two kinds of union are made cognate by their shared reliance on a verbal sign that can be performative or figurative, and

[29] Baumlin, *Rhetorics of Renaissance Discourse*, p. 174.
[30] See M. Thomas Hester, '"This Cannot be Said": a Preface to the Reader of Donne's Lyrics', *Christianity and Literature*, 39 (1990), 365–85, and Theresa M. DiPasquale, 'Receiving a Sexual Sacrament: "The Flea" as Profane Eucharist', in *John Donne's Religious Imagination: Essays in Honour of John T. Shawcross*, ed. by Raymond-Jean Frontain and Frances M. Malpezzi (Conway: University of Central Arkansas Press, 1995), pp. 81–95.
[31] See the introduction, p. 3, above.

both situations have their attendant anxieties of interpretation. The drama
of the poem obscures its real concern, which is not whether or not the lady
will agree to go to bed with him, but whether a Catholic or a Protestant
formulation of such a consummation promises the nearer intimacy.

This interest is again evident in 'The Extasie'; if these modes of thought
are not so dominant here or so verbally explicit, the poem nonetheless has
an insistent eucharistic subtext.[32] The lovers recline side by side in an
erotically charged landscape, touching only at hand and gaze; but though
it roots them to the spot, neither the 'fast balme' of their mingled sweat nor
the iterated reflection that hovers in their lines of sight is enough to satisfy
their desire for closeness.

> As 'twixt two equal Armies, Fate
>   Suspends uncertaine victory,
> Our soules, (which to advance their state
>   Were gone out,) hung 'twixt her, and mee.
> And whil'st our soules negotiate there,
>   Wee like sepulchrall statues lay;
> All day, the same our postures were,
>   And wee said nothing, all the day.   (ll. 13–20)

If bodies even this near cannot achieve the dissolution of unity, then their
disembodied souls fare little better: the poem is no valorisation of a purely
spiritual connection, but a determined argument for the involvement of
both body and soul, as sign and sacrament, in the transfigurations of love.
The dialogue of the interinanimated souls (Donne's coinage for a process of
mutual vivification, a fusion of spirit into body that is also a transfusion
between the two lovers) must be incarnated in action, and the transfixed
bodies need to come together to seal the union brokered by their souls.

> To'our bodies turne wee then, that so
>   Weake men on love reveal'd may looke;
> Loves mysteries in soules doe grow,
>   But yet the body is his booke.   (ll. 69–72)

The reverence in this language of scriptural fulfilment and divine mediation
camouflages the eroticism of its counsel of voyeurism, which is also an
invitation to bed quite as ingenious if rather subtler than that in 'The Flea'.

---

[32] Regina Mara Schwartz calls it 'a paean to the body that resonates with eucharistic language and
sensibility' (*Sacramental Poetics*, p. 112). For a reading of the poem which explicates its philosophical
contexts, see Targoff, *Body and Soul*, 53–7; she draws on Arthur Marotti's influential account, 'Donne
and "The Extasie"', in *The Rhetoric of Renaissance Poetry from Wyatt to Milton*, ed. by Thomas
O. Sloan and Raymond B. Waddington (Berkeley: University of California Press, 1974), pp. 140–73.

The pun in 'Loves mysteries' (on *mysterion*, which is the Greek word for sacrament) points up another level of signification: 'The bodies of the lovers', Felecia Wright McDuffie recognises, 'act as "outward and visible signs of an inward and spiritual grace", as church tradition describes the sacraments.'[33] Once again, thinking about sex in terms of eucharistic participation – the physical act a sign and seal of spiritual grace – is more than a conceit; and the poem, the 'booke' which embodies the souls and makes flesh word by transcribing their dialogue for other eyes, claims for itself a sacramental efficacy that is unmatched in any of the divine poems.

That living bodies are not the only form of sacramental embodiment in Donne's verse is evident from his marked interest in the symbolic power of objects. In the context of Southwell's martyrdom, Chapter 1 explored the connection between sacrament and relic, and the two poets' shared imaginative inheritance suggests that this sense might, too, be at work in some of Donne's writing.[34] The efficacious deaths of the martyrs of his childhood, their rags of flesh and bloodstained clothes taken and venerated for relics, inform an interest in the powerful token, whether it stands in for the absence of parting, or death; the 'bracelet of bright haire about the bone' (l. 6) is only the most obvious of the charms that want to share in some of the energy of those who have 'found a lawfull way of Re-baptizing, even in bloud' (*Sermons*, v: 66). In the poem to which it belongs, 'The Relique', another vivid imagining comes into play: the resurrection of the body at the day of judgement. Anything that collected and cohered the fragments of an individual scattered during life and in death has an irresistible pull for Donne, and he returns time and again to the niceties of the doctrine.[35] Here, it is a sly ruse to snatch a moment together with his lover after many ages dead: she has to be complete in each atom, he reasons, so she will need to come and fetch back that braid of hair on his arm. 'This device might be some way', Donne suggests, with an infinitely tender tentativeness,

> To make their soules, at the last busie day
> Meet at this grave, and make a little stay.   (ll. 9–11)

As so many of his fictions, this seeks to outwit fate as well as to reverse the process of dissolution and decay: to retain a slightly subversive individuality in the face of the general union of the last judgement.

---

[33] Felecia Wright McDuffie, *To Our Bodies Turn We Then: Body as Word and Sacrament in the Works of John Donne* (New York: Continuum, 2005), p. 70.

[34] See pp. 59–61, above.

[35] See Carey, *John Donne*, pp. 219–30, and Targoff, *Body and Soul*, pp. 164–83.

The fantasy extends to the projection of a distinctly Catholic future, 'where mis-devotion doth command' (l. 13), and the wreathed bone is taken for saints' relics, or – the thought is so daring it is barely breathed – a fragment of Christ's body: 'Thou shalt be'a Mary Magdalen, and I | A something else thereby' (ll. 17–18). The miracle of these lovers, though, is their sexual abstinence, again expressed in the language of sacrament: 'Our hands ne'er toucht the seales' (l. 29). This arid posthumous conjunction is the only sense in which her hair might encircle his bone, a forthright pun that is also found, submerged, in the other poem where Donne acts 'Love's martyr' (l. 19), 'The Funerall'; this time, 'that subtile wreath of haire, which crowns my arme' is not just symbolic of a sexual eucharist, it is itself 'The mystery, the signe you must not touch' (ll. 3–4). The efficacy of this sign is disputed: the poet wants to take it as transubstantiatory, an earnest for her withheld flesh, but it is 'only an empty sign of the grace that might have saved him'.[36] The poem ends with a blustering attempt to take control of its significance: 'Whate'er shee meant by it' (l. 17), it will become a talismanic means to reassert some measure of influence over the lady who gave it. If it refuses to mean one kind of little death, it can mean another; and he ends on a vengefully performative locution: 'since you would save none of mee, I bury some of you' (l. 24). In these poems and others like them, the crisis of theological signification is relocated from the eucharistic Host to lovers' tokens; Donne invokes the whole spectrum of sacramental belief to try for an expression of faith that will transcend absence, but it is the deluded lovers, besotted or rageful, that turn out to be the best Catholics. There is an insistent sense that the kind of incarnationist sacramentalism they seek always threatens to subside into the merely figurative, whether they realise it or not, and the written nature of the sign is implicated in this feared failure. The lovers' rhetoric fluctuates between thinking itself truly transformative and a series of empty signs: these sacramentalised tokens want to crystallise and confirm the words they stand in for but, constituted of those words, they are subject to the same instabilities of meaning. 'A Jeat Ring sent' becomes, through the punning of its opening lines, specifically about this substitution and its limitations: 'Thou art not so black, as my heart, | Nor halfe so brittle, as her heart, thou art' (ll. 1–2). Chiasmic repetition underlines the double meaning of this 'art', so what is black and brittle, but not so black and brittle as what it represents, is both the ring and the inked words of this verse made circular by its rhetorical frame.

---

[36] DiPasquale, *Literature and Sacrament*, p. 160.

In 'A Valediction of my name, in the window', Donne moves one step further in his exploration of the ideas about language and materiality that are consequent on thinking about sacramental substitution in verse. What this lover leaves as his surety, to mitigate his absence and as a promise of his return, is not a ring or a lock of hair, but a word. Before leaving for a journey, he etches his name on the window of his beloved. 'My name engrav'd herein | Doth contribute my firmnesse to this glasse,' the poem begins; the charm, as he calls his scratched signature, is to keep him for ever in front of his mistress's eye (ll. 1–2). The qualities of glass allow elaborate visual paradox: it can be seen and seen through, so she can look at once at his name and at her own reflection. '[L]oves magique' brings the two pictures together, and her face appears to her overwritten with that possessive inscription: 'Here you see mee, and I am you' (ll. 11–12). At the fourth stanza, however, the name starts to insist on an eerie embodiment, straining at the bounds of its potential signification:

> Or if too hard and deepe
> This learning be, for a scratch'd name to teach,
>   It, as a given deaths head keepe
>   Lovers mortalitie to preach,
> Or thinke this ragged bony name to bee
>   My ruinous Anatomie.   (ll. 19–24)

Etching words on glass is difficult, even with a diamond; the writing that results is not smooth like an inked hand, but infinitesimally angular. To Donne's mind these uneven characters suggest a skeleton, and so the name takes shape as a cipher invested with the rights and influence of the man it signifies, a grotesque guarantee of his real presence. As this spindly scratched carcass remains with his lover, Donne argues, the rest of his physical constituents will be drawn irresistibly back in a sexual second coming:

> The rafters of my body, bone
> Being still with you, the Muscle, Sinew,'and Veine,
>   Which tile this house, will come againe.   (ll. 28–30)

It is a resurrection fantasy, played out with a synecdochic signature instead of a corpse; the 'scatter'd body' (l. 32) of the distant lover looks forward to the day of judgement, and the animated inscription acts in the meantime as a prop to a weak faith. Already, the note of confidence on which the poem opened is faltering, and the fear of infidelity prompts the proxy name to new prodigies of enactment:

> When thy'inconsiderate hand
> Flings out this casement, with my trembling name,

> To look on one, whose wit or land,
> New battry to thy heart may frame,
> Then thinke this name alive.   (ll. 43–7)

Suddenly vulnerable and easily overlooked, the name trembles with indignation as well as with cold when his mistress threatens to respond to another man's wooing. 'Then thinke this name alive' might be fearful, if it did not recognise so acutely its own impotence.

Once again, the lover's attempts to leave a sign that will evoke a Catholic sense of living presence are frustrated by a creeping scepticism, and the drama of the last stanzas is not of this writing's powerfully performative assurance of faith, but an almost farcical description of the skeleton-name's efforts to interpose its insubstantial self between mistress and rival. The name wants to be a vigorous earnest of and surety for fidelity, when all it can do is rely on the memory it evokes in the mind of the beholder; it is sign, not substitute, and finds itself thwarted by a receptionist theory of sacramental participation. By the end, both the name on the window and the words of the poem that record it are emptied of efficacy. Tired of the fantasy, and the futility of the token he has left, Donne abandons the conceit.

> But glasse, and lines must bee,
> No meanes our firme substantiall love to keepe;
> Neere death inflicts this lethargie,
> And this I murmure in my sleepe;
> Impute this idle talke, to that I goe
> For dying men talke often so.   (ll. 61–6)

Those histrionic final four lines falsify the promised bodily restitution; the poet starts ailing even before he has left his mistress's company, and 'substantiall' love – the word here is charged with its eucharistic subtext – is recognised as beyond the power of brittle glass or black lines to influence. Words are no substitute for physical presence, and the whole intricate edifice of the poem crumbles to its puncturing conclusion. Far from being a way of keeping the living man in the mind of his beloved, 'the engraved name', as Baumlin notices, 'becomes the poet's grave'; from the first line, this pun has shadowed the rhetoric of faith and unity, and predicted the otherwise startling sickening of the final stanza. It is the only performative word in the poem.[37]

The eucharistic rhetoric of Donne's love poetry is less often a device to achieve the old magic of presence-in-absence than a way to mark its distance

---

[37] Baumlin, *Rhetorics of Renaissance Discourse*, p. 183.

and mourn its loss. The world of his lovers is shaped by modes of thought displaced from traditional worship, but the acute problem of keeping faith prevents any untroubled nostalgic preservation of their protocols in the private realm. It is the suspicious or frustrated lover who tends to turn to quasi-Catholic patterns of belief and their forms of expression in an attempt to compel acquiescence or fidelity; this shows a double failure of apprehension, a misunderstanding not just of the operation of the sacraments, but of the nature of love. Among these lyrics, the more explicit eucharistic vocabulary is almost always invoked in a context of erotic heresy: the sourly parodic complaint of 'Twicknam Garden', for example, positions its speaker as a petulant recusant. There is an opening reference to 'the Roman Catholic sacrament of Extreme Unction' in the 'balmes' (l. 4) this lover seeks for eye and ear; more direct and more arresting, however, is Donne's reformulation of the Petrarchan commonplace of the disappointed lover as impervious to the charms of season or surroundings.[38]

> O, selfe traytor, I do bring
> The spider love, which transubstantiates all,
>   And can convert Manna to gall. (ll. 5–7)

The beauty of the garden is turned to poison by the festering obsession of unreciprocated, or more specifically unconsummated, love; this reverse eucharist takes manna, traditionally a typological anticipation of the Last Supper, and turns it instead into the bitter wine with which Christ's thirst was mocked on the cross. The 'transubstantiation' here is from communion to crucifixion, and the implication that frustrated passion has the power to effect it; 'spider love' signifies an absence of physical contact, so-called because the cold-blooded arachnid was thought to reproduce without sex. Eucharistic parody does not end there: after imagining himself a 'senseless peece' of the garden, petrified with his poison into an anthropomorphic 'mandrake' or weeping 'stone fountaine' (ll. 17–18), this unhappy lover becomes the sacrifice that is the test of others' faith:

> Hither with christall vyals, lovers come,
> And take my teares, which are loves wine,
> And try your mistress Teares at home,
> For all are false, that tast not just like mine. (ll. 19–22)

Again, this has a distinctively Roman Catholic flavour: 'loves wine' is offered reverently in elaborate chalices as 'a sacrament of envious nonfulfillment', 'a eucharist of suspicion' for successful lovers.[39] This malevolent

---

[38] Whalen, *Poetry of Immanence*, p. 27.   [39] DiPasquale, *Literature and Sacrament*, p. 164.

figure evokes a warped sacramentalism as substitute and revenge for the physical deprivation of his beloved's touch; just as the failure of friendship in Donne's sonnet to Thomas Woodward, so erotic failure is here framed in the terms of doctrinal error.

IMPLICIT SACRAMENTALISM: RHETORIC AND DIVINITY

Implicit in this argument is a sense that the divine poems cannot be neatly divided from the secular poems by interest, imagery or even theological significance: both are richly informed by the controversy over the eucharist and its implications for poetic language and efficacy. This is no longer a controversial stance, but it is perhaps worth quoting again Donne's views on the transferability of patterns of thought and expression. He speaks of King Solomon, a particularly resonant figure of conversion:

Salomon, whose disposition was amorous, and excessive in the love of women, when he turn'd to God, he departed not utterly from his old phrase and language, but ... conveyes all his loving approaches and applications to God, and all Gods gracious answers to his amorous soul, into songs, and Epithalamions. (*Sermons*, 1: 237)

To an extent, this is what Donne does too: the transition is, however, made easier by the distinctly religious bent of 'his old phrase and language', so the superimposed impression is not so awry and squint as it might have been. In the middle of weighing up his chances on judgement day, for example, Donne – like the amorously inclined Solomon – can smoothly recycle a line he formerly used to ask for a different sort of favour ('as in my idolatrie | I said to all my profane mistresses ...' (Holy Sonnet 9, ll. 9–10)): the incongruity is felt more keenly by readers than by the poet. I have touched on the difficulties of determining the order of Donne's works, and would not hazard an argument that rested on any degree of precision in dating; from evidence both external and internal like this, though, it seems clear that a number of poems specifically on religious subjects postdate those already discussed. The divine poems therefore, with which the last part of this chapter is concerned, will be considered primarily as contiguous with, and in some cases a development of, the secular lyrics with which the study began.

In the absence of a work which addresses sacramental operation directly either as a spiritual matter or from the perspective of polemic, Donne's understanding must be reconstructed, again, from its rhetorical traces. Punning is an obvious, though not the only, place to look: its potential to double and divide, to explore the limits of the language of signification, lends it to the expression or enactment of a sacramental dynamic. The other feature that is significant is what Redfern calls the 'Janus-faced' nature of puns: they turn a word to different uses by multiplying its meanings. In orthodox Protestant theology, this is precisely the function of the prayer of consecration, as McNees points out; she cites Donne's explanation of the nature of presence in support of an argument about its rhetorical application: 'We say the sacramental bread is the body of Christ', he writes, 'because God hath shed his Ordinance upon it, and made it of another nature in the use, though not in the substance' (*Sermons*, VII: 296). This, McNees believes, 'provides an analogy for Donne's use of divisive poetic figures, particularly pun and paradox'; these devices take their warrant from an understanding of eucharistic theology which they are occasionally employed specifically to express.[40] The sequence *La Corona*, while surprisingly restrained in its wordplay given its iterative structure, offers an excellent example. The last line of each of the seven sonnets forms the first line of the next, until the final line of the last turns out to have been the first line of the first: a pleasing circularity that has long been identified with the devotional practice of telling the rosary. In the fifth sonnet, 'Crucifying', the words start working free of their single significations: 'Whose creature Fate is, now prescribe a Fate' (l. 7); 'When it beares him, he must beare more and die' (l. 11): this is *antanaclasis*, where a word is repeated in two different senses, and the coincidences of meaning here are felt as profound religious ironies. The sonnet ends with a plea for a sign of salvation that is explicitly eucharistic: '*Moyst, with one drop of thy blood, my dry soule*' (l. 14). In the space between one poem and the next, after crucifixion and before resurrection, a transformation takes place; from an imperative, 'Moyst' becomes an adjective, as the assurance of grace the poet asks for is granted: '*Moyst with one drop of thy blood, my dry soule* | Shall', Donne writes, 'bee | Freed' (ll. 1–4). The figure takes on a sacramental function, and rhetoric and eucharist act as mutual guarantee: Donne's confidence in their powers of truthful conveyance depends, finally, on this analogy, and on the capacity of each to underwrite the other.[41]

In 'The Crosse', the pun is a governing conceit, and the poem is interested in visual coincidence as well as verbal play. Its context is the

---

[40] McNees, 'Anglican Doctrine', 103.
[41] DiPasquale identifies the liturgical significance of the pun: 'Donne does to a word what the Consecration does to the bread and wine – he changes its nature by changing its use' (*Literature and Sacrament*, p. 81).

controversy over whether the cross had any place in reformed churches as physical artefact or symbolic gesture, for example at baptism; the most radical Puritans thought not, because of the dangers of misapprehension – the sign taken for what it signifies – leading to idolatry.[42] As is evident from this (for him) relatively unusual contribution to contemporary liturgical debate, Donne did not agree, and the poem is framed as a defence of that holy shape in all its manifestations: 'Since Christ embrac'd the Crosse it selfe, dare I | His image, th'image of his Crosse deny?' (ll. 1–2). Donne walks in a world where nothing has only its own signification, and he is determined to hold on to its possibilities:

> From mee, no Pulpit, nor misgrounded law,
> Nor scandall taken, shall this Crosse withdraw,
> It shall not, for it cannot; for, the losse
> Of this Crosse, were to me another Crosse.   (ll. 9–12)

The wordplay here is complex; the sense of 'burden' or 'affliction' that 'Crosse' carries the second time around is of course derived from Christ's cross, first in this line and, the poem contends, the pattern of all others. There is sufficient disparity for the force of the pun to be felt, but the etymological relation seals the argument: even if the literal cross were completely suppressed, it would trace its shape in the metaphorical cross ('suffering') such suppression would constitute for believers. It is a pun' Donne is pleased with and uses elsewhere, often, as in the passage from a sermon that follows, to advocate an active imitation of Christ:

When my crosses have carried mee up to my Saviours Crosse, I put my hands into his hands, and hang upon his nailes, I put mine eyes upon his, and wash off all my former unchast looks ... I put my mouth upon his mouth, and it is I that say, *My God, my God, why hast thou forsaken me?* (*Sermons*, II: 300)

Donne imagines himself as a corporeal pun: a double or mirror for Christ, stretched along his sinews in an impersonation so intimate and intense that the tears of one wet the eyes of the other. He becomes a living sacrament, suspended by a verbal correspondence on the sign of his own salvation.

'The Crosse' pursues the same logic of sacramental enactment, though without the concentrated compassion of that vision of Calvary.

---

[42] For the background to this dispute and its relevance to Donne's poem, see P. M. Oliver, *Donne's Religious Writing: a Discourse of Feigned Devotion* (London: Longman, 1997), pp. 67–80. Oliver reads it as a specific – and aggressive – refutation of (in the event, unsuccessful) reforms put to James I at the Hampton Court conference of 1604.

> Who can blot out the Crosse, which th'instrument
> Of God, dew'd on mee in the Sacrament?
> Who can deny mee power, and liberty
> To stretch mine armes, and mine own Crosse to be?
> Swimme, and at every stroake, thou art thy Crosse.   (ll. 15–19)

The deliberation and devotion of assuming this cruciform posture begins to dissipate as opportunities multiply; it is hard not to perform an imitation of Christ if an enthusiastic breast-stroke counts. This is much more like a bad visual pun, the kind of *paronomasia* that pushes disparate words or images into unwilling accord, and the world starts to fill up with 'Crosses in small things' (l. 20), from ships' masts to the wing-spans of birds, everywhere the poet looks. As the poem proceeds, 'Crosse' becomes a verb as well as a noun: 'Crosse | Your joy in crosses', Donne warns those who might be in danger of enjoying these imitative afflictions (ll. 41–1); 'the eye needs crossing' (l. 49); 'Crosse and correct concupiscence of witt' (l. 58). The logic of the figure is strained by its successive iterations, its powers of signification threatened by being made to seem fragile and unstable. It is only a more modern sensibility, though, that would see meaning leached like this rather than confirmed in its proliferation; Donne here adopts the viewpoint I have elsewhere associated with his contemporary and colleague Lancelot Andrewes, of understanding the universe as verbal and seeing the world in a word: a pun, however contingent, is to be treasured as evidence of the remains of a divine order; there is no such thing as an accident.[43] Paul Harland recognises this as specifically sacramental: 'One takes up the crosses, abundantly provided by nature and circumstances, as "The Crosse" shows, so as to imitate Christ, not in a literal or mechanical way, but in order to reincarnate the real presence of Christ in the world.'[44] Despite its sometimes homiletic tone, this poem describes a system of incarnatory signification in which, through this wordplay, it can itself participate: in a textual universe, objects and concepts are subject to an intellectual alchemy which will find within them the traces of God.

The cross that dominates the panoramas of Donne's verse, though, is in a different poem, and for all its magnitude, he sees it only in his mind's eye. Carey's atmospheric characterisation of the poet's situation in

---

[43] Sophie Read, 'Lancelot Andrewes's Sacramental Wordplay', *Cambridge Quarterly*, 36 (2007), 11–31.
[44] Paul W. Harland, '"A True Transubstantiation": Donne, Self-Love, and the Passion', in *John Donne's Religious Imagination*, ed. by Raymond-Jean Frontain and Frances M. Malpezzi (Canway: University of Central Arkansas, 1995), pp. 162–80 (p. 170).

'Goodfriday, 1613. Riding Westward' is hard to improve on: 'He moves like a planet away from a giant crucifix, the landscape's only feature, which he dare not look at, and on which Christ hangs, watching him. In all the two counties, Donne and Christ are the sole figures.'[45] 'Goodfriday' is a puzzling poem, partly because the title and its subscription ('Mr J. Dunne goeinge from Sr HG: on good fryday sent him back this Meditacion, on the waye') lead one to expect something temporally or topographically specific, rather than this visionary, supernatural rumination; and partly because, right from the start, it lacks the scrupulous self-positioning that might be expected – from, say, a poet like Herbert. In this work Donne abandons the opportunities offered by the double-faced pun in favour of an internal conflict on a grander scale: the poem pulls against its own logic from the first line. The poet is on a journey when he should be in church, and his excuses are ingenious but not wholly convincing. He starts with the tone of one setting forward an analogical proposition – 'Let mans Soule be a Spheare' – and goes on to explain that, though its natural bent be towards the east, in devotional reverence, 'Pleasure or businesse' exert a stronger gravitational pull which is why he is travelling in a contrary direction (ll. 1, 7). This argument is specious, and proved so by what follows. The next lines picture the spectacle the truant might have seen if he were facing the right way, and seventeenth-century England collapses into first-century Jerusalem to create a metaphorical landscape where the normal operations of time and geography are suspended. As Donne describes the sight he will not look on, it transpires that the press of business is not the only reason for his turning away:

> Yet dare I'almost be glad, I do not see
> That spectacle of too much weight for mee.
> Who sees God's face, that is selfe life, must dye;
> What a death were it then to see God dye?
> It made his own Lieutenant Nature shrinke,
> It made his footstoole crack, and the Sunne winke.
> Could I behold those hands which span the Poles,
> And tune all spheares at once, peirc'd with those holes?
> Could I behold that endlesse height which is
> Zenith to us, and to'our Antipodes,
> Humbled below us? or that blood which is
> The seat of all our Soules, if not of his,
> Make durt of dust, or that flesh which was worne
> By God, for his apparell, rag'd and torne? (ll. 15–28)

[45] Carey, *John Donne*, p. 121.

Donne struggles with the paradoxes of the incarnation, unable to reconcile God's divine nature with his abjection in human flesh; the sight he turns away from is realised in vividly carnal terms, with no sacramental understanding allowed to mediate between the spiritual ('those hands which span the Poles') and the physical ('pierc'd with those holes'). God is imagined, like Donne, as pulled in two contrary and conflicting directions: a pun embodied, as incarnation and eucharist. Donne is not, even here, interested in the mysteries of the real presence: his mind's eye sees Christ's lifeblood pattering on the dry ground under the cross, turning the earth into red mud; the world withers, but no cherubim with chalices intervene to bear it away for the communion rites of posterity.

'At the center of the poem – early, late, throughout – is Donne as a curiously Janus-faced man. One face, of will, turns away from Christ. The other, of memory, looks toward him.'[46] Thomas Sloane identifies the God with the double aspect as a governing figure in 'Goodfriday', and in Donne's work more generally; the incarnate Christ, too, is Janus-faced, one human and one divine. Donne's project of imitation here takes the form of a splitting of the self into two: will that rides forward and memory that reaches back. The irresolution of the final lines is in part a matter of tense, because they are framed as future expectation and not present certainty; it is also, however, because they refuse to ask for a unity of these dual perspectives. A Donne revealed in the image of his God is still, it turns out, two-faced:

> Though these things, as I ride, be from mine eye,
> They'are present yet unto my memory,
> For that looks towards them; and thou look'st towards mee,
> O Saviour, as thou hang'st upon the tree;
> I turne my back to thee, but to receive
> Corrections, till thy mercies bid thee leave.
> O think me worth thine anger, punish mee,
> Burne off my rusts, and my deformity,
> Restore thine image, so much, by thy grace,
> That thou may'st know mee, and I'll turne my face.   (ll. 33–42)

The poet has admitted, in the first few lines of the poem, that his reasons for turning his back are nothing to do with feelings of unworthiness or humility; 'Pleasure or businesse' (l. 7) prompts his journey on this day of devotion, and weakness keeps his focus to the front ('I durst not looke'

---

[46] Thomas O. Sloane, *Donne, Milton, and the End of Humanist Rhetoric* (Berkeley: University of California Press, 1985), p. 40.

(l. 29)). To recast this attitude as one of penitent submission is at best sophistical; it is more knowingly self-serving, for example, than the swimmer claiming to perform the shape of the cross with each stroke. The wit in this conceit risks shading over into cunning, particularly when the poet's final promise is revealed to be contingent on the prior action of Christ. Purification happens not through confronting the lowering crucifix at his back, but in order that he may do so; and what he expects to see after this 'double reversal of double retrospection, which no one alive could ever actually write', is an image of himself.[47]

'Goodfriday' has ciphered within it more Donnes than one; this is also true, though in a rather different sense, of 'A Hymne to God the Father'. This poem has attracted a certain notoriety: 'critics are often uncomfortable with John Donne's blatant pun on his own name'.[48] Since it was pointed out that there may also be a less blatant pun on Donne's wife's maiden name ('More'), critics have been uncomfortable with that too, or sometimes instead; the pun on sun/son has usually been left alone, as endorsed by frequent use and hermeneutic tradition.[49] As this chapter has argued, the kind of egocentric wordplay that prompts such adverse reactions was clearly natural to the poet, as demonstrated by the end of the verse letter to Sir Henry Wotton ('I have, and you have DONNE'), or Izaak Walton's relation of the sardonic witticism Donne is said to have made on his socially disastrous marriage: '*John Donne, Anne Donne, Un-Donne*'. Critics, though, have felt it a mixed blessing that the pair of them had surnames which were homonymic with common English words, and have been made uneasy by the possible proliferations: when is 'done' not 'Donne', 'more' not 'More'?

> Wilt thou forgive that sinne where I begunne,
>   Which is my sin, though it were done before?
> Wilt thou forgive those sins through which I runne,
>   And doe them still: though still I doe deplore?
>   When thou hast done, thou hast not done,
>   For, I have more.   (ll. 1–6)

This may be a general confession, from original sin onwards; or it may be the specific admission of an idolatrous, uxorious love, one that prevents the

---

[47] This is A. B. Chambers's description of the final turn of the poem, which he considers 'problematic' (*Transfigured Rites in Seventeenth-Century English Poetry* (Columbia: University of Missouri Press, 1992), p. 205).

[48] Frederick Ahl, 'Ars Est Caelare Artem (Art in Puns and Anagrams Engraved)', in *On Puns: the Foundation of Letters*, ed. by Jonathan Culler (Oxford: Blackwell, 1988), pp. 17–43 (p. 22).

[49] See Harry Morris, 'John Donne's Terrifying Pun', *Papers on Language and Literature*, 9 (1973), 128–37.

poet's true turning to God: 'I have More.' David Novarr displays a scepticism that is, to an extent, a useful corrective; but his suspicious shuddering
betrays a fundamental reluctance either to credit coincidence or to allow for
a play of meanings within the lines: 'Can Donne have *more* both ways, as
more sins and as *Ann More?*' he asks: 'a reading based entirely on the pun is
both strained and contrary to Donne's customary practice'.[50] But the point
of a pun is to have things both ways, and one reading cannot cancel out the
other without loss. In Donne's sonnet on his wife's death, a similar thought
is framed, with the same serendipitous ambiguity; if the woman's name is
not heard behind this grieving resignation, the sense is not compromised,
but the feeling is: 'why should I begg more love, when as thou | Does wooe
my soule, for hers offring all thine?' ('Since she whom I lovd', ll. 9–10). The
pun in another context might be rejected as inappropriate or even interfer-
ing, but it is still there. More is at stake in this argument than just a disputed
reading; allowing puns as half-heard possibilities acknowledges a sacramental viewpoint from which world and text are both subject to transfiguration.
Judith Anderson has called this '(im)possible' punning, where a subsidiary
sense is activated even as it is discounted as 'far-fetched or grammatically
irrational', and she has identified it as a strategy capable of altering the verbal
and therefore the physical world.[51] Though she does not make the argument
directly, her terms are implicitly sacramental: 'In the simultaneity of
Donne's (im)possible punning', Anderson writes, 'the crossing of bounda-
ries, disruption of the everyday, and doubling of reference actually *transfigure* the world that we know, rather than merely reflecting, refusing, or
rising above it.'[52]

Donne's attempts to influence his fate through the force of his rhetoric
are striking; the puns in the 'Hymne' carry the weight of his claim to
salvation, and even if Anne's presence in the poem might be in doubt, her
husband's is not. Donne inhabits his lines with anxious equivocation,
negotiating forgiveness for sins conceived, committed and persisted in,
things ill done and done to others' harm, sins for 'A yeare, or two'
renounced, but 'wallowed in, a score' (ll. 9–10). Forgiveness must be infinite
to match the depth of the poet's depravities; each time God thinks he has
finished, his servant John Donne turns out to be in need of further shriving:
'When thou hast done, thou hast not done | For, I have more' (ll. 5–6). As in

[50] David Novarr, '*Amor Vincit Omnia*: Donne and the Limits of Ambiguity', *Modern Language Review*,
      82 (1987), 286–92 (291–2).
[51] Anderson, *Translating Investments*, p. 125.
[52] Anderson, 'Donne's (Im)possible Punning', *John Donne Journal*, 23 (2004), 59–68 (68).

'Goodfriday', the resolution of this impasse is in both a projected future and a historical past, conditional upon a promise Donne seeks to elicit while half acknowledging that, in the incarnation, it has already been made:

> Swear by thy selfe, that at my death thy Sunne
> Shall shine as it shines now, and heretofore;
> And, having done that, Thou hast done,
>   I have no more.   (ll. 15–18)

As in 'Goodfriday', too, a logically complex ending conceals a lurking blasphemy. '[H]aving done that': the syntax is poised between confidence and calculation, between stating a fact and striking a deal. The phonetic logic of these lines is, though, what tries to seal his assurance of salvation; the sun cannot but shine, so the promise made in the incarnate Christ stands. The poet reverses the significance of his ill-omened name, fits it into a rhetorical structure that lets it give itself to God: 'Thou hast done'; if the pun on his name is not felt here insistently, the reach of God's grace, his ability to save such a sinner, is brought shockingly into question. The same trick ('you have DONNE') ratified the sacrament of friendship sent to Henry Wotton; a single word with two meanings figures the dual substances of the Host, the dual natures of God, and the Janus-faced poet whose present cannot stamp out the impression of his past.

For underlying Donne's rhetorical art and its imperative to test the limits of representational language is an interest in the possibilities of conversion. The metaphor with which this chapter opened, of the mind of a religious convert as a twice-struck coin, finds its twin in Donne's description of the powers of rhetoric:

The way of Rhetorique in working upon weake men, is first to trouble the understanding, to displace, and to discompose, and disorder the judgement, to smother and bury in it, or to empty it of former apprehensions and opinions, and to shake that beliefe, with which it had possessed it self before, and then when it is thus melted, to powre it into new molds, when it is thus mollified, to stamp and imprint new formes, new images, new opinions in it. (*Sermons*, ii: 282–3)

Though the tone here is negative, Donne's excitement at the idea of being overwritten or reinterpreted by God is evident throughout his verse. A disdain for the 'Smithfield martyrdom' suffered by recusants such as Southwell does not mean he did not find his own way to emulate Christ: it is a textual imitation of a figure who was, for Donne, 'a *figurative*, a *metaphoricall God*'; who had 'contracted thine immensity and shut thyself within syllables'; whose presence on earth was 'not only a verbal but an actual manifestation'; whose death 'is delivered to us, as a *writing* . . . not onely given us to read, but to write over, and practise'.[53] For Donne, rhetoric offered a way to transfigure the Catholic sensibility that would have demanded a martyr's death to a Protestant understanding of sacramental efficacy that allowed him to transubstantiate with words; the poetic use he makes of the old forms of worship rather guarantees than falsifies this conversion.

TRANSUBSTANTIATING TRANSUBSTANTIATION

This argument will draw to a close with one last example of Donne's sacramental wordplay. The word 'transubstantiation' appears nowhere in the divine poems, nor do any of its cognates; it does, however, occur three times in the secular verse, each time wrested from its original scholastic signification. The 'spider love, which transubstantiates all' in 'Twicknam Garden' is discussed above; the other two instances make the word carry an alchemical sense. 'But you are gold, and Shee', Donne writes of Virtue and the Countess of Huntingdon, 'Us she inform'd, but transubstantiates you' ('Man to God's Image', ll. 25–6). In the 'First Anniversary', the lamented Elizabeth Drury does not quite manage this feat, but she comes close: 'though she could not transubstantiate | All states to gold, yet guilded every state' (ll. 417–18). Making the term figurative like this is entirely consonant with Donne's practice elsewhere, even in the sermons: it is a bold appropriation of a word that should be specifically Roman Catholic – denoting, as it does, the conversion of the whole substance of the bread and wine into the body and blood of Christ in the eucharist – but comes to be pressed into the service of a reformed theology by Donne's poetic imagination. He may intend contemptuous dismissal of both papistry and poetry when he puts the misapprehensions of one down to the deceptive allure of the other, but he uses the insight to devastating rhetorical effect.

[T]he Roman Church hath catched a *Trans*, and others a *Con*, and a *Sub*, and an *In*, and varied their poetry into a Transubstantiation, and a Consubstantiation, and the rest, and rymed themselves beyond reason, into absurdities, and heresies, and by a young figure of *similiter cadens*, they are fallen alike into error. (*Sermons*, VII: 296)

Christ's presence in the sacrament is detached from the physical and invested in the rhetorical; this has implications for poetry as well as for theology, because Donne believes in figurative language as a vehicle

---

[53] *Sermons*; *Devotions on Emergent Occasions*, Expostulation 19; *Essays in Divinity*, ed. by Evelyn Simpson (Oxford: Clarendon Press, 1952), p. 37; *Sermons*, III: 349; *Sermons*, X: 196.

for truth and an instrument of conversion. His thoughts about the type of all converts, Saul-Paul, follow explicitly eucharistic lines, and depend on this rhetorical redeployment of the trope of transubstantiation: 'Here was a true Transubstantiation, and a new Sacrament,' he writes of the encounter on the Road to Damascus; 'These few words, *Saul, Saul, why persecutest thou me,* are the words of consecration; After these words, *Saul* was no longer *Saul,* but he was Christ' (*Sermons,* VI: 209). Again, the 'true Transubstantiation' is something that happens not on the altar but in the believer: 'when I have received it worthily, it becomes my very soule' (*Sermons,* VII: 321).

Donne has split the word so it retains the sense of efficacy from its primary signification, and language becomes the ground of a spiritual and emotional apprehension of sacramental grace. Jeanne Shami recognises the importance of this device: 'In the end, metaphor is the fertile ground of Donne's religious imagination and of his belief that real conversion takes place internally – in the heart – but, more importantly, is effected by and transformed into the language with which the heart's knowledge is expressed.'[54] She sees that '[i]n itself, transubstantiation makes sense *only* as a trope', but is, I think, wrong to suggest that 'Donne's metaphorical redefinition of controversial terms rids them of their conventional polemical baggage'; here, as elsewhere, Donne works to retain a sense of the physical in the figurative, and the daring of his strategy is that in transubstantiating the word 'transubstantiation', he has kept its literal meaning while investing it with a new spiritual one.[55] In other words, it acts as a pun as well as a metaphor. Donne's work does not think conventionally about rhetoric: eucharistic tropes extend and complicate traditional rhetorical practice, and across the genres of his writing ideas of sacramental operation and efficacy inform his methods and modes of figuration. Anxieties about keeping faith, both religious and romantic, lead to a desire to instantiate the real presence of the beloved, or the self, in the flesh of language; this tests the limits of figurative representation, and explains Donne's frequent recourse to devices like the pun, with their possibilities of splitting and doubling, and their promise of reorganising the material world. In this, Donne is sharply distinguished from his older contemporary and sometime co-religionist Robert Southwell; the advantage he takes of new distances between signified and sign would have been impossible under the old dispensation, when the

---

[54] Jeanne Shami, 'Troping Religious Identity: Circumcision and Transubstantiation in Donne's Sermons', in *Renaissance Tropologies: the Cultural Imagination of Early Modern England,* ed. by Jeanne Shami (Pittsburgh: Duquesne University Press, 2008) pp. 89–117 (pp. 116).
[55] Shami, 'Troping Religious Identity', pp. 109, 91.

truest sense of sacrament was always physical. Donne's conversions, from Catholicism to Protestantism, and from eros to agape, left him a thoroughly Janus-faced poet; for a brief space in both personal and cultural history, he made it possible for eucharistic tropes to express without heresy or blasphemy the deepest concerns of the emotional life.

CHAPTER 3

Herbert and metanoia

Herbert was looking forward to the new academic year. 'The Orators place (that you may understand what it is) is the finest place in the University,' he writes to his stepfather, Sir John Danvers, of the appointment which he was working to secure; 'though', he adds with a hint of ruefulness, 'not the gainfullest'.[1] This was a concern, because, as a younger son, Herbert needed to make his own way in the world. He was born into a relatively prosperous and well-connected Protestant family in 1593, seventh of ten brothers and sisters; the eldest, Edward, was also a poet, and became the first Baron Herbert of Cherbury. His mother seems to have been a charismatic and resourceful woman; she brought up her many children alone after the early death of Herbert's father, until she married the 24-year-old Danvers in 1609: she was then in her late forties. According to Aubrey, Danvers married Magdalen Herbert 'for love of her witt'. John Donne, too, must have been rather captivated by it; he was a frequent visitor to the household, and he dedicated to her the sequence of poems known as his Holy Sonnets. Herbert's was a cultured, intellectual and devout upbringing; as well as Donne and Francis Bacon, the boy would have met the composers John Bull and William Byrd at his mother's house, and the historian William Camden. For his formal education, he went to Westminster School, then overseen by Lancelot Andrewes as Dean of Westminster, and later to Trinity College, Cambridge.[2]

It was from here, having received his Bachelor of Arts in 1613 and been elected to a major fellowship in 1616, that Herbert made his application for the post of University Orator, in effect the post of professional rhetorician. In another letter to Danvers some days after the first, Herbert confronts the misgivings of a family friend: 'I understand by Sir *Francis Nethersols* Letter, that he fears I have not fully resolved of the matter, since this place being

[1] Herbert to Sir John Danvers [September 1619], in *Works*, pp. 369–70.
[2] This biographical account is derived from Helen Wilcox's entry on Herbert in the *DNB* online.

civil may divert me too much from Divinity.'[3] As his immediate predecessor in the role (Herbert was duly elected in January 1619/20), Nethersole was in a position to judge, and the concern he voices reflects a belief widespread at the time: that rhetoric and religion sorted ill together. Herbert's initial response to Nethersole's uneasiness is uncharacteristically glib: 'this dignity, hath no such earthiness in it, but it may very well be joined with Heaven', he answers, before a revealing qualification suggests that he may in fact have been more keenly aware of the contradiction than he was then prepared to allow: 'or if it had to others, yet to me it should not, for ought I yet knew'.[4] Herbert spent his career as a poet striving to make good this tempered assertion: anxious from the start to demonstrate that the rhetoric of his poetic art could be bent to sacred ends. If Walton is to be believed, it was as a seventeen-year-old undergraduate that Herbert started writing sacred verse. He sent to his mother two sonnets declaring his rejection of the current vogue for love poetry and all its erotic clichés, and dedicating his talent instead to the praise of God: 'Doth Poetry | Wear *Venus* Livery? only serve her turn?' he asks; 'Why are not *Sonnets* made of thee?'[5] This was to be a lasting preoccupation. With a far greater self-consciousness than can be found anywhere in the works of Southwell, or even Donne, Herbert throughout *The Temple* shows himself aware that this enterprise is, at best, uncertain of success; he both wishes it were possible and suspects that it is not, and these contradictory impulses and contrasting voices characterise much of his verse.

Contemporary readers were not on the whole sensitive to such difficulties, preferring to see Herbert's as a straightforwardly pious poetic; John Legate, author of the prefatory verses to Christopher Harvey's respectfully imitative *The Synagogue, Or, The Shadow of the Temple* is typical both in his extravagant respect for Herbert's synthesis of the spiritual and the intellectual, and in his failure to reproduce that achievement: '*Herbert!*' he apostrophises, 'Whose every strain | Twists holy Breast with happy Brain.'[6] The question of whether or not Herbert actually did succeed in creating a genuinely sacred poetic, though – one which contrived to marry the artifice of rhetoric with the sincerity of religion – is less interesting than a consideration of how hard and in what ways he tried. That *The Temple*

---

[3] Herbert to Sir John Danvers, 6 October 1619, in *Works*, ed. by Hutchinson, p. 370. That the previous letter was written no more than sixteen days before can be surmised from the fact that Herbert gives Nethersole his title ('Sir *Francis*'); Nethersole was knighted on 19 September 1619 (B. C. Pursell, 'Nethersole, Sir Francis (*bap.* 1587, *d.* 1659)', *DNB* online).

[4] Herbert, *Works*, p. 371.

[5] Herbert, *Works*, p. 206. Future references to Herbert's poetry will be to this edition, and will be given as line numbers in the text.

[6] Poem postfixed to Christopher Harvey, *The Synagogue*, 2nd edn (London, 1647).

might in fact be a dramatisation of an irresolvable tension between form and content (a 'strain' and 'Twist' very different from that imagined by Legate) is a possibility raised, though not always considered in all its complexity, by some of the most astute of Herbert's more recent critics. In the discussion that follows, I will consider in some detail A. D. Nuttall's sceptical analysis of Herbert's rhetorical strategy in *Overheard by God* and the response to Nuttall's argument put forward by Elizabeth Clarke in her *Theory and Theology in George Herbert.*[7] Through a careful scrutiny of Herbert's deployment of a characteristic rhetorical trope – *metanoia*, also known as *correctio* – this chapter will explore a vexed issue in his critical reception: the diversity, even inconsistency, of his poetic representation of the eucharist. By extrapolating a habit of thought from the rhetorical structures of Herbert's verse, I intend to outline a way of reading that will reconcile the 'range of Eucharistic interpretations, from receptionism to full consubstantiation, that his Eucharistic imagery admits of'.[8] In doing so, I hope also to establish a less troubled relationship between the rhetorical mechanisms of Herbert's writing, the tropes and devices he carried with him from his time as Orator at Cambridge to the tiny country parish of Fugglestone-with-Bemerton, Salisbury, and the mysteries of his faith.

THE *METANOIETIC* IMPULSE: CORRECTION AND DECEPTION

If some critics have been over-eager to find flaws in Herbert's thinking, this impulse is more than counterbalanced by the school of readers that treats his work with a reverence approaching hagiography. A tendency to respond to the verse in a personal and emotional vein has, at times, seemed to preclude a critical viewpoint which would pursue the logic of its argument and allow for even an achieved failure on the part of the poet-priest. Consider, for example, this passage from Rosamund Tuve's hugely influential 1950s study, *A Reading of George Herbert*: 'The tone in this self-correction – "*mine*, alas!" ', she writes of 'The Jews', ' – is an example of that humility which gives such an endearing sweetness to Herbert's voice that it is not possible to read the poet without loving the man.'[9] What is

[7] A. D. Nuttall, *Overheard by God: Fiction and Prayer in Herbert, Milton, Dante and St John* (London: Methuen, 1980); Elizabeth Clarke, *Theory and Theology in George Herbert's Poetry: 'Divinitie, and Poesie, Met'* (Oxford: Clarendon Press, 1997).
[8] William Bonnell, '*Amnesis*: the Power of Memory in Herbert's Sacramental Vision', *George Herbert Journal*, 15 (1991), 33–48 (33).
[9] Rosamund Tuve, *A Reading of George Herbert* (London: Faber, 1952), p. 124.

obscured in Tuve's affectionate response to what she sees as the winning modesty of Herbert's lines is her implicit acknowledgement of their artfulness: 'this self-correction'. For the characteristic trick of assertion and retraction, the public revision of intent here taken as a sincere expression of humility, can also be read as a fundamentally duplicitous device: it enacts at the level of the line the contradictions inherent in the whole notion of sacred verse, and stands as a fitting exemplar of the problematic interface between rhetoric and religion.

Fitting, because this figure of mortification is one to which he was frequently and significantly drawn: '*Metanoia* or *Correctio*', Richard Strier remarks, 'is one of Herbert's favourite devices.'[10] Here I will prefer the Greek word, *metanoia*, because of its wider reach: it is a term not just of rhetoric but of theology, where its sense of a change of mind is deepened and extended to encompass a kind of thinking-beyond (the prefix *meta-* means 'beyond' or 'after', as in 'metaphysics'). More than a penitent impulse, in other words: a fundamental cognitive reorientation. St Paul experiences a *metanoia* on the road to Damascus when he is called violently to his ministry, and it is the word he uses in the gospels to signify real repentance. As Chapter 2 suggested, Donne's formulation for this is 'true Transubstantiation': both words carry a sense of fundamental and mystical alteration. Both, too, were vexed terms in post-Reformation theology. Tyndale attracted the wrath of Sir Thomas More for translating *metanoia* not as 'penance' but as 'repentance' in a polemical rejection of a Catholic works-based piety; 'Penance is a word of their own forging to deceive us withal as many other are,' he explains. His gloss brings out a cognitive dimension that transfers to its rhetorical sense: '*Metanoeite* in Greek, forthink ye, or let it forthink you.'[11] *Metanoia*, then, is a profound alteration of life, understood as the reconceptualisation on an intellectual as well as an emotional plane of an individual's relationship with God; this meaning, though it will be submerged in what follows and subsidiary to the rhetorical one, is deeply relevant. Herbert systematically makes poetry rethink itself and its motives, dramatised as his struggle to persuade the 'Lovely enchanting language' (l. 19) he mourns in 'The Forerunners' to reconsider its attachment to secular eroticism and come with him to the church; it is a pattern repeated at every level in his verse. The coincidence in terminology

[10] Richard Strier, *Love Known: Theology and Experience in George Herbert's Poetry* (University of Chicago Press, 1983), p. 240.
[11] William Tyndale, *The Obedience of a Christian Man*, ed. by David Daniell (London: Penguin, 2000), p. 115.

between the rhetorical and the theological here reflects a deeper conver-
gence in Herbert's thinking, and expresses once again the shared conceptual
framework of the two disciplines.

There is, however, an important distinction. In theology, *metanoia*
implies a categorical movement forwards, an epiphany from which there
is no return. In rhetoric, the figure exists as a narrative dramatisation of
doubt, and it is this potential for equivocation and elusiveness that so
attracts Herbert, interested always in the poetry of process. This rhetorical
possibility comes, though, with some ethical difficulty. To say something
and then audibly to think better of it, whether through a more careful
consideration or as a result of divine prompting, is to admit one's faults: in
many ways an act of penitence and humility. This, at least, is how George
Puttenham understands it in *The Arte of English Poesie*; 'Metanoia, or the
Penitent', in his definition, is when 'we speake and be sorry for it, as if we
had not wel spoken, so that we seeme to call in our word againe, and to put
in another fitter for the purpose: for which respects the Greekes called this
manner of speech the figure of repentance'.[12] Note, though, the element of
rhetorical distance: 'as if'; 'so that we seeme'. Peacham, in *The Garden of
Eloquence*, has little time for the notion of *metanoia* as an articulation of
penitence, but neither does he object primarily on the grounds of its
potential duplicity. His reservations, such as they are, centre on the need
for there to be error or solecism before it can be employed: 'The use of this
figure serveth the Orator, who either through rashnesse of affection, weak-
nesse of memorie, or imperfection of speech, he hath said some thing
amisse, to resume it, and amend it.' It is almost as an afterthought that he
adds the acknowledgement that an error might, after all, have been deliberate; that a speaker, 'under pretence of misliking', could 'take occasion to
express his minde more largely'.[13] John Hoskins, too, is alive to the
possibility; noting that the figure is convenient for one 'pretending a greater
vehemence of meaning', he observes that it is 'used when you would make
the thing more credible itself than in the manner of your utterance'.[14] This
problem of bad faith gestured at by Peacham and Hoskins is exacerbated
when the correction is not spoken, but written: if one can suspect a self-
adjusting orator of knowing what he was going to say all along, with a poet
one can be absolutely sure. The usual way to remedy a mistake on the page

---

[12] George Puttenham, *The Arte of English Poesie* (1589), ed. by Gladys Doidge Willcock and Alice Walker
    (Cambridge University Press, 1936; repr. 1970), p. 215.
[13] Peacham, *Garden of Eloquence*, 2nd edn (1593), p. 173.
[14] John Hoskins, *Directions for Speech and Style*, ed. by Hoyt T. Hudson (Princeton University Press,
    1935), p. 29.

is to erase it, not to leave it in place while presenting the reader with the possibility of a preferred alternative; that Herbert chooses so often to deploy the second strategy, despite the obvious rhetorical gloss in its mimicry of speech, suggests a profound appreciation of this complex dynamic.

Significant, too, is the prominence of the position he affords this device: the whole of *The Temple* is framed by a striking example of *metanoia*. 'Lord, my first fruits present themselves to thee,' are the opening words of the first poem in the volume, 'The Dedication'; 'Yet not mine neither: for from thee they came, | And must return' (ll. 1–3). At first, this seems a most abject stance for Herbert to adopt; his sense of unworthiness will not allow him to offer his poems to God on his own behalf, so he requires them to offer themselves ('whatever that might mean', as Clarke sensibly remarks of this puzzling manoeuvre[15]). Then comes the realisation that even such a self-effacing gesture might smack of presumption: the poems are, as indeed everything is, God's to begin with, and so there is no need for anyone (or anything) to offer them. The poet in his humility disappears completely from the equation. Nuttall reads this as an instance of Herbert's theology in logical freefall, as the poet starts to imagine God writing verses in praise of himself; the moral victory is then ultimately Herbert's, because humility is clearly more virtuous than self-glorification: 'Even something as apparently simple as a humble dedication cuts itself to pieces before our eyes,' Nuttall comments; and, later, 'Herbert really has nothing to give. Yet somehow he cannot let this paradox die, and allows the pathetic self-assertion to survive in the published poem.'[16] But it is as unwise to underestimate Herbert's rhetorical proficiency as it is to be taken in by it, as Tuve is; the point about *metanoia* is that it allows the poet to illustrate a process of emendation without entirely performing it: the erroneous element, for all that it has been corrected, remains, and the very mechanism that makes the lines empirically dubious rescues them from moral transgression. What 'The Dedication' describes is the devotional impulse of a pious but fallible man and his recognition of its inadequacy; because it is impossible to know what would be most pleasing to God ('I Cannot skill of these thy wayes,' Herbert acknowledges in 'Justice' (l. 1)), and because to present only the final position and not the stages of reasoning that led to it would be a misrepresentation, as well as making for a very brief poem, both alternatives are left before the reader's eyes. Having made his point, the poet reintroduces himself as a cautious pronoun: 'from Thee they came, | And must return. Accept of them and me.' It seems ungenerous to call this a 'pathetic self-assertion', but in doing so Nuttall at least acknowledges that

---

[15] Clarke, *Theory and Theology*, p. 236. [16] Nuttall, *Overheard by God*, pp. 32, 60.

Herbert has not, after all, written himself out of the poem in a convulsion of humility; here, the *metanoia* allows him to express the impulse without actually taking the step that would render God's position in the poem untenable, though it may compromise the poet's position in other ways.

Sometimes, it is true, the device seems to bear no such interpretative weight, and merely takes its place among other, similar kinds of rhetorical ornamentation; as for example in 'A Wreath', which is a sophisticated and elaborate paean to the virtues of simplicity. The poem is shaped by its governing conceit, which dictates that the first words of each line should echo the last words of the previous line; this figure is *anadiplosis*, and it performs the action of interweaving the lines so that they do indeed form a 'Wreathed garland of deserved praise' (l. 1). More importantly, though, its demand for repetition prompts revision, and the apparently rigid framework buckles as the words start to war with the formal properties of the poem:

> my wayes,
> My crooked winding wayes, wherein I live,
> Wherein I die, not live: for life is straight,
> Straight as a line   (ll. 3–6)

These lines deliberately and explicitly resist the idea of straightforward linear progression: the increasingly radical modifications turn them back upon themselves, creating a tortuous plea for simplicity whose failure on its own terms is the point of the poem. 'Wherein I die, not live': again, as in 'The Dedication', the *metanoia* called up by the movement of the verse is designed to stand for the mortification of the poet. Positioned as it is, though, in the cluttered rhetorical setting of the poem (with its measured *chiasmus*, its careful *polyptoton*), the dramatic reversal has an ersatz quality to it: the terrible realisation is a stage-paste. This is the effect for which Herbert is striving; he acknowledges the appeal of his figures while simultaneously pointing out their utter inadequacy to their divine subject: 'thee, who art more farre above deceit, | Then deceit seems above simplicitie'. It is a graceful expression of the predicament of the Christian artist, and an implied rebuke to the reader who would mistakenly value the highly wrought verse ('deceit') over its devotional intent ('simplicitie'). As Clarke notes, 'The connection between "deceit" and the complicated form of this poem is inescapable at this point'; Herbert has written a rhetorical *tour-de-force* which condemns itself for its own duplicity, and in doing so he inevitably exposes the very device he relies on so heavily in 'The Dedication'.[17]

---

[17] Clarke, *Theory and Theology*, p. 36.

Such a feat clearly argues a certain ambivalence towards the art of rhetoric; it would, at least, be wrong to read it either as a wholesale rejection of the figures and forms, or as an unwitting self-contradiction. While it might be an exaggeration to say, as Helen Vendler does, that 'It is scarcely credible that anyone could attribute to him more subtlety than he possessed,' the prudent approach is surely to look for a theoretical coherence in Herbert's use of *metanoia* throughout *The Temple*, despite this superficial evidence of a logical inconsistency.[18] To begin with, it is obvious that context is of utmost importance for Herbert in determining style: his ear was trained to catch every verbal nuance, and he was acutely conscious of the difference that a change in tone or register could make. In the one letter he wrote to Lancelot Andrewes now extant,[19] he excuses himself from visiting Winchester on the grounds that his duties as praelector in rhetoric are so pressing; in the postscript, he makes a significant apology for the mode in which he has chosen to write, and in particular for the lack of pomp in his signature: 'Pardon (most illustrious hero) the fact that my forenames fall so boldly in this letter.' Herbert goes on to defend his decision to avoid what he calls the vain and luxurious style of the age, something he might easily have adopted – 'I could have crammed my lines with honours, with magnificence, with highness' – in favour of a simpler and more graceful approach; he flatters his correspondent that Andrewes's extensive reading in the classical authors will have taught him to prefer the 'Roman elegance' of this spare style.[20] What makes this postscript important is its explicit demonstration of Herbert's concern for the forms of appropriate address; his facility with words, he implies, allows him to adopt any rhetorical mode, and he follows his own natural inclination against fashionable floridness

[18] Helen Vendler, *The Poetry of George Herbert* (Cambridge, MA: Harvard University Press, 1975), p. 5.
[19] Considering Herbert's letter to Andrewes that is *not* now extant, this one is rather disappointing; Izaak Walton describes a lengthy communication in Greek, 'which Letter was so remarkable for the language, and reason of it, that after the reading it, the Bishop put it into his bosom, and did often shew it to many Scholars, both of this, and forreign Nations; but did alwaies return it back to the place where he first lodg'd it, and continu'd it so near his heart, till the last day of his life' (*The Lives of Dr John Donne, Sir Henry Wotton, Mr Richard Hooker, Mr George Herbert* (London, 1670), pt II, pp. 26–7).
[20] Herbert to Lancelot Andrewes [*c.*1619], in *Works*, pp. 471–3 (p. 473). The relevant Latin text reads: 'Ignosce (Heros illustrissime) quòd pronomina mea adeò audacter incedant in hâc epistolâ: potui refercire lineas Honoribus, Magnif., Celsitud., sed non patitur, vt mihi videtur, Romana elegantia, periodíque vetus rotunditas. Quare malui seruire auribus Tuis, creberrimâ Antiquitatis lectione tersis atque expolitis, quàm luxuriae saeculi, ambitionísque strumae, non adeò sanatae ab optimo Rege nostro quin turgescat indies, atque efferat se, indulgere.' I am very grateful to Katherine Harloe for help with the translation.

only when he has a sufficiently high regard for the taste of his interlocutor to be sure that his plainness will not be misinterpreted as discourtesy.

Applying this insight to the poems in *The Temple* is not straightforward. The question of to whom they may in fact be directed (God? the fallen reader?) is a vexed one; it is by no means clear, indeed, that the poems all have the same notional addressee. When it was first published after Herbert's death in 1633, *The Temple* bore a subtitle: *Sacred Poems and Private Ejaculations*. This does not appear at the head of either manuscript copy of the work, indicating that it was perhaps devised not by Herbert but by Nicholas Ferrar, who acted as his literary executor; nevertheless, it is a suggestive formulation. The idea that there might be two distinct kinds of writing in the work, one (the 'sacred poems') that struggles visibly with the difficulties of reconciling rhetoric with religion from which the other (the 'private ejaculations') considers itself exempt, is seductive. Following Louis Martz, some critics have associated these 'ejaculations' with Augustinian ejaculatory prayer; the *OED* has as one sense of the word: 'a short prayer darted up to God. A short, hasty emotional utterance.'[21] It is an appealing theory, because if some of the poems in *The Temple* might be thought of as sharing in the status of prayer, the ambivalence of Herbert's attitude towards the art of rhetoric is some way to being explained: he can express derision for the figures in which he elsewhere puts such faith because in this scheme it is the addressee who determines their potency, and not the originator. If such a contingent sanctification of rhetoric seems far-fetched, consider these words by Andrewes on the importance of the *form* of a prayer, as opposed to its content: 'we must pray in such manner and forme, as hee requireth', the bishop directs;

God doth heare us many times even, *quando petimus malum* [when we ask for bad things]: in as much as he doth not give us the hurtfull things, which we ignorantly aske. But hee will not heare us, *cum petimus male* [when we ask badly], *yee aske and receive not, because yee aske amisse.*[22]

This stress on the way a prayer should be framed argues a belief in the efficacy of correct expression, as God will not even listen to a petition, however just, ineptly put; but it also implies that when a prayer is granted, the very arrangement of its words is retrospectively invested with power and significance: rhetoric is redeemed by the direct intervention of God.

[21] Martz, *The Poetry of Meditation*, p. 254; *OED*, 'ejaculation', *n.*, 4b. See also Clarke, *Theory and Theology*, pp. 100–26; I am indebted to her comprehensive discussion of the history and possibilities of this word.
[22] Lancelot Andrewes, *Scala Coeli. Nineteene Sermons Concerning Prayer* (London, 1611), pp. 39–40.

Andrewes and Herbert did not always agree on matters of rhetorical propriety, however. In *The Country Parson* Herbert advocates a simple style, and explicitly derides Andrewes's invariable practice of breaking the scriptural text into lexical fragments; it would be rash, then, in this instance to assume that they are in accord.[23] To propose an uncomplicated identification of individual poems with this kind of prayer (which may, anyway, be rather different from the ejaculatory prayer with which they are identified by the subtitle) is ultimately an unsustainable argument, though in the course of considering it some suggestive points are raised. That Herbert does, in *The Temple*, operate in two distinct rhetorical registers is clear; the first is self-conscious, concerned with its own integrity as sacred verse, and on some level hostile to, or at least suspicious of, the rhetoric it nevertheless necessarily deploys. To the group of poems written in this register might belong, for example, 'A Wreath', 'Jordan (I) & (II)' and 'A true Hymne'; all incline with varying degrees of success towards simplicity and, ultimately, a kind of silence: all forsake themselves through the medium of verse. 'Must all be vail'd,' Herbert asks in 'Jordan (I)', 'while he that reades, divines, | Catching the sense at two removes?' (ll. 9–10); his claim, though, that he is content 'plainly [to] say, *My God, My King*' (l. 15) is clearly given the lie by the fourteen lines of verse that precede it. The second type of poem seems not to feel the need to interrogate or to undermine itself in this way; the poet displays no anxiety about the possible contradictions of the enterprise, or about the potential for artifice and duplicity in the rhetorical devices he uses. 'Giddinesse', 'Nature' and 'Repentance' look not at, but beyond themselves, to their divine audience; their language is sanctified by its object, and untroubled by its motives.

The situation is more complicated than such a neat binary division might suggest, particularly if the distinction is held to be analogous to that between poetry and prayer. There is, to begin with, the difficulty of distinguishing between the two kinds of poem using anything but arbitrary and external criteria; put simply, not all of the poems notionally addressed to God in the imperative mood (those that introduce a correction with 'make', or 'let', for example) avail themselves of the rhetorical amnesty that one might expect would be accorded to prayer. Furthermore, some poems seem to employ both registers at once. 'Good Friday', for example, is framed as an address to God, but almost from the first line questions its own fitness to treat of its subject: 'How shall I measure out thy bloud', Herbert asks; 'How shall I count

---

[23] '[T]he other way of crumbling a text into small parts, as, the Person speaking, or spoken to, the subject, and object, and the like, hath neither in it sweetnesse, nor gravity, nor variety, since the words apart are not Scripture, but a dictionary' (Herbert, *Works*, p. 235).

what thee befell, | And each grief tell?' (ll. 2–4). It signals its self-accusation through a series of puns, which point up the slipperiness of words: 'How shall I measure?' means both 'How can I calibrate?' and 'How can I render in verse?'; 'count', 'tell', 'number' and 'score', which appear in subsequent lines, can also all be taken in a poetic (or indeed musical) as well as a numeric sense.[24] The *metanoia* that ends the first part cannot, however, be read convincingly here as a device conscious and critical of its own duplicity, since it works by claiming to sweep away the false assertions of poetic conceit. The idea that Christ's sacrifice can find a calibration or a counterweight in enemies, in stars, leaves or fruit, is rejected in favour of a more inward measure: each hour of the poet's life shall stand for one grief. This resolution is itself then corrected as an impulse towards self-glorification, and replaced at last with a true reckoning:

> Then let each houre
> Of my whole life one grief devoure;
> That thy distresse through all may runne,
> And be my sunne.
>
> Or rather let
> My severall sinnes their sorrows get;
> That as each beast his cure doth know,
> Each sinne may so.   (ll. 13–20)

'Between this third stanza and the last, Herbert realizes, with mortification, that this whole Good Friday meditation has been an exercise in self-aggrandizement': Vendler allows the poet the theatrical touch of a revelation in the white space between stanzas; 'In a sudden bitter "turn" ', she goes on to remark, 'Herbert places himself at last "correctly" vis-à-vis the Passion.'[25] For all Herbert's initial emphasis on the inadequacy of his measures, the point of the poem is surely lost if this corrective turn is intended to be read as an empty rhetorical flourish; and while the device may seem to conflict with the sentiments of the preceding lines, it is clear that it is not intended wholly to be undermined by them.[26]

If the poetry/prayer division does not hold up to close scrutiny, an alternative explanation must be found for the disjunction, and also for

---

[24] For a discussion of the importance of these puns in Herbert's writing here and more generally, see Kathleen J. Weatherford, 'Sacred Measures: Herbert's Divine Wordplay', *George Herbert Journal*, 15 (1991), 22–32.

[25] Vendler, *Poetry of George Herbert*, p. 149.

[26] Strier picks up on something of this when he describes it as 'the only instance in *The Temple* in which Herbert's use of a *correctio* at the end of a poem . . . provides a weaker rather than a stronger ending' (Strier, *Love Known*, p. 54).

what is a striking feature of Herbert's rhetorical practice: the frequency with which *metanoia* occurs in the imperative mood, in the notional form of an appeal (a prayer?) to God. These climactic lines from 'Giddinesse', a lament for the imperfections of man, are a good illustration of the point: 'Lord, mend or rather make us: one creation | Will not suffice our turn' (ll. 25–6). It is a drastic plea for continual regeneration, and the need for correction by the hand of God (or, in fact, for complete rewriting) is demonstrated even in the moment in which it is desired. Strier recognises the importance of the lines, though he does not explore the mechanism by which they achieve their effect: 'Herbert's use of *correctio* here', he writes, 'is, as his use of this device almost always is, deeply significant theologically: men must be remade, not merely mended, by God.'[27] Clarke goes further, seeing in the device not just an explanation of the problem, or indeed a demonstration of it, but an enactment of its solution: 'The *correctio* of the poem simulates the divine process at work'; Herbert, it seems, has answered his own prayer.[28] This notion of the divine author being implored to revise his recalcitrant creation appears, too, in 'Nature', a poem which traces a similar trajectory to that of 'Giddinesse'; this time, the plea is more personal, an 'I' as opposed to a 'we': the poet stands, 'Full of rebellion' (l. 1), and confesses the frailty of his faith. He asks, once again, to be mended or remade:

> O smooth my rugged heart, and there
> Engrave thy rev'rend Law and fear;
> Or make a new one, since the old
> > Is saplesse grown,
> And a much fitter stone
> To hide my dust, then thee to hold. (ll. 13–18)

The movement from insurgency to the supplication of a self-correcting appeal is a familiar one; what is at first more surprising is the ambiguity that attaches to the lines. While Herbert presumably means to ask God to make him, Herbert, a new heart, he could (grammatically, at any rate) equally be asking God to make a new Law; the adjective 'saplesse', though perhaps more readily applicable to the hardened heart of a man conscious of sin, could also refer without too much of a wrench to the Law that oppresses him with that consciousness.[29] Herbert's primary meaning, it

---

[27] Strier, *Love Known*, p. 11.   [28] Clarke, *Theory and Theology*, p. 235.

[29] See *OED*, 'sapless', *a.*, 2c: 'Of immaterial things, ideas, sayings, etc.: Destitute of inner worth, insipid, trivial, pointless.' Of particular relevance, because of their theological frame of reference, are the citations from 1664 and 1850: 'It is to make the Prophecy guilty of a sapless and useless Tautologie' (Henry More, 1664); 'The evangelical principles of the Reformation had begun to decline . . . into a dry and sapless orthodoxy' (John Marsden, 1850).

might be argued, is made clear in the biblical source of this notion; his plea for a new heart to replace the one of 'stone' in his breast is derived from a book of the Old Testament: 'A new heart also will I give you, and a new spirit will I put within you: and I will take away the stony heart out of your flesh, and I will give you a heart of flesh' (Ezekiel 36:26). Herbert, however, is alluding to these verses in asking God to 'Engrave' on his heart: 'I will put my laws into their mind, and write them in their hearts.' The passage continues in a vein which seems at least to authorise the alternative reading proposed: 'In that he saith, a new *covenant*, he hath made the first old. Now that which decayeth and waxeth old *is* ready to vanish away' (Hebrews 8:10–13). Here, it is a new Law, and not a new heart, that is called for. But it is one thing for God to decree a new Law; quite another for man to request it. Herbert's ambiguous syntax conflates the two passages, and in doing so demonstrates rhetorically the state of mind that the poem describes. The 'rebellion' of the opening phrase, it transpires, has not entirely been put down, and continues to 'lurk' beneath the submissive surface of the lines: the corrective motion of the *metanoia*, which had appeared to represent absolute humility in the face of God's will, leaves in its wake another error, a deliberate error, to demonstrate the fallibility of man.

Perhaps the most extreme example of this dynamic of the revised appeal, though, comes at the end of 'Clasping of Hands'. The poem is a riddling and disorientating riot of pronouns: in its twenty lines, the words 'I', 'me' and 'mine' appear twenty-eight times; 'thou', 'thee' and 'thine', nineteen. The assault on the reader's inner ear is compounded by the repetition and precise reversal, from one stanza to the next, of the rhyme terms which end each line: 'mine / thine', 'more / restore'. This formal patterning has the peculiar effect of lending the *metanoia* at the poem's denouement a prosodic inevitability quite at variance with its import; the urgent revision which ends in the poet's startled and startling cry for an identity completely submerged in God's is, at least on a phonetic level, anticipated by the lines which precede it. It is worth, here, quoting the poem in full:

> Lord, thou art mine, and I am thine,
> If mine I am: and thine much more,
> Then I or ought, or can be mine.
> Yet to be thine, doth me restore;
> So that again I now am mine,
> And with advantage mine the more,
> Since this being mine, brings with it thine,
> And thou with me dost thee restore.

> If I without thee would be mine,
> I neither should be mine nor thine.
>
> Lord, I am thine, and thou art mine:
> So mine thou art, that something more
> I may presume thee mine, then thine.
> For thou didst suffer to restore
> Not thee, but me, and to be mine,
> And with advantage mine the more,
> Since thou in death wast none of thine,
> Yet then as mine didst me restore.
>   O be mine still! still make me thine!
>   Or rather make no Thine and Mine!   (ll. 1–20)

Anticipated, and rendered unachievable; without the words 'thine' and 'mine', the tongue-twisting, logic-chopping poem could not exist. The rhetorical dexterity with which this aspiration towards self-annihilation (of both poet and poem) is simultaneously expressed and resisted is remarkable. Herbert quibbles like a sophist on the concept of possession, and then sweeps all away in his prayer to be remade, or perhaps unmade, by God; once again, he relies on the device of *metanoia* to finesse the words into a dual signification.

THE DIVINE VOICE

There is another problem raised by a scheme that attempts to explain the complex deployment of *metanoia* throughout *The Temple* by distinguishing two rhetorical registers and investing one of them with the performative powers of prayer: what happens when the correcting voice is not Herbert's, but God's? This question requires immediate qualification: it would perhaps be less contentious to say 'when the voice is figured as coming from an external source which is, presumably, divine' – a dynamic described neatly in the Williams MS poem, 'Perseverance', itself about the act of writing. Herbert refers to 'the poore expressions of my Love', which are composed 'as for the present I did move, | Or rather as thou movedst mee' (ll. 1, 3–4). The *metanoia* allows, even encourages, a confusion between the promptings of the poet's imagination and his divine inspiration, a confusion which recalls the logical impasse of the 'Dedication': how, with propriety, to offer to God words which he has in effect written himself? And this is by no means the only occasion on which this rhetorical device is required to withstand such logical and devotional strain. 'The Holdfast' is a troubled poem, for all the reasoned resolution implied by its sonnet shape;

throughout, Herbert works to expose the futility of human language in the face of divine utterance, while approaching dangerously close to a demonstration of their interdependence. The very title is suggestively ambiguous: the 'Holdfast' is both the tenacious believer, miserly of his faith, and that to which he cleaves; it is both Herbert and God.[30] The poem opens in characteristically militant style: 'I Threatned to observe the strict decree | Of my deare God with all my power & might' (ll. 1–2) There is complacency as well as fervour in this display of energy and resolve, and the reader is not surprised when the voice of authoritative scepticism intrudes:

> But I was told by one, it could not be;
> Yet I might trust in God to be my light.
> Then will I trust, said I, in him alone.
> Nay, ev'n to trust in him, was also his. (ll. 3–6)

The argument takes a similar direction to that of 'The Dedication', into an impending circularity: all that a man might offer to God is his already, even the capacity to believe; again, the paradox is expressed through the figure of *metanoia*.

> We must confesse that nothing is our own.
> Then I confesse that he my succour is:
> But to have nought is ours, not to confesse
> That we have nought. (ll. 7–10)

Each attempt to fasten on a verb and make it performative – 'I trust', 'I confesse' – is frustrated by the corrective voice, which repeats and so reclaims the word for divine use. The consternation that this silencing causes ('amaz'd' here carries the sense of 'stunned' or 'stupefied') is alleviated only when the speaker is prompted to a higher level of comprehension; human models of ownership and exchange cease to be relevant, and in this new scheme man retains his moral agency:

> I stood amaz'd at this,
> Much troubled, till I heard a friend expresse,
> That all things were more ours by being his. (ll. 10–12)

Perhaps predictably, this explanation has not proved satisfactory to Herbert's more sceptical readers. 'What if the line serves merely to express the need to evoke the mere outward shape of the wished-for answer,' Nuttall asks, 'and really offers no substantial resolution at all?' His 'merely' and 'mere' suggest what he might think of a poem which indulges in such

---

[30] *OED*, 'holdfast', *n.*, 3 and 2.

rhetorical *legerdemain*. For Nuttall, the self-correcting impulse of 'The Holdfast' is sophistical; he regards its logic, like that of 'The Dedication', as irredeemably flawed: 'Herbert piously blurs his own reasoning to make God seem better.'[31]

This anxiety betrays a rationalist reluctance to believe in the rhetorically enforced notion that something can be two things at once, in this case both 'ours' and 'his': the 'outward shape' of the answer that Herbert provides proves rather too protean for comfort. Primarily, though, Nuttall's objections reflect a fundamental lack of sympathy with the Calvinist doctrine of grace which underpins the poem: an unempathic reading such as this sees only conflict, because it cannot allow the resolution of faith that the correction implies. Nuttall's theoretical and theological agenda ('Jesus was mad', is the somewhat surprising conclusion of his argument[32]) leads him to attach more significance to the positions of ignorance, mutiny or insurgence that Herbert adopts and then theatrically rejects than to the words which correct them and constitute the poem's final position, particularly when these are imagined as coming from an external divine source ('I heard a friend expresse'). This critical stance results in an ingenious if slightly wilful misreading of Herbert's revisionary impulse, which calls irresistibly to mind Peacham's warning on the dangers of the figure of *metanoia*: 'It behoveth the Orator to take heede that he utter no heinous, wicked and slanderous words, with entent to correct them, for a word of offence is like a wilde bird which hath escaped thy hand and cannot be called againe.'[33] The 'fierce and wilde' (l. 33) words which escape the anguished speaker of 'The Collar' are a case in point; while the poem deploys no *metanoia* in the strict sense of the figure, it nonetheless describes a familiar trajectory of rebellion quelled by the corrective voice of God. It might be thought of as exemplifying the general tendency towards transparent revision, the practice of leaving in place alternative readings, of which the use of the figure of *metanoia* constitutes an important though restricted part.[34] So the poem opens with an assertion of intellectual and spiritual independence, a wish for freedom from God's law and will: 'I Struck the board, and cry'd, No more. | I will abroad' (ll. 1–2). By far the greater part of the poem is taken up with an expression of and expansion on this theme of dissatisfaction with the hardships of the devotional life, a railing against the anxiety and anguish

---

[31] Nuttall, *Overheard by God*, pp. 70–1. [32] Nuttall, *Overheard by God*, p. 142.
[33] Peacham, *Garden of Eloquence*, p. 173.
[34] 'One of the particular virtues of Herbert's poetry', Vendler notes, 'is its provisional quality. His poems are ready at any moment to change direction or to modify attitudes' (*Poetry of George Herbert*, p. 31).

of faith, and a determination to serve the self and not God. When it finally comes in the penultimate line, the resolution is sudden, swift and, for the poet, utterly effective:

> But as I rav'd and grew more fierce and wilde
> > At every word,
> Me thoughts I heard one calling, *Child!*
> > And I reply'd, *My Lord.*   (ll. 33–6)

It has been called 'the supreme Calvinist poem', a dramatization of the soul in a state of depravity which is redeemed by the intervention of an ultimately powerful God.[35] There is no argument here, no reasoned refutation of the speaker's complaints; all that is needed to exact instant submission is a single word, and, initially, even that is of doubtful provenance ('Me thoughts I heard one calling'). It is easy to see how this response to what are viscerally felt and energetically expressed doubts might fail to satisfy a sceptical reader, how the impression left by the first thirty-two lines of the poem, those 'heinous, wicked and slanderous words', might outweigh that produced by the single syllable of correction; but this, of course, would be to miss the point as far as Herbert is concerned. This one word figured as coming from God is not just enough, it is supremely performative, a recognition and a redemption.

Once again, the same logical objection to this way of dramatising doubt surfaces: if that one divine utterance is necessary and sufficient, what is the point of the rest of the poem? As with 'Jordan (I)' or 'A true Hymne', Herbert gestures in a few words towards a poetic of simplicity which is compromised, or at least complicated, by the surrounding verses. '*My God, My King*' ('Jordan (I)', l. 15); '*My joy, my life, my crown*' ('A true Hymne', l. 5); '*My Lord*' ('The Collar', l. 36): these successive restatements describe his fascination with the idea of the word that will render all others obsolete, while demonstrating in their variousness the impossibility of ever finding such a word. This list of near-synonyms recalls the act of definition-by-metaphor that Herbert performs in 'Prayer (I)', and leaves the reader with the same sense that if any were truly successful the poem would stop; as it is, the concluding phrase of that poem, 'something understood', is perfectly judged, for it catches at the essence of the thing by suggesting that in some cases words are inadequate to spiritual or cognitive process, though it is only through words that such inadequacy can be articulated. Critics who have

---

[35] Gene Edward Veith, *Reformation Spirituality: the Religion of George Herbert* (Lewisburg, PA: Bucknell University Press, 1985), p. 34.

remarked on this tendency are inclined to see it as 'an aspiration to muteness'.[36] 'As always', Clarke writes, 'Herbert is in the paradoxical position of
having to use words to create the effect of silence.'[37] This, though, is
seriously to misrepresent Herbert's intention. The ardent *aposiopesis* of the
final cry of 'The Thanksgiving' might seem a good example: 'Then for thy
passion – I will do for that – | Alas, my God, I know not what' (ll. 49–50).
These lines, however, only pretend to be a faltering failure of expression, a
lapse into silence: what they in fact achieve is a careful articulation of fervour
tempered with humility. Devices like *aposiopesis* and *metanoia* mimic the
processes of divine revelation and poetic composition, allowing Herbert to
present himself as a tentative poet, fumbling for grace or inspiration as he
revises and rethinks his work in public.[38] The description of *The Temple* as
'a picture of the many spiritual Conflicts that have past betwixt God and my
Soul' is illuminating in this context; to figure correction, hesitancy, speech-
lessness, is to create poems of process which are, nonetheless, fully
achieved.[39] Far from inclining straightforwardly towards 'muteness' or
'silence', such rhetorical strategies seek rather to invest the words which
constitute them with an extra-semantic meaning, a significance that is
beyond their bare signification.

METANOIA AND THE EUCHARIST

I have talked above of a misrepresentation of Herbert's 'intention', a
concept fraught with all kinds of hermeneutic dangers; in this case, though,
the dangerous enterprise of attempting to determine what an author might
have thought about what he was doing seems justifiable. With the usual
caveats, to consider *why* Herbert writes is, in an important sense, to further
an understanding of *what* he writes. It is hard to judge the accuracy of the
only surviving external account of Herbert's own professed opinions on his
poetry, from which its characterisation as a 'picture' of 'spiritual Conflicts' is
excerpted: it appears in the form of a deathbed conversation with Edmund
Duncon in Izaak Walton's *Lives*, which was published more than forty years
after the event. Duncon was still alive at that time, however, and is believed

---

[36] Robert B. Shaw, 'George Herbert: the Word of God and the Words of Man', in *Ineffability: Naming the Unnamable from Dante to Beckett*, ed. by Peter S. Hawkins and Anne Howland Schotter (New York: AMS, 1984), pp. 81–93 (p. 82).

[37] Clarke, *Theory and Theology*, p. 234.

[38] For a discussion of Herbert's hesitant persona, see Stanley Fish, 'Catechizing the Reader: Herbert's Socratean Rhetoric', in *The Rhetoric of Renaissance Poetry from Wyatt to Milton*, ed. by Thomas O. Sloan and Raymond B. Waddington (Berkeley: University of California Press, 1974), pp. 174–88.

[39] Walton, *Lives*, pt II, p. 74; italics omitted.

to have given the story to Walton first-hand; to think of it as truthful to the
spirit if not to the letter of the exchange does not seem too rash, particularly
as parts of the account are consistent with attitudes expressed elsewhere in
Herbert's writing.[40] In handing over the manuscript of what was to become
The Temple for Duncon to convey to Nicholas Ferrar, Herbert is supposed
to have said: 'desire him to read it; and then if he can think it may turn to the
advantage of any dejected poor Soul, let it be made publick; if not, let him
burn it, for I and it, are less than the least of Gods mercies'.[41] It is a
suggestive anecdote, and not just because of the interesting implication
that for Walton at least, if not for Herbert, the truly pious poet must be
prepared to make a bonfire of his life's work; he ought also, if possible, to be
dead or dying, innocent of any desire to profit in reputation or advancement
from the exercise of this skill in sacred verse. What is significant in this story
is the way Herbert is situated with regard to his imagined reading public: he
is of them, in his rebelliousness, his fallibility and his struggles with his faith;
and yet he is also apart from them. *The Temple*, a reproduction in verse of
his spiritual experiences, is understood as an exemplum for anxious or erring
souls, but it is not only that Herbert, having emerged from the darkness of
doubt into the 'perfect freedom' of submission to God's will, is in a position
to offer comfort or solace to those less fortunate (a stance which would
involve an awkward degree of superiority, however humbly claimed or
conferred).[42] His attitude incorporates, too, something of a professional
interest: it is, at times, as a priest that he writes, and he asks that his words
share in the privileged status of priestly utterance – a mode of expression
different from private prayer, and one which encompasses the licence to
ventriloquise and to interpret the Word of God which so troubles Nuttall.
Seen in this light, the imperative 'make' and 'let' which so often herald a
metanoietic turn become something akin to the Hebrew jussive: words
which carry the force of a command as well as a plea.[43]

---

[40] 'The Dedication', for example, clearly expresses a similar wish that readers should profit spiritually
from the poems: 'Turn their eyes hither, who shall make a gain;' See also the Williams MS poem
'Perseverance', in which Herbert wonders 'whither these my words | Shal help another' (ll. 5–6). This
correspondence, however, could equally, in fairness, be adduced as evidence for a view of Walton's
account as inauthentic and derivative. That it reproduces exactly words ascribed to Herbert in the
preface to *The Temple* ('Lesse then the least of Gods mercies') is clearly not accidental, and an
argument using one to validate the other risks circularity (Herbert, *Works*, p. 5).

[41] Walton, *Lives*, pt II, pp. 74–5.   [42] Walton, *Lives*, pt II, p. 74.

[43] Ahouva Shulman establishes a distinction between the two which rests on the relative status of the
speaker: 'When used by a superior speaker, [third-person jussive forms] have the force of a command,
as in Gen 1:3: "And God said: 'Let there be light', and there was light" . . . In situations where the
speaker does not have the power or the ability to impose his desire upon the doer of the action, the
speaker's desire must be interpreted as a wish' ('The Function of the "Jussive" and "Indicative"

To observe that Herbert was for a brief time a priest as well as a poet, and to suggest that the pursuit of one occupation might well have informed his approach to the other, is in some ways rather an obvious point to make; but this circumstance has specifically rhetorical implications which deserve close attention. That there is a division of register in *The Temple* which manifests itself as a sporadic unease about the validity of religious verse is evident; I have so far resisted presenting an alternative to the poetry/prayer model which proved inadequate, but want now to suggest that this difficulty might be overcome and the divergence reconciled when Herbert assumes a priestly authority over his words and towards his readers. Yet another caveat is necessary here. Herbert was ordained deacon probably in 1624, when he was thirty-one; rather unusually, it was not until 19 September 1630, just three years before his premature death, that he was ordained into the priesthood. As Helen Wilcox observes, the reasons for this delay are not clear, although she suggests some possible explanations, including 'long-term financial uncertainty, a sense of unworthiness . . ., continuing interest in a secular career – academic or courtly – and his chronic ill health'.[44] Though the details must remain a matter for speculation, it seems likely that the decision was a considered one, and that Herbert meditated seriously on the functions and responsibilities he would assume as a priest. Chief among these – what a priest could do and a deacon could not – was the celebration of the eucharist, and I shall return to the possible implications of this below. It may be, however, that when Herbert assumes a priestly authority in his verse, he is trying out the role that he will eventually adopt, and in which he will subsequently be remembered.[45]

Evidence of Herbert's thoughtful approach to his ministry can be found in *A Priest to the Temple, or, The Countrey Parson*, a kind of manual or handbook which was written in the 1630s, though not published until 1652. In it, he attaches a great deal of importance to the art of the sermon: 'The Countrey Parson preacheth constantly,' he explains; 'the pulpit is his joy

---

Imperfect Forms in Biblical Hebrew Prose', *Zeitschrift für Althebraistik*, 13 (2000), 168–80 (177–8)). This, however, is something of a simplification, in that it ignores the nuance of performativity that attaches to this formulation regardless of the speaker's authority. Relevant here is J. L. Austin's *How to Do Things with Words*, 2nd edn (Oxford: Clarendon Press, 1975; repr. 1980), despite his conviction that poetry is always 'infelicitous' – that is, can never be truly performative in this sense.

[44] Wilcox, *DNB* online.

[45] The difficulty of dating Herbert's poems, none of which was published in his lifetime, compounds these uncertainties; it is likely, however, that many of the new poems in the later extant manuscript were 'probably written towards the end of his life', that is, after his ordination as a priest (Wilcox, *DNB* online; see also her discussion of the various source-texts of *The Temple* in *The English Poems of George Herbert*, ed. by Wilcox (Cambridge University Press, 2007), pp. xxxvii–xl).

and his throne'.[46] In this context, Herbert does not feel anxiety about the seductive power of rhetoric: when he expounds his theory of preaching, there is none of the wariness of that 'Lovely enchanting language, sugar-cane' ('The Forerunners', l. 19) that colours so many of the poems in *The Temple*. Though it is true that Herbert favours a plain style for sermons (one which is 'not witty, or learned, or eloquent, but Holy'), he certainly does not believe or suggest that this simplicity is simply achieved: 'When he preacheth', Herbert advises, the parson 'procures attention by all possible art', which presumably includes mode of expression as well as gesture and aspect.[47] What allays the doubts that such an artful approach might be expected to raise in other circumstances is the necessary authority conferred on he who preaches the Word of God in God's name; such status becomes a guarantee not only of motive, but of means. In assuming the protective mantle of the church, the priest can use words with confidence, regardless of the man's frailty or uncertainty; something of this dynamic is expressed in the assurance of the final line of 'Aaron', when, self-doubt at last resolved, the priest calls his congregation to worship: 'Come people; Aaron's drest' (l. 25).

With authority comes power. That Herbert borrows (or perhaps antici-pates, or redeploys) a priestly voice in his verse offers a means of interpreting its self-scrutinising rhetoric, but it also has wider implications for the way in which rhetoric works. Herbert evidently believed that a minister of the church should preach as often as the opportunity arose, and the certainty of a sermon can be caught in some of his writing; it is, however, a verbal act that the priest was required to perform considerably less frequently (*The Countrey Parson* recommends 'at least five or six times in the year') that has the greater significance for his poetic practice: the rehearsal of the words of institution which precedes the administration of the sacraments in Holy Communion.[48] It is nothing new to identify a sacramental impulse in Herbert's verse. 'At the heart of George Herbert's poetry', Jeanne Clayton Hunter writes, 'lies the Eucharistic Christ.'[49] Martin Elsky argues for its presence at a structural level, reading the moment in 'Superliminare' when poetry is spoken of as 'The churches mysticall repast' (l. 4) as evidence that *The Temple* follows a liturgical trajectory: '[this image] thus holds the entire collection of poems together as a Eucharistic offering'.[50] Other critics have

---

[46] Herbert, *Works*, p. 233.   [47] Herbert, *Works*, p. 232.   [48] Herbert, *Works*, p. 259.

[49] Jeanne Clayton Hunter, '"With Winges of Faith": George Herbert's Communion Poems', *Journal of Religion*, 62 (1982), 57–71 (57).

[50] Martin Elsky, 'The Sacramental Frame of George Herbert's "The Church" and the Shape of Spiritual Autobiography', *Journal of English and Germanic Philology*, 83 (1984), 313–29 (316).

found a preoccupation with the concept of the eucharist in the verbal texture of the verse; Robert B. Shaw sees the instruction in 'Jordan (II)' to 'copie out only that' (l. 18) as analogous to the celebration of the sacraments, evidence of a spiritual grace made manifest in an outward sign: 'A briefer way of saying that in Herbert's poetry signs strain toward union with what they signify', Shaw concludes, 'is to say that his language is sacramental.'[51] There is, then, something of a critical consensus on the matter: it is evident from Herbert's writing that he was profoundly interested in and influenced by a eucharistic model, even before he himself had the authority to preside at the ceremony. To attempt to determine precisely what such a sacramental imagination might consist in and how it is expressed at a rhetorical level, however, it is necessary to move beyond what are in most cases either rather general statements or unhelpfully nebulous formulations.[52]

The first difficulty is in placing Herbert within the broad spectrum of post-Reformation thought on the subject.[53] In his poems, there are several more or less direct statements about the nature of his belief in the eucharist, but these admit of (and have been subject to) a variety of different inter-pretations, from something like a Calvinist doctrine of virtualism to a position just short of a fully Catholic understanding of Christ's transub-stantiated presence as body and blood under the accidents of the Host. The principal grounds for dispute are two poems in which Herbert appears to advocate directly contrary views: 'Love Unknown' and 'The Invitation'. The first is clearly receptionist in its assertion that the communicant must have faith in order to receive: 'while many drunk bare wine, | A friend did steal into my cup' (ll. 42–3). Herbert takes a similarly careful stance when describing the experience of communion in 'The Agonie': 'Love', he writes, 'is that liquour sweet and most divine, | Which my God feels as bloud; but I, as wine' (ll. 17–18). In 'The Invitation', however, Herbert speaks of wine 'Which before ye drink is bloud' (l. 12), a formulation that suggests a belief in the inherent efficacy of the words of institution, regardless of the worthiness of the communicant, which is tantamount to subscribing to the Catholic doctrine of transubstantiation. It is hints such as this that prompt R. V. Young to conclude that Herbert 'intimates a sense of awe in the presence of the sacrament that is appropriate only to a belief in the real

[51] Shaw, 'The Word of God and the Words of Man', p. 89.

[52] This, for example, from Heather A. R. Asals: 'The poetry is eucharistic because it consecrates the "creature" of language as the ontological bridge to the divine' (*Equivocal Predication: George Herbert's Way to God* (University of Toronto Press, 1981), p. 6).

[53] This has been a contentious question for decades, if not centuries, and the brief account that follows does not pretend to be comprehensive.

presence in some substantial mode'.[54] Robert Whalen agrees, though with a
cautious emphasis on the potential orthodoxy of such a position: 'Herbert
thus shares with his English Protestant contemporaries a concern that the
Eucharist involve Real Presence.'[55] These critics find themselves facing the
same difficulties and indeed opportunities of terminology as the Reformation
theologians they follow; the phrase 'real presence' asserts something more
than a figurative or symbolic understanding of the eucharist, though it stops
(somewhat counter-intuitively) short of intending Christ's actual presence in
the Host, as Cranmer was careful to make clear.[56] It becomes possible,
therefore, to ascribe to Herbert a belief in a substantial sacramental presence
that yet does not compromise his Protestant faith. This is not necessarily a
mistaken view, but it does risk a failure to confront all of the implications of
Herbert's position. Donald R. Dickson takes a straightforward acknowledgement as the starting point of his more nuanced account: 'Some poems', he
admits, 'seem to attribute a materiality to the sacrament that is Lutheran if
not Roman Catholic in its theology.'[57] Dickson goes on to remark, however,
that to interpret this as an inconsistency is to miss the point of what Herbert
was trying to do, or rather what he was *not* trying to do: these poems seek to
convey a powerful and immediate understanding of the spiritual and sensory
experience of communion; they do not aim either at a clear explication of
Herbert's own views, or at a resolution of contemporary doctrinal disputes
over the issue.

This is a very sensible admonition. But Herbert *did* write poems which
specifically address the controversy over the eucharist, as well as those which
are interested simply in what it is to receive communion; 'The
H. Communion' and 'Divinitie' in *The Temple*, and the earlier Williams
MS version of 'The H. Communion' all concern themselves with the
matter, and it does not seem unreasonable to look here for some kind of
statement of Herbert's eucharistic beliefs. It is immediately apparent, however, that these doctrinal poems are if anything even less helpful than the
others in establishing a coherent stance. They share what ultimately
amounts to an extraordinarily determined tendency completely to sidestep
any issues of substance (in both senses), and unanimously evince a wilful

[54] Young, *Doctrine and Devotion*, p. 115.
[55] Robert Whalen, '"How Shall I Measure out thy Bloud?," or, "Weening is Not Measure": *TACT*,
     Herbert, and Sacramental Devotion in the Electronic *Temple*', *Early Modern Literary Studies*, 5
     (2000), paras. 1–37 (para. 11).
[56] See the introduction, pp. 14–27, for a fuller discussion of this.
[57] Donald R. Dickson, 'Between Transubstantiation and Memorialism: Herbert's Eucharistic
     Celebration', *George Herbert Journal*, 11 (1987), 1–14 (1).

disengagement with the terms of the debate. These lines from 'Divinitie' are representative:

> But he doth bid us take his bloud for wine.
>   Bid what he please; yet I am sure,
> To take and taste what he doth there designe,
>   Is all that saves, and not obscure.   (ll. 21–4)

Herbert states quite clearly that he sees no difficulty of interpretation: to receive communion is to enter into a state of grace, and though he does not consider the mechanism of this transaction in any detail, he can assert with suspicious complacency that the mystery is 'not obscure' – a less than illuminating comment in context. It is significant that he revises, here, the words of institution: the phrase 'take and taste' replaces the biblical 'take and eat'.

While the change may in this instance stem from a pragmatic impulse (one can hardly 'eat' wine, and 'taste' here does have a pleasingly alliterative quality, as well as echoing Psalm 34, 'O taste and see how gracious the Lord is'), it is notable how frequently Herbert resorts to the terminology of taste and smell, as opposed, for example, to that of consumption and digestion, in describing the experience of communion. 'Taste and fear not', he enjoins in 'The Invitation': 'God is here' (l. 16); and 'Love (III)', whose narrative frame of a weary traveller approaching an inn turns on the submerged host/Host pun, ends with a similar injunction: 'You must sit down, sayes Love, and taste my meat' (l. 17). 'The Odour' is a curiously synaesthetic poem which treats the sacrament obliquely, imagining it as a 'broth of smells, that feeds and fats my minde' (l. 10). It shares with 'The Banquet' a eucharistic image-complex of 'smell', of 'perfumes' and 'sented' pomanders, though the second poem goes further in its rhetoric of latent violence:

> Doubtlesse, neither starre nor flower
>   Hath the power
> Such a sweetnesse to impart:
> Onely God, who gives perfumes,
>   Flesh assumes,
> And with it perfumes my heart.
> But as Pomanders and wood
>   Still are good,
> Yet being bruis'd are better sented:
> God, to show how farre his love
>   Could improve,
> Here, as broken, is presented.   (ll. 19–30)

Christ's body is crushed for its eucharistic efficacy, like a pomander or a piece of perfumed wood. Herbert shows himself quite drawn to the paradox of scent, where beauty comes from violence in processes of both manufacture and consumption: intincture, enfleurage, distillation; crushing, bruising, burning. He allows himself to be enrapt by scent as a means of figuring a divine translation, more intimate and less apprehensible than other modes of consumption, something infused or transfused, a cipher for the sacrament that flushes the blood without having to negotiate mouth, tongue, teeth. This is a Christ of orris or of oud, and the image has to be brutal as well as beautiful; the divine broken body is aestheticised but not sanitised, its very fractures and lacerations ('bruis'd', 'broken') the source of its salvific perfume. There are all sorts of ironies here, in using something as closely associated with Catholic devotional practice as perfume to understand the workings of the sacrament; but it is not so out of place in a poem that again engages in a rhetorical flirtation with the idea of the real presence: the 'God, who gives perfumes | Flesh assumes', which is not a particularly reformed locution. This interest in divine scent is characteristic of Herbert's deliberate and consistent failure to address the material implications of receiving the Host (the notion that Christ's body is routinely chewed and swallowed by the faithful); he retreats from the grounds of contention by positing a means of consumption that is direct and efficacious without, however, involving anything quite so physical as the teeth.

While 'Divinitie' maintains that the mystery of the sacrament is 'not obscure', 'The H. Communion' is unusual among Herbert's works in that it nonetheless appears to go some way towards attempting to clarify its technicalities. What seems like it might offer a plain statement of belief, however, turns out on closer analysis to represent at most a highly ambiguous position on the doctrine of the real presence. For the first two stanzas of the poem the figurative and the actual are held in a careful rhetorical balance, and Herbert exploits the tension between them to describe (without exactly explaining) what happens once the communicant receives the Host: 'by the way of nourishment and strength | Thou creep'st into my breast' (ll. 7–8). The two abstract nouns are designed to be understood in either material or spiritual terms, or indeed both; Herbert is perhaps recalling the advantage that Cranmer took of the same possibility in his formulation of the reformed position: 'And as every man is carnally fedde and nourished in his body by meat and drinke,' the archbishop writes, 'even so is every good christian man spiritually fed and nourished in his soule, by the flesh and bloud of our Savyour Christ.'[58] Again, the poem's siege conceit

[58] Cranmer, *An Aunswere*, p. 37.

forcefully suggests a physical dimension while permitting an absolutely figurative interpretation; Christ, metonymically presented as the 'small quantities' of sacramental substance ingested by the believer, is imagined as invading the body like an army: the elements 'spread their forces into every part' (l. 11). At the division of the first section of the poem, however, comes a significant clarification:

> Yet can these not get over to my soul,
> > Leaping the wall that parts
> Our souls and fleshy hearts;
> > But as th'outworks, they may controll
> My rebel-flesh, and carrying thy name,
> > Affright both sinne and shame.   (ll. 13–18)

Herbert seems here at last to be maintaining the expected distinction between flesh and spirit, in stating that straightforward transaction between them is impossible. This he does, though, with a surprisingly tentative turn of phrase ('can these not' could almost be a question, as opposed, for instance, to the equally possible and rather more definite 'these can not'), and with a confusing contortion of imagery. Veith founders in essaying a paraphrase: 'Herbert denies that the physical elements can "leap the wall" between the soul and the flesh. They can, however, function as "outworks", that is, fortifications outside the wall (OED), which, in their physicality, can subdue "My rebel-flesh" by frightening sin and, significantly, shame.'[59] Unless Herbert intends 'outworks' in the sense of 'hors-d'oeuvres', an intriguing though sadly wholly unlikely possibility, Veith is right to interpret the word as a military term; what he doesn't remark, however, is that an outwork is an exclusively defensive edifice, 'an outer defence':[60] as the invading elements turn into outworks, the siegers and the besieged collapse elegantly into one. There is, further, a useful elision of terminology in this stanza: an argument which posits an insuperable divide between 'souls' and 'fleshy hearts' (a divide predictably imagined in the very concrete terms of a wall) does not actually preclude the possibility that the substance that has influence over the 'rebel-flesh' is itself flesh – the Word made flesh. Herbert does not have to decide whether it is bread or body that must remain on the material side of his wall, particularly as, in the next stanza, he finds a way to scale it: 'Onely thy grace, which with these elements comes, | Knoweth the ready way' (ll. 19–20). Grace, it transpires, can effect the transition from flesh to spirit and open 'the souls

---

[59] Veith, *Reformation Spirituality*, p. 215.   [60] *OED*, 'outworks', *n.*, 2 and 1a.

most subtile rooms' (l. 22), and the eucharist retains both its efficacy and
its mystery.

Herbert's communion poems, then, witness a deliberate retreat from theological contention to a position of faith and prayer. His determined refusal
to engage with the debate is nowhere made clearer than in the Williams MS
version of 'The H. Communion', which dismisses the question of Christ's
real presence in the Host with facetious wit:

> ffirst I am sure, whether bread stay
> Or whether Bread doe fly away
>   Concerneth bread, not mee.   (ll. 7–9)

Even what amounts to an unambiguous statement of a Calvinist understanding presents some difficulties of interpretation in the light of the rest of
the poem: 'That fflesh is there', protests a suddenly pragmatic Herbert,
'mine eyes deny' (l. 31). This attempt to quell discord by recourse to a
heartily commonsensical approach is reminiscent of the sweeping claim in
'Divinitie' that the matter is 'not obscure', and about as convincing.[61] The
poem's final lines encapsulate his double-thinking agility in the rhetorical
device best suited to its expression:

> This gift of all gifts is the best,
> Thy flesh the least that I request.
>   Thou took'st that pledg from mee:
> Give me not that I had before,
> Or give mee that, so I have more;
>   My God, give mee all Thee.   (ll. 43–8)

This climactic *metanoia* does not accomplish the looked-for transition from
obscurity to clarity, or from faction to unity: it is as hard to follow as the
winding complexities of the doctrinal exposition that precedes it. The conventional reformed view, that Christ's flesh was given in the incarnation ('before')
and will not be present on earth again until the Second Coming, is allowed to
stand alongside a Lutheran longing for the experience of Christ's real presence
in the eucharist: 'Or give mee that,' the poet asks: 'give mee all Thee.'

[61] Dickson points out that the poem only masquerades as the logical presentation of a reasoned case: 'it
becomes clear', he notices, 'that [Herbert] is merely enumerating theological arcana and not advanc-
ing an argument that will accommodate all these positions' ('Between Transubstantiation and
Memorialism', 9).

This is an early work, supplanted in the published version of *The Temple* by the poem of the same name discussed above; its sardonic tone certainly smacks more of the disputatious undergraduate than of the dignified priest who voices others of Herbert's works, as he tries out that role in his poetry. It is, nonetheless, highly significant for an understanding of his eucharistic theology: not just in what it says, which is in fact remarkably little for a specifically doctrinal poem of almost fifty lines, but for the way in which it avoids saying it. The corrective turn of the final stanza is not, here, simply an expression of humility, an acceptance of the possibility of human error; it facilitates a duality of thought which is neither tentative nor evasive, but creative. *Metanoia* is a figure of possibility which allows alternatives to coexist in the mind and on the page; Herbert's recourse to it at this moment represents an attempt to combine an intellectual response to the mystery of the sacrament with the intuitive understanding that is authorised by his faith. The attempt is not fully realised, and the poem is (at least in an aesthetic sense) unsuccessful; hence, presumably, its radical revision into the unrecognisable version that turns up in *The Temple*; but the rhetorical mechanism that contrives to encompass something which both is and is not true, something which remains itself while turning into something else, continues profoundly to inform the way Herbert thinks and writes about the eucharist. The distinctive mood of his poetry is one that is alive to alternatives, self-correcting, *metanoietic*: 'A poem by Herbert', Vendler notices, 'is often "written" three times over, with several different, successive and self-contradictory versions co-existing in the finished poem.'[62] As provisionality is the characteristic temper of Herbert's verse, so the eucharist is its chief preoccupation,[63] and to consider one in the context of the other begins to suggest a way of reading Herbert that resolves the vexed doctrinal contradictions into a mode of belief with a compelling internal logic. I want to draw attention once again to the coincidence of terminology whereby what St Paul calls a *metanoia* is described by Donne as a 'true Transubstantiation'. The concept moves beyond the verbal level of rhetoric, beyond the device described by the term 'correctio', into a wider sense that can comprehend also mode of understanding and a way of thinking. The shape of the figure is, as I have already suggested, replicated on a cognitive plane; this is not straightforwardly *metanoia* in its theological sense, as a spiritual watershed that confirms a turning to God, but something at once more elusive and less

---

[62] Vendler, *Poetry of George Herbert*, p. 29.
[63] C. A. Patrides calls it 'the marrow of his sensibility' (*The English Poems of George Herbert*, ed. by C. A. Patrides (London: Dent, 1974), p. 17).

teleological: a minor poetic figure that comes to structure and express a form of sacramental belief.

John Pettavel has written a short meditation on the reach of the word; it is a devotional rather than a scholarly work, but it outlines a theory of signification germane to this discussion. *Metanoia*, he argues, 'implies, among many other possible meanings, the passage of one sort of thinking, one level of thinking, to another':

'Horizontal' thought cannot deal with more than one meaning at a time, whereas 'vertical', 'metanoietic' thought works differently. ... This form of perception-thought or insight will harmonize opposed aspects of ideas where the either-or form of thinking will divide. A rise in level of thought, as well as quality of thinking, will make concordant what at first sight seems contradictory.[64]

A modified version of this *metanoietic* model of thought serves as a way of understanding Herbert's response to contemporary eucharistic controversy. The view of Herbert as a poet not in control of the theological implications of his verse still has some critical currency; that there is a degree of inconsistency in the poetic presentation of Herbert's eucharistic beliefs, however, need not demonstrate doctrinal confusion or a latent Catholicism. If Herbert might instead be credited with an inclusive theology that admits no contradiction in different understandings of the communion experience, the tension disappears. Just as, on a rhetorical plane, the device of *metanoia* allows the error to coexist with its correction, so the same framework transposed to a conceptual level (Pettavel's 'vertical' model of thought) makes possible a poetics that can posit a number of mutually exclusive doctrinal positions without having to decide between them. The poet retreats in humility from the need to formulate a consistent viewpoint, preferring rather to have faith in, than a precise understanding of, the mysteries of the sacrament.

[64] John Pettavel, *Metanoia: Essays in the Interpretation of Certain Passages in the Gospels* (Haslemere: Phene Press, 1983), pp. 8, 5.

CHAPTER 4

Crashaw and metonymy

Herbert's careful equivocations won for him a broad readership. His early death in 1633, at the age of forty, obviated the necessity for siding with either Parliament or king in the turbulent years that followed. Neither faction secured an ideological monopoly on his works; the seeming simplicity of its verse recommended *The Temple* to Puritans as well as to Calvinists, and Herbert was read on both sides of the contention throughout the seventeenth century, and indeed beyond. Richard Crashaw, the younger man, was not so fortunate in his chronology or his reception: the vagaries of politics and theology inflicted a damage on his poetic reputation from which it has, even now, barely recovered.

In recent years, there has emerged a tendency to open discussions of Crashaw by remarking on the propensity of other critics to open such discussions with a defence of his verse against the imputations of 'bad taste' that have dogged it since at least the first half of the nineteenth century.[1] This is to be no exception. The preoccupation with 'taste' (in both its literal and figurative senses, as an examination of the terms of the debate will make clear) is a legitimate response to one of the central concerns of Crashaw's writing: an attempt to imagine rhetorically the implications of Christ's presence in the eucharist. Both before and after his conversion to Catholicism following exile from England in 1643, Crashaw was writing devotional verse which expresses a profoundly sacramental imagination; by

---

[1] See, for example, the introductory paragraphs of: Eugene R. Cunnar, 'Crashaw's "Sancta Maria Dolorum": Controversy and Coherence', in *New Perspectives on the Life and Art of Richard Crashaw*, ed. by John R. Roberts (Columbia: University of Missouri Press, 1990), pp. 99–126 ('It has become almost obligatory to begin an essay on Crashaw by explaining his disparaging treatment at the hands of critics over the years'); Lorraine Roberts, 'Crashaw's Epiphany Hymn: Faith out of Darkness', in *'Bright Shootes of Everlastingnesse': the Seventeenth-Century Religious Lyric*, ed. by Claude J. Summers and Ted-Larry Pebworth (Columbia: University of Missouri Press, 1987), pp. 134–44; Michael McCanles, 'The Rhetoric of the Sublime in Crashaw's Poetry', in *The Rhetoric of Renaissance Poetry*, ed. by Thomas O. Sloan and Raymond B. Waddington (Berkeley: University of California Press, 1974), pp. 189–211.

exploring his rhetorical habit, and in particular his employment of the figure of the reflexive turn (and the trope of metonymy on which the figure depends), this chapter will try to understand how his devotional imperatives are expressed in his verse, and why their expression may have proved quite so unsettling for generations of readers.

CRITICISING CRASHAW: A MATTER OF TASTE

It is not difficult to find possible explanations for the deep suspicion with which the man and his work were regarded for so many years. Crashaw was born in 1612/13, the son of a fairly well-to-do clergyman and Puritan controversialist, William Crashaw. He was schooled at Charterhouse, and in 1631 went up to Pembroke College, Cambridge, as a pensioner. Four years later, he became a fellow of Peterhouse. Peterhouse at that time was very high church indeed; although Nicholas Tyacke writes that St John's in the 1630s 'emerged as second to none in the lavishness of its new chapel furnishings', he adds: 'Only Peterhouse Chapel, under the mastership of the Arminian John Cosin, can challenge comparison with that of St John's.'[2] There is every reason to believe that Crashaw found it a congenial environment; when the discord between king and Parliament intensified in the early 1640s, Crashaw's strongly royalist and Laudian sympathies, and those of the institution to which he belonged, caused trouble for them both. The Parliamentary Commissioners visited the college in late 1643 to tear down its graven images; a few months later Cosin and five of Peterhouse's fellows, including Crashaw in his absence, were expelled. It is at this point or shortly before that the poet left England for good; he travelled in Holland and France before making his way to the papal court in Rome in search of preferment; passed over and disappointed, he died in Loreto in 1648 at the age of thirty-seven.[3] It is unclear precisely when during the course of these adventures Crashaw converted to Catholicism; although it was certainly before the publication in 1646 of his first major devotional work, *The Steps to the Temple*, it was undoubtedly after much of the verse collected in that volume was written.

The critical implications of this biography are wide-reaching. To the nineteenth-century palate, Crashaw's was a life that may have been lived, and that certainly ended, in very bad taste: not just in a foreign land, but in a foreign religion, too. Alison Shell makes clear the association: 'to them', she

[2] Tyacke, *Anti-Calvinists*, p. 194.
[3] This brief account is derived from Thomas Healy, 'Crashaw, Richard (1612/13–1648)', *DNB* online.

writes of 'critics of the more distant past', 'the baroque was a Catholic fashion; and for many of them – in a symbiosis of religious and aesthetic prejudice – the baroque equated to blowsy emotionalism and dropsical bad taste'.[4] Shell perhaps has in mind such commentators as Henry Southern, who asserted in the *Retrospective Review* of 1820 that some of Crashaw's verse was 'so gaudy and flowery, as to be disgusting to the simpler taste of a good Protestant'.[5] This judgement anticipates much later criticism, both in its aversion to its subject, and in the terms in which that aversion is expressed. It might perhaps be argued that words like 'disgusting' or indeed 'taste' used in an aesthetic context such as this have long since forgotten their meta-phorical origins, and should not be made to bear the charge of the senses that underwrite them. But even a brief consideration of the criticism reveals a persistent confusion of the oral with the aesthetic that smacks of an intuitive recognition of some quality of Crashaw's verse. Consider, for example, Paul G. Stanwood on his predecessors: 'Some commentators have dismissed "The Weeper" ... as a collection of mere *bon-bons* and not even delectable ones';[6] or Young on the same subject: '[Crashaw] is often described as a kind of poetic confectioner, specialising in rococo cake decoration.'[7] The tenor of observations such as these recognises a pervasive critical unease: one that absorbs and reflects Crashaw's disturbing preoccu-pation with the edible, and, in particular, with the potential edibility of the body of Christ.

Stanwood and Young catch at another marked feature of Crashaw's interest in food: bon-bons and icing are both very sugary, and the impos-sible sweetness of some of the verse is quite striking. 'Musicks Duell', to take an example from among the secular poems, employs the word 'sweet' and its cognates ('sweetness', 'sweetly' and so on) twenty-two times in 168 lines. It tells the story of a contest between a lute-player and a nightingale, each trying to out-do the other with the beauty of their music. As so often with these challenges, the nightingale comes off rather worse: she expires in a moment of creative ecstasy. The sweetness of the song that kills her is arrestingly imagined as a tangible, liquid thing: the 'Sweet-lipp'd Angell-Imps' can 'swill their throats | In creame of Morning *Helicon*', while the

---

[4] Shell, *Catholicism, Controversy and the English Literary Imagination*, pp. 56–7.
[5] Quoted in Lorraine M. Roberts and John R. Roberts, 'Crashavian Criticism: a Brief Interpretative History', in *New Perspectives on the Life and Art of Richard Crashaw*, ed. by John R. Roberts (Columbia: University of Missouri Press, 1990), pp. 1–29 (p. 10).
[6] Paul G. Stanwood, 'Time and Liturgy in Donne, Crashaw, and T. S. Eliot', *Mosaic*, 12 (1979), 91–105 (101).
[7] Young, *Doctrine and Devotion in Seventeenth Century Poetry*, p. 158.

nightingale 'lets loose a Tide | Of streaming sweetnesse'.[8] It is easy to see how this excess might strike readers with ready access to a surfeit of sugar as syrupy almost to the point of sickliness, and how distaste can be transmuted into an accusation of bad taste. Food is not felt as a fit subject for lyric poetry, and the discomfort is naturally exacerbated when the food imagery itself is the stomach-turning combination of sweet and creamy that Crashaw often seems to favour.[9]

For some, distaste can swiftly become disgust. Robert Martin Adams's notorious 1950s article on the subject of Crashaw's bad taste identifies his fondness for food-related metaphor as a deliberately unsettling tactic: 'the fact that there is something slightly nauseating about the terms of this extension', he writes of 'The Weeper', 'is not wholly apart from Crashaw's intent'.[10] It is the fourth and fifth stanzas of the poem that are responsible for inducing feelings of critical queasiness; prominent, again, is that characteristic mixing of images of sugar and cream:

> Upwards thou dost weepe,
> Heavens bosome drinks the gentle streame.
> Where th' milky rivers meet,
> Thine Crawles above and is the Creame.
> Heaven, of such faire floods as this,
> Heaven the Christall Ocean is.

> Every morne from hence,
> A briske Cherub something sips
> Whose soft influence
> Adds sweetnesse to his sweetest lips.
> Then to his Musicke, and his song
> Tastes of this breakfast all day long.   (1646; pp. 79–80)

It is worth quoting almost in full Adams's response to these lines, both because it is a concise elucidation of some of the central issues raised by the

---

[8] 'Musicks Duell' (1646), ll. 75–7, 93–4, in Crashaw, *The Poems English, Latin and Greek, of Richard Crashaw*, ed. by L. C. Martin (Oxford: Clarendon Press, 1927), p. 151. All references are from this edition; page numbers, and in the case of lineated poems, line numbers, will appear in the text in parentheses. Where relevant, the year of publication is indicated; poems first published in 1648 (the second, revised, edition of *Steps to the Temple*) are usually given in their 1652 versions (*Carmen Deo Nostro*), following Martin.

[9] 'To mention food in a lyrical context calls into question the doctrine of good taste': Jocelyne Kolb, *The Ambiguity of Taste: Freedom and Food in European Romanticism* (Ann Arbor: University of Michigan Press, 1995), p. 11.

[10] Robert Martin Adams, 'Taste and Bad Taste in Metaphysical Poetry: Richard Crashaw and Dylan Thomas', *The Hudson Review*, 8 (1955), 61–77 (67).

imagery of eating, and because it has been very influential on subsequent readings of 'The Weeper'.

One aspect of Crashaw's 'bad taste' is the deliberate injection of a homely word or circumstance amid lofty spiritual reflections . . . The transformation of salt tears to milk is queer; raising the butterfat content to make it cream is odder yet. The delicacy of 'sippes' gives us a slight respite; but the domestic word 'Breakfast' in congruence with the idea of aftertaste (the whole image being underlain by notions of cud-chewing, angelic saliva, and a delicate series of cosmic belches) would seem to be in the worst possible taste.[11]

Adams's droll anatomisation of the workings of Crashaw's metaphorical frame is in some ways deft and acute, but in others curiously selective; he is quite right to point out the unsettling effect of the unstable salt–cream liquid, but his extrapolations ('underlain by notions') seem to have only the very vaguest warrant in the text: it is hard to identify an unambiguous reference to cud-chewing. Adams ignores the more subtly disquieting effect of, for example, these lines – 'Where th'milky rivers meet | Thine Crawles above and is the Creame'; 'floats' would seem a more natural choice than the sluggishly alliterative 'Crawles' in this context, as Crashaw himself admitted when he revised the poem for the second edition of 1648. Notable, though, is the poet's reluctance to lose either the alliteration or the disquiet, which is clearly part of his design: 'Where th'milky rivers creep, | Thine floates above; & is the cream' (p. 309). Whether the milk tears are creepy or crawly, the effect remains the same: the disjunction provokes in the reader a sense of faint disgust.

Perhaps most surprisingly of all, Adams does not explore the logical curiosities of 'Heavens bosome drinks the gentle streame'. What is strange about the line is its self-enfolded quality; 'the gentle streame' of the Magdalene's tears presumably becomes one of the 'milky rivers' that are imagined as constituting the vault of the sky. If 'milky rivers' is read as carrying a suggestion of a pun on 'mothers' milk' – a suggestion strengthened by the inevitable association for the classically educated of these milk-running heavens with the myth of the Milky Way – then this leaves us with the oddity of a milk-drinking bosom. And further, if Heaven *is* the crystal ocean of (presumably 'composed of'?) such fair floods, Heaven's bosom is in fact drinking its own substance, itself. The image becomes even more problematic when the brisk cherub arrives for his breakfast: it is not he, but 'his song' which 'tastes of' – both 'sips' and 'has the flavour of', hence

[11] Adams, 'Taste and Bad Taste', 66–7.

Adams's 'cosmic belches' – these sweet milky tears, and Crashaw's deliberate catachresis once again has a slightly discomfiting effect. The hint of
eroticism, too, is another complicating element; the disturbing effect of
these lines can in part be located in their shifting frame of reference, and the
inappropriate mixing of edible and inedible. There is here a deliberate
confusion, at least for a morbidly sensitive reader, of hunger with desire:
of one kind of appetite with another.

OUTRAGEOUS APPETITES: THE EROTICS
OF THE EDIBLE CHRIST

For Crashaw, the overwhelmingly important appetite is a spiritual one, and
his craving for God is a constant and complicated presence in his verse. But
to make a neat distinction between the religious and the gastronomic is not
always possible. The recurrent trope of sweetness mentioned above, for
example, has a liturgical, and more specifically a Catholic, significance:
'Jesu, Dulcis Memoria' is a twelfth-century hymn attributed to St Bernard
of Clairvaux, the aptly named Doctor Mellifluus (the *OED* gives the
primary meaning of 'mellifluous' as 'Flowing with, exuding, or containing
honey or a honey-like substance; of the nature of or resembling honey;
sweetened with or as with honey'). It describes Christ as 'super mel et
omnia', 'above honey and everything', and was sung to celebrate the Feast
of the Holy Name of Jesus, a feast excluded from the Protestant liturgy
with the introduction of Cranmer's Prayer Book in 1549. That this mystical
association of the body of Christ with the taste of honey was familiar to
Crashaw and appealed to him is evident from his own take on the subject,
'To the Name Above Every Name, the Name of Jesus, a Hymn'. This
poem first appeared in the revised and expanded version of *Steps to the
Temple* in 1648 (pp. 239–45), and can with some assurance be ascribed to
the post-conversion period of Crashaw's career. In the course of the poem
he invokes 'each severall kind | And shape of sweetnes' (ll. 37–8), 'every
sweet-lipp't Thing' (l. 47), 'soft ministers of sweet sad mirth' (l. 62); he
unearths a 'store | Of Sweets' (ll. 66–7), 'hidden Sweets' (l. 122), a 'Hoard
of Hony' (l. 158), a '(Clowd of condensed sweets)' (l. 168). Crashaw's
crowning superlative is worth remarking for its magnificent peculiarity
and disarming specificity; he trumps Bernard's 'super mel et omnia' with a
metaphor of ecclesiastical bureaucracy: 'Hourly there meetes | An univer-
sall Synod of All sweets' (l. 176).

    Not that the religious dimension of his food imagery or its sacred
precedent can redeem Crashaw's verse from accusations of tastelessness,

however; quite the reverse, in fact: 'To conventional taste', as David Reid remarks, 'the blending of devotional and erotic feeling is one of the embarrassments of Crashaw's art.'[12] He might have added that there is a particular problem when a more prosaic kind of appetite is also thrown into the equation, and that Crashaw seems to have a distinct relish for the mixture of all three. In these lines from 'On a prayer booke sent to Mrs M. R.', the fairly commonplace tactic of figuring heavenly in terms of earthly love is taken to unsettlingly explicit extremes.

> O let that happy soule hold fast
> Her heavenly armefull, shee shall tast
> At once, ten thousand paradises
>   Shee shall have power,
>   To rifle and deflower,
> The rich and roseall spring of those rare sweets,
> Which with a swelling bosome there shee meets
> Boundlesse and infinite————————
> ————————————bottomless treasures,
>   Of pure inebriating pleasures,
> Happy soule shee shall discover,
>   What joy, what blisse,
>   How many heavens at once it is,
> To have a God become her lover.   (1646; ll. 105–18, p. 130)

It is not a great surprise to notice the confusion of the sensual and the sensory that allows the lady in question to 'tast' the 'rare sweets' of a book that is also her lover; that she might become inebriated by this activity is perhaps a little odd, but again not particularly remarkable. What does give pause is the idea of Mrs M. R., presumably a respectable married woman, in the role of rapacious sexual-spiritual aggressor – 'hold[ing] fast' to the 'heavenly armefull' that she, with her 'swelling bosome', can 'rifle and deflower'. And the poet, as mediator between the lady and her lover, also occupies a slightly dubious position; to Reid, it 'sounds as if Crashaw were pimping for God'.[13] Finally, the most arresting typographical features of the lines – those mute, reaching dashes – are strangely suggestive. They are a silent articulation of the limits of sensation, a representation of devotional climax which seems both to conceal (as if the lines score out inadequate or censorable words beneath) and to invite alternative inscription: their blankness is a challenge. By 1652, they are gone. The short lines sit, indented, neatly on top of one another:

---

[12] David Reid, 'Crashaw's Gallantries', *John Donne Journal*, 20 (2001), 229–42 (238).
[13] Reid, 'Crashaw's Gallantries', 238.

                              Boundles & infinite
                              Bottomles treasures
                      Of pure inebriating pleasures.   (1652; ll. 118–20, p. 331)

Much of the erotic charge is lost.

   But this very faintly disturbing set of imagery barely registers on the
Crashavian scale of outrage. Conventional and indeed contemporary taste
can be forgiven for recoiling from some of Crashaw's bolder eroti-religio-
gastronomic experiments; take, for example, the epigram on Luke ii,
'Blessed be the Paps which Thou has sucked':

              Suppose he had been Tabled at thy Teates
              Thy hunger feeles not what he eates:
              Hee'l have his Teat e're long (a bloody one)
              The Mother then must suck the Son.   (1646; p. 94)

The difference between feeding from a body, as the thirsty cherub does, and
feeding off a body, as the faithful Catholic communicant does, is not one
Crashaw is usually keen to confront: the outrage of this jumbled concate-
nation of unthinkable syllogism, though, cannot but be deliberate. In four
short lines, Crashaw manages to imply that the incarnation combines
elements of hermaphroditism, incest and cannibalism: the paradox that
Mary, having succoured her son with her milk, will in turn be saved along
with all humankind by virtue of the blood he sheds at the crucifixion, is
expressed in a luridly explicit analogy of exchange that rams home the very
shocking implications of Christ's real presence in the eucharist. It carries
something of the flavour of those medieval Catholic stories which tell of
Jews and other sceptics being converted to the true faith by perceiving the
Host as gobbets of flesh, or as a baby being torn limb from limb. Something
of the flavour, and something of the confrontation, too: in these stories it is
the faithless who are punished with such disturbing cannibalistic visions;
only to believers does the Host appear in its reassuring guise as bread.[14]

   Crashaw's fiercely conformist father would presumably not have
approved. William Crashaw was something of a Puritan controversialist;
he amassed a considerable library of theological works, and himself made a
few robustly anti-Catholic contributions to contemporary debate in the
early years of the seventeenth century.[15] One of these, *The Spotted Jesuite*,
contains a passage that becomes significant in the light of his son's evident

---

[14] For an account of such stories, their origins and implications, see Clark, *Eucharistic Sacrifice*,
   pp. 410–34, and Duffy, *The Stripping of the Altars*, pp. 95–108.
[15] See Crashaw, *Poems*, pp. xv–xxi.

fascination with the relationship between Christ's blood and Mary's milk; it is hard to see how the poet's devotional interest in the appraisal of blood and milk might be reconciled with his father's abhorrence of the idea. Crashaw Senior exclaims with pious disgust against those who

> compare together his bloud and her milke, and upon comparison find them so equall, that they mix them together, and in the mixture find the milke so excellent, that they preferre it afore the bloud, as a thing more pretious, and with which, they may not be so bold as with the bloud of Christ, and feare not to affirme that the corruptions of our Nature, and sinnes of our soule are healed and helped as well by her milke as Christs bloud.[16]

The notion of *mixing*, of blending together the edible and the inedible (and in this case, as William Crashaw tries to suggest, the inappropriate combination of liquids of vastly different orders of significance), once more provokes a powerful reaction of disgust. This fulmination serves to demonstrate, too, that such unseemly amalgamation was regarded in some quarters as a distinctively Catholic, or at least Jesuitical, phenomenon: the water, wine, blood, tears, sweat and milk that wash in such quantities through Crashaw's verse might be read as bearing eloquent witness to his eventual confession.

There is a clear liturgical significance in this running theme of liquids that combine together or change into one another: by employing such conceits the poet can aspire to the actions of the priest at communion, mixing water with wine and speaking the words of institution which turn it into blood. For Crashaw, who was ordained as such a priest, this is, in all its complexity, a recapitulation on a literary level of an authorised (and still Protestant) liturgical act.[17] Crashaw's absorption in the mysteries of the incarnation is reflected in the recurrent metaphorical themes of his verse; his insistence on the mutability of substances, their potential to melt, dissolve, solidify or be

---

[16] *The Bespotted Jesuite whose Gospell is Full of Blasphemy against the Blood of Christ . . . Which Erronious Doctrine is Fully and Cleerly Laid Open and Reproved* by W. C. (London, 1641), p. 5. And compare Crashaw's epigram 'Upon the Infant Martyrs': 'To see both blended in one flood | The Mothers Milke, the Childrens blood, | Makes me doubt if Heaven will gather, | *Roses* hence, or *Lillies* rather' (1646; p. 95).

[17] Jeffrey Johnson has noticed the devotional implications of Crashaw's liquid imagery: 'This persistent blending and confusing of substances', he writes, 'is the expansive method by which Crashaw celebrates, liturgically, the paradoxes found in Immanuel (God with us)' (' "Til We Mix Wounds": Liturgical Paradox and Crashaw's Classicism', in *Sacred and Profane: Secular and Devotional Interplay in Early Modern British Literature*, ed. by Helen Wilcox, Richard Todd and Alasdair MacDonald (Amsterdam: VU University Press, 1996), pp. 251–8 (p. 252). Stanwood, too, comments that 'Crashaw is a poet of the liturgical mode, where the Incarnation informs his every gesture and speech' (Stanwood, 'Time and Liturgy in Donne, Crashaw and T. S. Eliot', 99).

transformed, reveals and allows a quite individual understanding of the eucharist.

The intimacy and intensity of tasting God, the experience which so much of his verse strives to replicate, could easily be seen as shocking by a reader who does not share in such an understanding. The last two stanzas of 'On the wounds of our crucified Lord', which describe a compellingly unstable trajectory of ultimately sacramental images, provide a challenging example. The poem opens with a characteristic apostrophe to the bleeding gashes on Christ's body, in which Crashaw contrives to establish through artful confusion an equivalence between a drop of blood, a kiss and a tear: 'O These wakefull wounds of thine! | Are they Mouthes? or are they eyes?' (ll. 1–2). He goes on to imagine Christ and the grieving Magdalene engaged in a peculiar economy of exchange:

> This foot hath got a Mouth and lippes
>   To pay the sweet summe of thy kisses:
> To pay thy Teares, an Eye that weeps
>   In stead of Teares such Gems as this is.
>
> The difference onely this appears,
>   (Nor can the change offend)
> The debt is paid in *Ruby*-Teares,
>   Which thou in Pearles did'st lend.   (1646; ll. 13–20, p. 99)

She kisses his feet and is kissed back by their wounds; she weeps, and in return for her tears receives drops of Christ's blood: his injuries are both mouths that kiss and eyes that cry. The poem is obsessed with the exchangeability and interchangeability of salt-water, blood and kisses, but where the first two harden into jewels ('*Ruby*-Teares' and 'Pearles'), the kisses resist such a change of state; they remain awkwardly outwith the easy commerce of blood and tears, for a kiss is a debt repaid in the very instant it is incurred. The kisses, too, share (though in a minor key) some of the disturbingly vampiric overtones of transgressive eating and eroticism that are such a striking feature of the epigram on Luke 11; as Empson helpfully remarks of the concluding couplet of 'Blessed be the Paps which Thou has sucked', 'a wide variety of sexual perversions can be included in the notion of sucking a long bloody teat which is also a deep wound'.[18] Both poems seek to surprise

---

[18] William Empson, *Seven Types of Ambiguity* (London: Chatto and Windus, 1930; repr. London: Penguin, 1995), p. 257. Empson emphasises his point by borrowing the adjective 'long' from the previous clause where it applies, presumably, to time ('e're long') and using it to describe the teat itself. His (understandable) confusion mirrors the unsettling instability at the centre of the quatrain.

a reader into an absolutely visceral understanding of Christ's presence in the Host, and they do this by effacing the interim stages between crucifixion and communion: the blood-and-water that streams from the wounded Christ is shockingly figured as flowing directly into the mouths of the faithful: 'This is my blood indeed.'

CRASHAW'S SELF-CONSUMING ART

Christ bleeding on the cross is a subject to which Crashaw repeatedly returns. He is fascinated by the mystical logistics of the eucharist, by its scale and transhistoricity, and there is something slightly literal-minded in the awe with which he persistently imagines the channels, rivers, seas, floods and deluges of blood emanating from Christ's wounds: as if it were in itself enough, perhaps, to fill all the communion chalices of all the churches in the world, day after day, for thousands of years. Crashaw clearly believes in the impossibility of overstatement; this, and his conviction that Christ's blood must be requited by Magdalene's tears, lead to such idiosyncratic images as this one, from the revised version of 'The Weeper': Christ is 'follow'd by two faithfull fountaines; | Two walking baths; two weeping motions; | Portable, & compendious oceans' (1652; p. 312). But mere hyperbole ultimately proves inadequate to the expression of Crashaw's wonder at this act of self-sacrificing generosity. It is another rhetorical trick, a characteristic and complicated pattern of imagery which Christopher Ricks, after Empson, calls variously 'the short-circuited comparison' or 'self-inwoven simile', and Reid 'the reflexive turn', that Crashaw uses with such subtle force to convey most acutely his understanding of Christ's presence in the sacrament.[19] In the discussion that follows, Reid's coinage will be adopted as the less restrictive term; though Crashaw's images often carry an implicit sense of comparison, they rarely constitute anything so formal as a simile. 'A reflexive turn', Reid explains, 'is a figure of speech that involves something in paradoxical self-referentiality, usually through comparison or metonymic association and usually with the use of reflexive pronouns or of "own".'[20]

This figure can be found frequently in Crashaw's eucharistic poems, where it carries a particular theological weight – as it does, for example, in these lines from 'On the bleeding wounds of our crucified Lord' (1646;

[19] Christopher Ricks, 'Andrew Marvell: "Its Own Resemblance"', in Ricks, *The Force of Poetry* (Oxford: Clarendon Press, 1984), pp. 34–59; Empson, *Seven Types of Ambiguity*, pp. 160–1; David S. Reid, 'The Reflexive Turn in Early Seventeenth-Century Poetry', *English Literary Renaissance*, 32 (2002), 408–25.
[20] Reid, 'The Reflexive Turn', 408.

pp. 101–2): 'Thy restlesse feet . . . swim, alas! in their owne flood' (ll. 5, 8). It also occurs later in the poem, as Crashaw asserts Christ's humanity and his divinity, as well as his real presence in the eucharist:

> Thy hand to give thou canst not lift;
> Yet will thy hand still giving bee;
> It gives, but ô it self's the Guift,
> It drops though bound, though bound 'tis free.   (ll. 9–12)

The torrent does not just come from Christ, it *is* Christ: he deliquesces, and there is no distinction between the body on the cross and the blood that flows from it. This is couched in rather similar terms to a lyric of Southwell's, and the differences are telling:

> That which he gave, he was, O peerelesse gifte
> Both god and man he was, and both he gave
> He in his handes him selfe did trewelye lifte.
>
> ('Of the Blessed sacrament of the Aulter', p. 23 (ll. 7–9))

Crashaw is far more interested in the bloody logistics of the event than is his Jesuit predecessor. Where Southwell marvels reverently at the sacrifice, Crashaw confronts it: the pun in the last line which points to the irony of the drooping hand dropping blood skulks on the very edges of propriety, and it is not one Southwell would have made. Both poets are struck by the same thought, but Crashaw's expression has a mordant fervour quite alien to the earlier work.

In his influential essay on Andrew Marvell, 'Its Own Resemblance', Ricks compares the ways in which Marvell and Crashaw employ this mirroring figure and finds Crashaw sadly wanting. Marvell, Ricks argues, is wittier and more mysterious, because his images elegantly exploit an existing congruence rather than attempting to surprise unlike things into accord. Marvell's conceit of a drop of dew wept by itself, which 'Shines with a mournful light, | Like its own Tear', is 'unimaginable and yet is more than clear, is plausible, because of that shared liquidity of shape [between eye and tear]'.[21] Crashaw, on the other hand, does not always respect the integrity of the substances of which he writes, as has already been seen, and this proves problematic for Ricks; these lines from 'Wishes. To his (supposed)

---

[21] Ricks, 'Andrew Marvell', p. 37; Ricks quotes from 'On a Drop of Dew', *Miscellaneous Poems by Andrew Marvell Esq.; Late Member of the Honourable House of Commons* (London, 1681), p. 5. Though it is not certain when Marvell's poem was composed, it was probably after the publication of *Steps to the Temple*; Nigel Smith gives the most likely date as 'the late 1640s' (*The Poems of Andrew Marvell*, 2nd edn (Harlow: Longman, 2007), p. 39).

Mistresse' are reminiscent in their deliberate phase state uncertainty of the kisses, blood and tears imagery of 'On the wounds of our crucified Lord' (quoted above):

> Each Ruby there,
> Or Pearle that dare appeare,
> Bee its owne blush, bee its owne Teare. (1646; ll. 62–4, p. 196)

Ricks sets this charming and compact image of jewels shamed because outshone by the hair they adorn against the gently arresting pathos of Marvell's drop of dew weeping itself for sorrow at being separated from the sky:

> What is missing from the lines of Richard Crashaw which Marvell probably knew … is such a sense of awed transposition, for there is no haunting interminability, such as exists when we try to imagine a drop of water wept by itself, between a pearl and 'its own Teare'; instead of Marvell's fluid windows, we are handed something that crystallizes as cleverness.[22]

Marvell does, it is true, come off better from this particular comparison: Crashaw's little bit of mannered whimsy cannot compete with the liquid grace of Marvell's simile, even if one acknowledges that this crystallisation (or, perhaps more accurately here, this dissolution – Ricks's choice of term recalls once more the bon-bons of fond critical memory) is a deliberate rhetorical ploy.

But it is not a fair fight. Ricks might have chosen instead to compare Marvell's lines from 'On a Drop of Dew' with, for example, this graver and more complex self-inwoven simile from 'To *Pontius* washing his blood-stained hands': 'Each drop's a Teare that weeps for her own wast' (l. 11). Crashaw writes of the water with which Pilate tries symbolically to eradicate his responsibility for sentencing Christ to death; the hands will never be clean, though the drops are defiled by his 'Adult'rous touch':

> Leave, leave, for shame, or else (Good judge) decree,
> What water shal wash this, when this hath washed thee.
> (1646; ll. 15–16, p. 95)

---

[22] Ricks, 'Its Own Resemblance', p. 38. Ricks's gentle disparagement calls to mind Eliot's more generous estimation of Crashaw's cognitive powers: 'it is a deliberate conscious perversity of language, a perversity like that of the amazing and amazingly impressive interior of St Peter's. There is brain work in it' (T. S. Eliot, 'A Note on Richard Crashaw', in *For Lancelot Andrewes: Essays on Style and Order* (London: Faber and Gwyer, 1928), pp. 117–25 (p. 123)).

Defiled, and incarnadine; this shame, 'these sullied cheeks this blubber'd face' (l. 4), is an ugly grief far removed from the flush of a ruby or the tear of a pearl. The reader is asked to imagine a drop of water which must also be both an eye and a tear: a tear that weeps itself in distress at being squandered on Pilate's bootless attempts to secure absolution. Further, the tear has a tear-stained ('blubber'd') face – is stained with itself, as well as with the taint of Pilate's hand. 'What water shal wash this', Crashaw questions, and the image corkscrews to a 'haunting interminability' of a kind, as the impossibility of remedy underwrites the magnitude of the sin. 'Each drop's a Teare that weeps for her own wast': it is an ornate conceit, and lacks the lightness of touch that irradiates Marvell's 'Like its own Tear', but it approaches that simile more nearly both in phrasing and in feeling than the lines from 'Wishes. To his (supposed) Mistresse' that Ricks decided to use as his comparison. For Ricks could always, of course, have chosen instead to set Marvell's lines against those of Crashaw from which they are an almost verbatim steal; to complain that the earlier poet's figure lacks the 'sense of awed transposition . . . such as exists when we try to imagine a drop of water wept by itself' seems a little ungenerous given that Marvell lifted the whole conceit straight from another of Crashaw's poems, 'The Teare'. Here, what causes the tears to cry themselves in distress is the sadness of parting from Mary's eye:

> Each Drop leaving a place so deare,
> Weeps for it selfe, is its owne Teare.   (1646; p. 84)[23]

Both poets make a devotional point with the image; Marvell's simile ('Like its own Tear') seems to recommend itself by maintaining a philosophical distance from its subject – by demonstrating, that is, less 'blowsy emotionalism and dropsical bad taste'.[24]

Another point of correspondence to remark here is the pastoral image of flood from 'Upon Appleton House' which Ricks also singles out for praise, admiring 'the astonishment which Marvell's figure delights to recognize': 'The River in it self is drown'd, | And Isl's th'astonish'd Cattle round.'[25] The paradox of a river losing itself by becoming more than itself is elegantly and economically expressed; the thought, though, is again not an original one. A

---

[23] There is another correspondence that makes it almost certain that Marvell did know 'The Teare', or at least that he and Crashaw share a common source: in both poems, the drops of water fall on roses. 'Such a Pearle as this is | (Slipt from *Aurora's* dewy Brest) | The Rose buds sweet lip kisses' (p. 84). I am grateful to Jane Partner for pointing this correspondence out to me; see 'Poetry and Vision in England, 1650–1670' (unpublished doctoral thesis, University of Cambridge, 2005), pp. 83–6.

[24] Shell, *Catholicism, Controversy and the English Literary Imagination*, pp. 56–7, quoted above.

[25] Ricks, 'Its Own Resemblance', p. 41; Marvell, *Miscellaneous Poems*, p. 92.

comparison with Crashaw's admittedly less agile use of the same turn neatly illustrates the fundamental differences in style between the two poets:

> Rain-swolne Rivers may rise proud
> Threatening all to overflow,
> But when indeed all's overflow'd
> They themselves are drowned too.   (1646; ll. 33–6, p. 102)

Characteristically, when Crashaw employs the image, it is the rivers of blood emanating from Christ's body that he has in mind: these lines are from a poem called 'On the bleeding wounds of our crucified Lord'. The restrained sense of wonder that Marvell conjures is lost in the devotional imperative. For Crashaw, the important paradox is that salvation can come from crucifixion, that a man must be immersed in blood lest he should be sunk in sin: 'A deluge least we should be drown'd' (l. 40). His recourse to the reflexive turn is on one level a way of figuring the mystery through unthinkable hyperbole. To follow the logic of the poem is to conceive of an ocean of liquid Christ so vast that it cannot be contained: this has subtle polemical implications for a theology of the eucharist.

It may seem an obvious ploy, to change a secular for a devotional poem – to substitute 'To *Pontius* washing his blood-stained hands', or 'On the bleeding wounds of our crucified Lord', for 'Wishes. To his (supposed) Mistresse' – and then stand back and admire the inevitable increase in gravitas and inscrutability, but in the case of this poet it is a more than justifiable manoeuvre: it is essential. Crashaw uses the reflexive turn above all to express his conception of the central mysteries of his faith, and to watch it at work only in a courtly context is to miss its point in his writing. This is not to suggest that Ricks was not sensible of such an application; implicit in the terms which he uses to describe the reach and flexibility of the figure is an understanding of how valuable it might prove to a sacramental imagination: 'literal reflections also catch the light', he writes, 'with their paradoxes of identity and difference, transposition, unreal reality and substantial insubstantiality'.[26] If the paradoxes Ricks identifies inform and enable this rhetorical trick, they also lie at the heart of the transformation of the elements in the Host and its relation to Christ's death on the cross. A hand that gives the gift of itself, which is the gift of salvation: Crashaw's rhetoric rehearses on an infinitesimal scale and on a lyric plane the divine action of transubstantiation; his reflexive turns are a smoke-and-mirrors presentation of substances that are both themselves and something other,

---

[26] Ricks, 'Its Own Resemblance', p. 35.

mysteries which must be apprehended by their effects, and which stand in metonymical relation to their source.

Crashaw's figures have devotional aspirations; even in their falling short, they reverently express the distance between divine immanence and human apprehension. This dynamic, and the odd disjunctions to which it gives rise, can be seen at work in a frankly rather peculiar verse on Christ's wounds. 'On our crucified Lord Naked, and bloody' imagines the incarnated son of God as sort of divine clothes closet. The wounds, which have in other poems been eyes and mouths, are here, in a touchingly homely metaphor, presented as cupboard doors:[27]

> Th' have left thee naked Lord, O that they had;
> This Garment too I would they had deny'd.
> Thee with thy selfe they have too richly clad,
> Opening the purple wardrobe of thy side.
>   O never could bee found Garments too good
>   For thee to weare, but these, of thine own blood.   (1646; p. 100)

As so often, the blood is figured as an intriguingly ambivalent substance; it is both Christ and covering: by metonymic substitution of his blood for Christ, the thing hidden and the thing hiding (Ricks's 'identity and difference'). It performs its customary trick of congealing into another substance altogether: in this case becoming quite literally, in a very submerged pun, material – the garment that covers Christ ('substantial insubstantiality'). It shares in the moral ambiguity of an act simultaneously cause for lament and celebration, at once gory evidence of a shaming barbarity and an ennoblingly regal, or perhaps episcopal, rich purple raiment ('transposition'). Finally, it is Christ and 'too good' for Christ ('unreal reality'). The reflexive turn contrives to replicate rhetorically in its double-thinking structure the familiar but elusive paradoxes associated with the doctrine of transubstantiation, where wine and bread become, in substance, blood and body while remaining, in appearance, themselves. The logical and verbal mechanics of its operation offer a way of expressing a faith in impossibility (one that stops just short of heterodoxy) which Crashaw delights in exploiting. 'Thee with thy selfe they have too richly clad': he restates with some rhetorical flair what

---

[27] It is the literal-minded way in which Crashaw explores it that is odd, not the conceit itself: there is some scriptural warrant for such an image. 'But put ye on the Lord Jesus Christ' (Romans 13:14); 'For in this we groan, earnestly desiring to be clothed upon with our house which is from heaven: If so be that being clothed we shall not be found naked' (II Corinthians 5:2–3). Compare also Joseph Hall on the character of the faithful man: 'when he goes in, to converse with God, he weares not his owne clothes, but takes them still out of the rich Wardrobe of his Redeemer' (*Characters of Vertues and Vices: In Two Books* (London, 1608), p. 20).

proves to be the paradox of the poem's title, a paradox signified most subtly with a comma: 'On our crucified Lord Naked, and bloody'. Within the terms of the poem, clearly, it is impossible that he should be both.

The reflexive turn is not a device traditionally valued highly in poetry. Empson, in identifying it and placing it within the scope of his fifth type of ambiguity, the 'fortunate confusion', speaks a little slightingly of 'so limited an instrument as the short-circuited comparison', and it can indeed seem at times an exasperatingly slippery and imprecise mode of expression.[28] Why Crashaw was so drawn to it can, as I have tried to suggest, be explained at least in part by the potential coincidence of its formal properties with a way of approaching eucharistic theology: it allowed him to imagine and to express a transubstantial dynamic on a rhetorical plane – without, that is, involving the necessary contradiction of a structure of belief which was still, just about, Protestant. There is, however, another concern, so closely related that it might look in some lights like a facet of the first, which is also distinctively Crashavian and which the reflexive turn also voices. At the beginning of this chapter I located a certain critical disdain for Crashaw's work in his pervasive preoccupation with the edible, a preoccupation reflected in the topoi of eating and tasting to which the verse returns again and again. (This seems to have been an intellectual rather than a physical interest: 'What he might eate or weare he tooke no thought,' Thomas Car piously testifies in the laudatory verse that prefaces *Carmen Deo Nostro*; 'His needfull foode he rather found then sought.')[29] The theological and gastronomic concerns are parallel because, finally, what Crashaw finds fascinating is the transformation of substance through ingestion: the reflexive turn is a rhetorical device which might in some sense be thought of as transforming its terms by instituting an act of self-consumption, as at least one of those terms – the thing or itself – must ultimately vanish if the image is pursued to its logical conclusion. 'Here food it selfe is fed' ('On the miracle of the multiplyed loaves', 1646; l. 4, p. 86): this might be paraphrased as 'Here food is fed to itself', for the substance that is fed is, by definition, food; one reaches a clear cognitive impasse in trying to imagine what, if anything, might be left behind once food has eaten itself.

---

[28] Empson, *Seven Types of Ambiguity*, pp. vi, 191. It should be noted, however, that William Keach has advanced an argument defending Shelley (in Empson's opinion the worst offender) from accusations of lexical opportunism and woolly thinking: 'when not able to think of a comparison fast enough', Empson writes, 'he compares the thing to a vaguer or more abstract notion of itself' (p. 190). For Keach's response see 'Reflexive Imagery in Shelley', *Keats–Shelley Journal*, 24 (1975), 49–69, and *Shelley's Style* (London: Methuen, 1984), pp. 79–117.

[29] 'Crashawe the Anagramme', 1652; ll. 29–30, p. 234.

METONYMY AND CHRISTIANITY

The poem that unites all of these elements in a design both complex and intriguing is 'An Apologie for the Precedent [or 'Fore-going'] Hymne', which follows Crashaw's panegyric on St Teresa. When reprinted posthumously in *Carmen Deo Nostro*, the apology is revealingly elucidated (though presumably not by Crashaw himself); the Hymn needs excuse, it is explained, for 'having been writt when the author was yet among the protestantes'. That it exists at all suggests that Crashaw's conversion was not simply the legitimisation of already-held beliefs; he was himself aware that poems written before his conversion (though all published afterwards, of course) might give expression to theological views not necessarily consistent with those he had since embraced. Any lack of proper Catholic feeling in the earlier poem, however, is more than compensated for by the distinctively Roman liturgical movements of the later one; 'it constitutes a criticism of the "Hymn"', Walter R. Davis remarks, 'and, at the same time, exemplifies a different kind of poem – not only highly emotional, but embracing an act analogous to the Eucharist and thus an action in its (the poem's) own right'.[30] The 'act' to which Davis refers is the verbal act by which Teresa's words are transformed, by degrees, into Christ's blood: 'O 'tis not spanish, but 'tis heav'n she speaks!' (l. 23). Crashaw opens the poem with a description of how Teresa's foreign 'names & wordes' have influenced his English ones; he goes on to identify her Spanish tongue with Spanish sack, a white wine, but revises the comparison to establish instead an equivalence with 'strong wine of love', the wine of the eucharist: both words and wine cause his soul to 'swell' in religious ecstasy. And then comes the moment of transubstantiation:

> we will pledge this SERAPHIM
> Bowles full of richer blood then blush of grape
> Was ever guilty of, Change we too 'our shape
> (My soul,)   (1652; ll. 30–2, p. 323)

This protean substance is now the blood of Christ. There follows a passage of praise and wonder at the mystery, lines which stand in their contemplative awe as a sort of verbal counterpart to the elevation of the Host;[31] finally, the instant of communion is enacted in a deft self-reflexive turn:

---

[30] Walter R. Davis, 'The Meditative Hymnody of Richard Crashaw', *English Literary History*, 50 (1983), 107–29 (111).
[31] In *Poetry of Meditation*, p. 347, Louis L. Martz uses the notion of the elevation of the Host to describe the few lines following l. 161 of 'To the Name above every Name'; that insight seems, if anything, even more relevant here.

> Wine of youth, life, & the sweet Deaths of love;
> Wine of immortall mixture; which can prove
> It's Tincture from the rosy nectar; wine
> That can exalt weak EARTH; & so refine
> Our dust, that at one draught, mortality
> May drink it self up, and forget to dy.   (ll. 41–6)

'The notion of being too drunk to remember to die is certainly a charming one,' is Reid's comment on the conceit, though he is clearly sensible of the intricacy of the image: he acknowledges that 'Mortality drinks itself up by complex synecdochic and metonymic equivocation.'[32] Metonymic, certainly: mortality is an attribute of, and so a metonym for, sinful humankind, and here it must also stand for the blood that issues from Christ's mortal wounds as he hangs dying on the cross. An admittedly somewhat unwieldy paraphrase might run something along the lines of 'by drinking mortality (the wine of the eucharist that is the blood of Christ's dying), mortality (humankind) will lose its mortality (will be granted eternal life)'. Shades of Lethe underwrite the image. Crashaw has once again performed his devotional conjuring trick, this time by choosing to designate something by an attribute that will be made to vanish. Reid concludes: 'It is the wine of divine love that triumphs in this reflexive turn; the mortality that drinks itself up simply disappears.'[33]

The trope on which all of this turns is metonymy: a trope to which Crashaw is peculiarly drawn, and which is an extremely important, if not the dominant, weapon in his rhetorical armoury. Peculiarly, because its centrality to Crashaw's art (both on its own and as a facilitating notion for the reflexive turn) might be considered slightly surprising if one subscribes to the view put forward by Roman Jakobson in his seminal essay on the subject; Jakobson distinguishes between the two principal modes of metaphor, which he describes as leading from one term to another by similarity, and metonymy, where the relationship between the two terms is one of contiguity. It is helpful here to draw on I. A. Richards's distinction between tenor and vehicle, where tenor is the literal element that is being figured – the first term – and vehicle the element which figures it – the term which is eventually used, and to which the first term leads either by similarity or contiguity (though in both cases there must clearly be a perception of disparity for the trope to work).[34] 'The principle of similarity underlies poetry,' Jakobson writes; 'Prose, on the contrary, is forwarded essentially by

---

[32] Reid, 'The Reflexive Turn', 419.   [33] Reid, 'The Reflexive Turn', 419.

[34] 'A first step is to introduce two technical terms to assist us in distinguishing from one another what Dr Johnson called the two ideas that any metaphor, at its simplest, gives us. Let me call them the tenor and the vehicle' (I. A. Richards, *The Philosophy of Rhetoric* (Oxford University Press, 1936; repr. 1965), p. 96).

contiguity. Thus, for poetry, metaphor, and for prose, metonymy is the line
of least resistance and, consequently, the study of poetical tropes is directed
chiefly toward metaphor.'[35] This might be broadly true, but there are
notable exceptions, and Crashaw is prominent among them.[36]

That it is both characteristic and unusual, at least according to Jakobson's
scheme, suggests that the deployment of metonymy in Crashaw's verse
warrants careful critical attention. The *OED* describes the trope as 'a figure
in which the name of an attribute or adjunct is substituted for that of the
thing meant, e.g. *sceptre* for *authority*'; Lanham's *Handlist of Rhetorical
Terms* gives a broadly similar definition, though with a difference in
emphasis: 'substitution of cause for effect or effect for cause, proper name
for one of its qualities or vice versa'.[37] What is outside the compass of both
of these works, however, is the theological potential of such a trope. 'Meta-
nymy' is, literally, 'after name', or 'above name'; if one is to concur with
Aquinas in supposing that a name is a sign of an intelligible concept, and
that knowing must therefore come before naming, it follows that an understanding of God is in some sense a metonymic process because he must be
named for the effects he causes. But that Crashaw felt so strongly the pull of
this rhetorical trope might argue a particular cast of mind, and not simply a
generally devout temper; 'Metonymy is not just a way of speaking,' Asals
maintains, 'it is a characteristic Catholic way of thinking.'[38] Her argument is
that the Catholic mode of worship confers a sacred status on certain objects
because of their association with, that is, their contiguous relationship to,
other objects: a theological metonymy. In support of this position, she
quotes the Jesuit apologist who refuted William Crashaw's denial that the
nails which had pierced Christ's flesh should be considered sacred because
of their contact with his body: 'we ought to worship the Crosse of Christ',
he writes, '*as also a relique that touched his sacred flesh*'.[39] The situation
is more complex, though, than Asals's straightforward equation between
Catholicism and metonymy suggests. 'Metonymy', Judith Anderson reminds

---

[35] Roman Jakobson, 'Two Aspects of Language and Two Types of Aphasic Disturbances', in Jakobson
and Morris Halle, *Fundamentals of Language* ('S-Gravenhage: Manton, 1956); reprinted (partially) in
Modern Theory and Criticism: a Reader, ed. by David Lodge (London: Longman, 1988), pp. 57–61
(p. 61).

[36] '[M]etonymy is a characteristic mark of the poetry of Richard Crashaw' (Heather A. R. Asals,
'Crashaw's Participles and the "Chiaroscuro" of Ontological Language', in *Essays on Richard
Crashaw*, ed. by Robert M. Cooper (Salzburg: Institut für Anglistik und Amerikanistik, 1979)
pp. 35–49 (p. 41)).

[37] Richard A. Lanham, *A Handlist of Rhetorical Terms*, 2nd edn (Berkeley: University of California Press,
1991), p. 102.

[38] Asals, 'Crashaw's Participles', p. 42.   [39] Asals, 'Crashaw's Participles', p. 43.

us, 'is the figure invoked by reformers of different stripes and with different intentions perhaps more often than any other to explain the words of institution'; as a survey of sixteenth- and seventeenth-century rhetorical handbooks reveals, the figure is in fact a distinctively Protestant tool for the right interpretation of Scripture.[40] If the action of the sacraments can be explained metonymically, the notion of Christ's real presence in the Host ceases to be necessary: believers can trust both their senses, which tell them that bread and wine remain substantially unchanged even after the priest has spoken the words of institution, and the Bible, which tells them that those same elements do indeed become body and blood ('this is my body, which is broken for you', 1 Corinthians 11:24). Metonymy allows Scripture to retain its integrity in the face of a changing understanding: Protestant thinkers can interpret its truth as a figurative truth.

Asals's notion of metonymy and Catholicism as necessarily united by a shared concern with contiguity is clearly in need of some amplification. To this end, one might consider the work she adduces as chief evidence for her view, a poem that first appears in the 1648 edition of *Steps to the Temple* (suggesting that it is a post-conversion composition). Of 'The Flaming Heart, upon the Book and Picture of the seraphicall saint Teresa, (As she is usually expressed with a Seraphim beside her)', Asals writes: 'one way of seeing what the poem is about is that it defies the *per se* existence of everything it touches, making definition stand as effect'.[41] Another way of seeing what the poem is about is to think of it as contrasting the truth-claims of language and picture: the poem's rhetorical complexity derives from its aim of determining the theological potential of the written word. It consists in a series of images whose ostensible object is to establish which of the things painted by the artist are fitting accoutrements for St Teresa, and which are proper to the seraphim next to her; it borders on the unimaginable in its relentless contradiction.[42] For the artist, it appears, has got it wrong: 'Painter, what didst thou understand', Crashaw asks, 'To put her dart into his hand!' (l. 13) The whole poem deals with questions of contiguity, with the attributes of hearts, blushes and wounds and the adjuncts of veils, darts and flames, and their right relationship to the two central figures; this grand theme is played out at a rhetorical level.

---

[40] Anderson, *Translating Investments*, p. 53. See the introduction, pp. 10–12, 24 above, for examples from Swynnerton, Fenner, Prideaux and Cranmer.

[41] Asals, 'Crashaw's Participles', p. 43.

[42] Reid talks of the 'wonderful metonymic preposterousness' and 'magnificent absurdity' of the lines ('Crashaw's Gallantries', 237, 240). Eliot, too, finds some of Crashaw's images 'entirely preposterous' ('Note on Crashaw', p. 123).

in love's feild was never found
A nobler weapon than a WOUND.
Love's passives are his activ'st part.
The wounded is the wounding heart.
O HEART! the æquall poise of lov'es both parts
Bigge alike with wounds & darts.
Live in these conquering leaves; live all the same;
And walk through all tongues one triumphant FLAME.

(1652; ll. 71–8, p. 326)

The grammatical metaphor ('passives', 'activ'st') serves, in a slightly self-conscious move, to focus attention on the verbal mechanics of the lines; Crashaw delights in the learned paradox of participles whereby the passive ('wounded') heart is defined by the effects it actively causes ('wounding'). The heart undergoes a series of transformations; it becomes a womb, pregnant with the unlikely offspring of 'wounds & darts', and is then imagined as the words of Teresa's writings ('Live in these conquering leaves'). Finally, the heart grows legs (it already presumably has arms, as Crashaw earlier refers to 'the Hand of this great HEART' (l. 36), and walks through tongues no longer as a heart but, in yet another example of Crashaw's terminally unstable imagery, as a flame.

What is most striking about these lines is their quality of defiant illogicality; and if the images seem absurd or preposterous, it is because of the confusion of rhetorical tropes that Crashaw employs. To paraphrase the imperative 'HEART ... walk through all tongues one triumphant flame' is just about possible (a plausible, if somewhat reductive, reading might be: 'Teresa's works will be understood in all languages'), but to construe the line rhetorically is much more difficult because the metaphoric, metonymic and synecdochic elements constantly leach into one another. 'HEART' is a synecdoche for the saint – a part of her standing for the whole – but it is also a metonymy: the saint, as represented by her heart, stands for her works. 'Tongues' is primarily metaphorical, but with synecdochic and metonymic aspects: the image comprehends tongues from mouths and tongues of fire as well as tongues in the (here) more obvious sense of languages, or of speaking in tongues. Finally, 'flame' is a metonymy of a synecdoche of a metonymy: it is an attribute of the ('flaming') heart that stands for Teresa (who stands for her works) throughout the poem. None of these devices involves anything so straightforward as substitution, but rather all depend on deletion; leaving aside for a moment one level of metonymic representation, what we are left with can be regarded as a contraction of the notional line: 'the heart of St Teresa walks through foreign tongues as a flame of the heart of St Teresa'. An expression of great figurative complexity results because the elements dropped are not logically the most dispensable, which has been identified as a defining quality of such rhetorical devices: 'Metonymy and synecdoche are produced by deleting one or more items from a combination, but not the items it would be most natural to omit.'[43] Metonymy, then, is characterised by unnaturalness and illogicality; or to express it in less pejorative terms, by its potential for impossibility and its ability to efface the constraints of the material universe. Crashaw's favoured trope may reflect his Catholic sensibility in part, as Asals maintains, through a common stake in contiguity; more importantly, though, the leap of faith required by a metonym allows it to approximate rhetorically the workings of the eucharist.

COMMUNION IN ONE KIND: EUCHARISTIC ACCOMMODATION

At the start of this chapter I described a critical tradition which reacted to Crashaw's poetic extravagancies – the imagery of eating, the wildly unstable substances, and, above all, the incessant mixing, generic, liturgical and rhetorical – with a distaste bordering on disgust. It should perhaps not be surprising that the most interesting of Crashaw's works from a doctrinal point of view are those that are in the worst imaginable taste, because those aspects of his verse which are most likely to provoke critical squeamishness are precisely the grounds on which he tries to build a subtly alternative conception of the eucharist.

For Crashaw's religious verse aspires to be more than just a poeticisation of established doctrine. It is in itself both an act of devotion and – this is true, at least, of the pre-exile works – an attempt to find a way of worshipping that will reconcile his deep sense of the mysteries of his faith with current orthodoxy. I particularly do not want to suggest that Crashaw's eventual conversion to Catholicism was either inevitable or necessary; pre-Civil War Protestantism was a broader church than is sometimes imagined, and the historical accident of Crashaw's turning to Rome should not be allowed to obscure the subtle accommodations that verses written before this conversion seek to make. Ross reads Crashaw only half-right when he

---

[43] David Lodge, *The Modes of Modern Writing: Metaphor, Metonymy, and the Typology of Modern Literature* (London: Edward Arnold, 1977), p. 76. Lodge presents a very useful gloss on and expansion of Jakobson's theories.

describes him as 'ravished by the sensuous surfaces of the Church', and his eucharistic poetry as 'faithful to the very accents of Aquinas'.[44] Such a judgement correctly acknowledges Crashaw's obvious Catholic leanings, but ignores the subtle doctrinal innovations of his devotional verse. His disconcerting interest in edibility, in the physical sensation of tasting God, is, significantly, largely confined to communion in one kind, and this is particularly true of the poems in the 1646 edition of *Steps to the Temple*; it is the blood that fascinates him, not the flesh; the wine that catches hold of his imagination, not the bread. As Reid observes, Crashaw is 'one of the great topers of English verse: drinking and being drunk (in both senses) are motifs he keeps returning to'.[45] Crashaw confounds the reformed literalism that would reject transubstantiation as an alimentary outrage on the body of Christ by, ultimately, imagining a fluid Host that need not be chewed, digested or excreted. It is a refined response to the persistent Protestant horror of the communicant's teeth; to the outrage voiced early by Cranmer, who quotes first Cyprian and then Augustine in support of his assertion that Christ in the eucharist is 'not eaten, swalowed, and dygested with oure teeth, tungues, throtes and bealyes'. '[W]e whette not our teethe to byte but with pure faith we breake the holy breade,' he writes; 'Prepare not thy jawes, but thy hert.'[46] In *De Doctrina Christiana*, Milton's fierce rejection of the notion of physical presence takes a scatological turn: the implications of his polemical Puritan response are discussed in Chapter 6, below. Crashaw's devotional imperative, however, prompts him to a subtler negotiation of the difficulty: liquid Christ evidently presents far fewer practical problems of ingestion.

Crashaw's communion in one kind sidesteps, without answering, the objection that it is unthinkable for the body of Christ to be torn and crushed in the mouth; it retains, therefore, without needing to confront, the possibility of an actual divine presence in the Host. In the same way, figuring the wound in Christ's side as the source of an unstanchable sacramental torrent allows Crashaw to imagine that there might, just theoretically, be enough blood to go round – thus obviating the need to

---

[44] Ross, *Poetry and Dogma*, p. 241.
[45] Reid, 'The Reflexive Turn', 418. He is perhaps thinking of lines such as these, from 'Sancta Maria Dolorum': 'O let me suck the wine | So long of this chast vine | Till drunk of the dear wounds, I be | A lost Thing to the world, as it to me' (1652; p. 287).
[46] Cranmer, *Defence*, pp. 91, 92 (italics omitted). This notion is also, of course, expressed by Calvin in the *Institutes*, where he calls it 'that perverse error that Christ is annexed to the element of bread': 'we are not to dream of such a presence of Christ in the sacrament as the artificers of the Romish court have imagined, as if the body of Christ, locally present, were to be taken into the hand, and chewed by the teeth, and swallowed by the throat' (*Institutes*, trans. by Beveridge, IV. xvii. 12 (pt II, pp. 564–5)).

interrogate the inconceivable dynamic of transubstantiation, and preserving, just, an accommodation between Catholic sensibility and Anglican orthodoxy. The fleshly equivalent would presumably have involved either a very large Christ or a body that renews its suffering, Prometheus-like, for eternity: in any case, a more difficult concept to swallow. Though a singular imagining, Christ as the source of an inexhaustible river of blood is by no means unique. The Italian painter and sculptor Gian Lorenzo Bernini (1598–1680) engraved, towards the end of his life, the vision of the sixteenth-century Florentine mystic, Maria Maddelena di Pazzi. She saw, and he pictured, the martyred Christ: the wounds in his wrists, feet and side stream into an ocean of blood that rills and foams below a magically suspended cross, and washes towards a lowering horizon. Cherubs flock, swept by a supernatural storm; the grieving Magdalene holds up her hands to this haemophiliac Christ, trying in vain to catch the liquid that spurts from his side. It is the visual rendering of a reflexive turn: Christ's restless feet 'swim, alas! in their own flood'.[47] This way of conceiving of the eucharist is important for Crashaw at the level of form as well as substance. His theological understanding expresses itself, as Herbert's does, in the rhetorical structures of his verse, and in particular in his characteristic recourse to the reflexive turn. The attraction of this device is that it carries within it a potential for assertion through logical impossibility which both allows and is made possible by faith without necessary scrutiny. Put simply, it offers Crashaw a way to articulate a eucharistic theology distinct from, but consistent with, both the memorialism of reformed orthodoxy and the transubstantiation of the Roman Church: a theology that relies on the power of faith to render such distinctions ultimately irrelevant. 'Faith is my skill. Faith can believe,' he writes in 'The Hymn of Sainte Thomas in Adoration of the Blessed Sacrament'; 'Faith is my force. Faith strength affords | To keep pace with those powrfull words' (1652; ll. 13–14, p. 292). This stance recalls Herbert's persistent refusal to subject his understanding of eucharistic theology to rational explanation – the mystery which, he insists, 'Concerneth bread, not mee' ('The H. Communion', l. 9). Civil war, however, prevented Crashaw from taking refuge in this position of retreat; when the English Church no longer allowed his faith to keep pace with the 'powrfull words' of institution, he chose conversion and exile rather than

---

[47] Although Crashaw's poetry has frequently been compared with baroque art in general, and Bernini's work in particular, this conceptual correspondence has not been remarked. It goes unmentioned, for example, in Robert T. Petersson's monograph on the subject: *The Art of Ecstasy in Teresa, Bernini, and Crashaw* (London: Routledge and Kegan Paul, 1970). I am grateful to Alex Dougherty for drawing my attention to this picture.

Figure 4.1 'Sanguis Christi', Francesco Spierre after Gian Lorenzo Bernini, *c.*1669–70.

face the permanent absence of God on earth. Crashaw's doctrinal attitude is pervasive and eccentric, and no reading of his poetry can avoid confronting it. This expedient idea of drinking God is in some ways the chief unsettling aspect of his poetic, because it is the one where all others converge: the erotic, the gastronomic, the Catholic, and even the feminine, for such passive devotion – standing under the cross with an open mouth – can be seen as opposed to a strenuous masculine searching for God. The most interesting elements of Crashaw's verse are also most problematic and disconcerting; this goes some way towards explaining a critical fascination that gingerly persists, despite the amply documented and colourfully expressed recoilings of generations of squeamish readers.

CHAPTER 5

Vaughan and synecdoche

In the foregoing chapters, I have attempted to demonstrate the particular and pervasive influence of four writers' conceptions of the eucharist on their writing practices. I have outlined some poetic limitations of Southwell's Catholic literalism, and described Donne's playful exploitation of the rhetorical opportunities offered by a move towards a more figurative sensibility. I have suggested that Herbert's distinctive vacillation between the scholastic and the mystical can be traced in his preference for the double-speaking figure of *metanoia*, both at the rhetorical level of the line and in the structures of his thought; and that Crashaw's disturbingly fluid metonymical imagery finds its source in the poet's associative and literalising sacramental imagination. For all of these men, the eucharist was absolutely central to both life and work. In their various holy orders, the recusant missionary, the court preacher, country parson and pre-conversion college priest celebrated communion as the highest rite and mystery of the church; the transformative power invested in them of pronouncing the words of institution came, in diverse ways, to animate by analogy their devotional writings.

Henry Vaughan's is a slightly different case. He was born in Breconshire, Wales, in 1621 (or perhaps in early 1622), and it was not he but his twin brother, Thomas, an alchemist and also a writer, who was ordained.[1] As they reached maturity, civil war broke out. Vaughan fought on the royalist side, and several poems in an early secular collection, the *Olor Iscanus*, remember bloody conflicts and dead comrades; it is likely that he lost his younger brother, William, in a battle in 1648, during the final phase of a war that was to end in bitter defeat for Vaughan's side. The upheaval proved devotional

---

[1] This very brief biographical sketch is derived from F. E. Hutchinson, *Henry Vaughan: a Life and Interpretation* (Oxford: Clarendon Press, 1947) and Alan Rudrum, 'Vaughan, Henry (1621–1695)', *DNB* online. See also Rudrum, *Henry Vaughan* (Cardiff: University of Wales Press, 1981) and, for a rather more impressionistic account, Stevie Davies, *Henry Vaughan* (Bridgend: Poetry Wales Press, 1995).

as much as it was political; it was in terms of shut churches and abandoned rites that Vaughan was to mourn the downfall of the king and the established order he fought for. Following the early republican victories, the *Book of Common Prayer* (which had been in continual use since 1559) was replaced in 1645 by the *Directory for Public Worship*, a stripped-down rite that dispensed with Cranmer's familiar set forms of prayer.[2] For some, this represented a painful dispossession. Morrill explains the tenacious appeal of the old order: '[A]fter eighty years of maturation', he writes, 'a hybrid church, thoroughly if murkily reformed in its doctrines, unreformed in its government, a mish-mash in its liturgy, had achieved not only an intellectual self-confidence but a rhythm of worship, piety, practice that had earthed itself into the Englishman's consciousness and had sunk deep roots in popular culture.'[3] In any event, this mish-mash liturgy proved hard to extirpate; the Prayer Book went abroad in the Interregnum, as various exiled clergymen – John Cosin, the master of Crashaw's old college, Peterhouse, prominent among them – continued to keep its use alive on the continent until the restoration of the monarchy in 1660.[4] As late as 1657, too, John Evelyn records a clandestine service in England, its Christmas Day communicants menaced in the devotional act by republican forces: 'as he was giving us the holy Sacrament, the Chapell was surrounded with Souldiers,' Evelyn relates; 'These wretched miscrants, held their muskets against us as we came up to receive the Sacred Elements, as if they would have shot us at the Altar.'[5]

Vaughan was one of those resistant to the Prayer Book's eclipse, and he too made efforts to preserve and disseminate its text. The disruption of the old rhythm of worship that turned Crashaw towards Catholicism had a different but no less profound effect on the younger man, but Vaughan's was an emotional rather than a physical exile. His mind was anyway more naturally attuned to the Old Testament sociability of man with angel, and occasionally with a distant and occluded divinity, than to commerce or conversation with a living (or indeed dying) Christ; Vaughan wanders a make-believe landscape lit and shadowed with a reverent nostalgia, looking for someone who has left hieroglyphics, codes and cryptograms but no part

---

[2] For a more detailed account, see the introduction, pp. 34–5 above.

[3] Morrill, 'The Church in England, 1642–1649', in *Reactions to the English Civil War, 1642–1649*, pp. 89–114 (p. 113). See also Charles H. George and Katherine George, *The Protestant Mind of the English Reformation, 1570–1640* (Princeton University Press, 1961), pp. 348–63.

[4] See Brian Cummings, 'Introduction', in Cranmer, *Book of Common Prayer*, pp. xl–xliii.

[5] Entry for 25 December 1657, *The Diary of John Evelyn*, ed. by E. S. de Beer, 6 vols. (Oxford: Clarendon Press, 1955), III. 203–4.

of Himself behind. The face that Donne so anxiously studies in 'What if this present were the world's last night?', and the crucified body he and Herbert imagine as their own in 'Spit in my face, you Jews' and 'The Sacrifice', and which Crashaw approaches with an eager blood-catching cup in so many of his lyrics, are veiled from Vaughan. Pilgrims and animals decipher the Book of Nature; poets hold out hands and words to one another across the generations for comfort and society. The incarnate sacrificial Christ, though, is not to be found. Here and there can be heard echoes of the child's voice, but 'stunted eternally like Peter Pan', Malcolm Mackenzie Ross remarks, this figure will never 'fit his little limbs along the High Cross'.[6] After 1645, the sacrament of the eucharist as he understood it could no longer be openly administered in the churches of England and Wales, and this represented for Vaughan a devastating rupture of continuity with the liturgical and literary past.

It turned him, I shall argue, into what has been termed a poet of real absence. Crashaw, unable to worship in the way he wanted, converted to Catholicism and left Cambridge for Europe where he could exercise his religious views in safety. Vaughan held similar high-church beliefs; instead of exile and the momentous step of conversion, however, he chose Anglican recusancy; like the outlawed Catholics to whom Southwell ministered half a century before, he stayed where he was and tried to keep the old ways of worship alive. The similarity in the way the two poets imagine their work is worth remarking. For an Anglican in the 1650s, as for a Catholic in the 1590s, the scarcity of priests of the right confession and the impossibility of ordaining any new ones made books a necessary surrogate: Southwell and Vaughan, as so often in the ironic reversals of those volatile times, found themselves in a similar position though ideologically divided, and both came to understand their writing as part of a mission to minister to their respective recusant communities. The 1650 and expanded 1655 collections of verse published under the title *Silex Scintillans*, upon which this chapter will concentrate, are a crucial part of this project. They seek to recuperate the rupture made by the Interregnum, and to stand in, in an important sense, for divine service.

There is, however, an odd omission: Vaughan's verse is strangely dis-engaged from the possibility of Christ's presence, the mysteries of word made flesh and bread made body that so fascinated the previous generation of devotional writers. This is surprising, in part, because of their paramount importance for the poet whose works Vaughan took as inspiration and

[6] Ross, *Poetry and Dogma*, pp. 96–7.

archetype for *Silex*: 'the blessed man, Mr *George Herbert*'.[7] (His verbal, metrical and figurative borrowings from *The Temple* are legion; I don't propose to discuss them in exhaustive detail here because the issue has already received a great deal of accomplished critical attention, but this should nevertheless be noted as a significant discrepancy.[8]) Louis Martz, in his influential study *The Paradise Within*, ponders the strange lack at the core of Vaughan's sensibility; he reads the opening poem of *Silex* beside that of *The Temple*, and observes that, in marked contrast to 'The Sacrifice', '[t]here is in "Regeneration" not a single reference that could be called eucharistic'. The disparity leads him to characterise Vaughan's understanding of communion with God as individual rather than communal, and this he constructs as a response to the ecclesiastical depredations of the age: 'it is as though the earthly church had vanished, and man were left to walk alone with God'.[9] This is not, though, an entirely happy state of affairs for Vaughan. He is absolutely aware of his inability even imaginatively, let alone physically, to participate in the sacrament: it is a felt absence, and one that consistently and extensively informs the symbolic landscape of *Silex*. The strategy he conceives to supply the deficiency involves a somewhat oblique approach: Vaughan reaches for communion through the mediatory devices of other texts (the writings of Scripture, *The Temple*) and other events (the manna left for the Israelites in the desert, Christ's incarnation on earth). His typological imagination allows him to offer what has gone before for what will come after, and the frequent borrowings from his textual sources allow him to recreate in *Silex* a sense of the whole of the lost tradition and liturgy by quite literally preserving parts of it. Finally, and most importantly, Vaughan refigures his understanding of how divine presence might be experienced in his time; debarred from sensory encounter with the wine and bread of the eucharist,

---

[7] Preface to *Silex Scintillans* (hereafter *Silex*) (1655), in Vaughan, *Works*, p. 391. I discuss the eucharist as the 'marrow of [Herbert's] sensibility' in Chapter 3, p. 118, above.

[8] In his edition of Herbert's *Works*, Hutchinson remarks that one 'never comes to the end of the verbal parallels' (p. 42). For an account of Herbert's influence on Vaughan, see, among others, E. C. Pettet, *Of Paradise and Light: a Study of Vaughan's 'Silex Scintillans'* (Cambridge University Press, 1960); Jonathan F. S. Post, *Henry Vaughan: the Unfolding Vision* (Princeton University Press, 1982), pp. 70–156; Graeme J. Watson, '*The Temple* in "The Night": Henry Vaughan and the Collapse of the Established Church', *Modern Philology*, 84 (1986), 144–61; Gerald Hammond, '"Poor Dust Should Lie Still Low": George Herbert and Henry Vaughan', *English: the Journal of the English Association*, 35 (1986), 1–22; and Frances M. Malpezzi, 'Dead Men and Living Words: Herbert and Revenant in Vaughan's "The Garland"', *George Herbert Journal*, 15 (1992), 70–8.

[9] Louis Martz, *The Paradise Within: Studies in Vaughan, Traherne and Milton* (New Haven: Yale University Press, 1964), pp. 12–13.

he imagines instead a sacrament capable of reception by other means: a grace made present to the eye of the believer as rays of divine light.

THE SYNECDOCHE OF THE FLASHING FLINT

These relations are governed by what comes to stand as a controlling figure throughout the two collections of verse: synecdoche. In recent years, there has been some confusion about wherein precisely lies the difference between this figure and that of metonymy, with which it undoubtedly has much in common.[10] It is a difficulty which does not seem to have occurred to the Renaissance rhetoricians, however; they are generally agreed that, while by metonymy we are to take the name or attribute of a thing for the thing itself, and vice versa, synecdoche involves what might be thought of as a more tangible connection. Puttenham expresses the consensus in describing synecdoche as when 'by part we are enforced to understand the whole, by the whole part, by many things one thing, by one, many, by a thing precedent, a thing consequent'.[11] In considering the levels of synecdoche in *Silex*, I intend to follow Puttenham's definition, but with an extension and refinement of possibility suggested by Kenneth Burke, the twentieth-century American critic. 'We might say', he says, 'that representation (synecdoche) stresses a *relationship* or *connectedness* between two sides of an equation, a connectedness that, like a road, stretches in either direction.'[12] It is this idea of connection which is so enduringly important to Vaughan: of the child to the man, of the man to God, of the Old Testament to the New, of a book to its reader, of the public worship of the past to the private liturgy of the present.

The title page of the 1650 edition of *Silex* bears a curious emblem (see Fig. 5.1). It is the flashing flint: a heart of stone that turns flesh enough to weep, bleed and flame at the punitive and salvific hand of God striking directly out of the clouds. The sparks that fly from this contact, the tiny

[10] Gareth B. Matthews goes so far as to conclude, perhaps a little peremptorily, that 'lexicographers and rhetoricians suggest no very interesting distinction between "metonymy" and "synecdoche"' ('Sensation and Synecdoche', *Canadian Journal of Philosophy*, 2 (1972), 105–16 (110)).

[11] Puttenham, *The Arte of English Poesie*, p. 185. Puttenham is probably following Quintilian here, who writes that synecdoche works by 'letting us understand the plural from the singular, the whole from a part, a genus from a species, something following from something preceding, and *vice versa*'. He goes on to add that 'it is but a short step from synecdoche to *metonymy*' (Quintilian, *Institutes*, quoted in Angus Fletcher, *Allegory: the Theory of a Symbolic Mode* (Ithaca: Cornell University Press, 1964), pp. 85–6).

[12] Kenneth Burke, 'Four Master Tropes', in Burke, *The Grammar of Motives* (New York: Prentice-Hall, 1945), pp. 503–17 (p. 509).

Figure 5.1 Frontispiece to Henry Vaughan, *Silex Scintillans* (London, 1650).

fragments of stone or light struck from the flinty heart, are identified by its title as the poems that constitute the volume of verse. Despite its prominent position, the emblem's absence from the 1655 edition – which is simply a number of additional poems bound with the leftover sheets from the earlier imprint, and so might be expected to be substantially the same up to the start of the new material – has led some critics to dismiss its importance as an interpretative device. Barbara Kiefer Lewalski recognises the image as being 'based on Herbert's synecdoche of the stony heart', but she dismisses the idea that it might have much significance for Vaughan's work: 'the elimination of the emblem and emblem poem from the 1655 volume, and the avoidance of most such imagery in Part II', she asserts, 'indicate Vaughan's recognition that this Herbertian motif is only a minor theme for him.'[13] I am not, here, going to speculate on why the figure was dropped from the expanded edition of *Silex*, except to suggest that the decision could equally have been a pragmatic as a symbolic one, given the air of thrift which surrounds the venture. I am, however, going to begin by presenting an argument for the illuminative value of the concept of the flashing flint for at least those poems to which it stood preface in the 1650 edition of *Silex* – even if it should, ultimately, highlight only what is missing from that collection. In the terms of Vaughan's synecdoche, these poems are figured as parts of the poet's obdurate heart, both the function and the means of its conversion into flesh. Through them, the reader is invited to understand the inner experiences of the unworthy seeker after God; the result is something rather different from either Herbert's raw spiritual anguish or the assurance and command of his priestly voice. It is the intimacy of a poetry of failure where each verse performs flint and flesh in the moment of transformation: 'not a bright, static vision', James D. Simmonds makes clear, but 'a fierce tension, a dynamic struggle, a delicate balance – always lost, always renewed'.[14]

This beleaguered heart has a further significance. It acts also as a eucharistic symbol at one remove, forming a typological connection between the Old and New Testaments, and between the writings of Scripture and the life of the believer. It is the rock of Horeb, from which God caused water to spring to sustain his people in the desert, and it is Christ the true rock, from whose pierced side flowed the blood and water of the sacraments. Donald R. Dickson argues for the emblem as evidence of Vaughan's desire to re-enact this typological dynamic; 'As Christ', he explains, 'was the true rock split open, so must the hard rock of the believer's heart be split open so

[13] Lewalski, *Protestant Poetics*, p. 318.
[14] James D. Simmonds, *Masques of God: Form and Theme in the Poetry of Henry Vaughan* (University of Pittsburgh Press, 1972), p. 21. For a discussion of Vaughan as a poet of failure, see Matthew Prineas, 'The Dream of the Book and the Poetry of Failure in Henry Vaughan's *Silex Scintillans*', *English Literary Renaissance*, 26 (1996), 333–55. Also relevant here is Sharon Cadman Seelig's comment: 'He is a poet . . . of disappointments' (*The Shadow of Eternity: Belief and Structure in Herbert, Vaughan and Traherne* (Lexington: University Press of Kentucky, 1981), pp. 53–4).

that living water can flow from it.'[15] The flashing flint presents, with synecdochic economy, a number of resonant connections at the very outset of *Silex*: the poems are introduced as luminous fragments by which the reader is to understand the whole of the poet's heart; that heart is, too, a 'thing consequent', in Puttenham's terminology, which calls to remembrance Christ's passion and, in turn, its Old Testament antitypes. As Lewalski notes, the device is also a compact reference to that other great inspirational force for Vaughan, the works of George Herbert; from almost the beginning of *The Temple*, when he laments in 'The Altar' that 'A HEART alone | Is such a stone', this is a recurrent image for the earlier poet.[16] It is undoubtedly a richly suggestive frontispiece, but what Lewalski questions is not its intrinsic interest but its relevance to the volume of verse to which it serves as introduction; an exploration of related imagery in the poems themselves will go some way towards answering such scepticism.

Before embarking on the attempt I want to turn briefly to an essay by Geoffrey Hill on one of the finest achievements of the second instalment of *Silex*: 'The Night'. 'The Night' tells the story of the Pharisee Nicodemus who seeks Jesus out one night to listen to his teaching; it establishes a parallel between this biblical figure and Vaughan himself, setting up a connection between past and present as times of spiritual struggle – 'that land of darkness and blinde eyes' is both first-century Jerusalem and Interregnum England.[17] But while Nicodemus can simply leave his tent and visit his teacher, Vaughan faces graver difficulties; he imagines 'God's silent, searching flight', 'His still, soft call; | His knocking time', but cannot find him in the 'loud, evil days' of the present (ll. 31, 34–5, 37). The poem ends with a familiar longing: 'O for that night! Where I in him | Might live invisible and dim' (ll. 53–4). Hill's concern is with the mechanics of Vaughan's verse, and in particular, his reasonable rhymes.[18] He reads 'The Night' as a poem of conversion, as Nicodemus is converted to Christianity by what he hears; opposing ideas are held by Vaughan's careful measures at once together and apart. 'Conversion is the key to the metaphysics of *Silex Scintillans* and to the poetics of "The Night",' Hill explains; 'Coldness,

---

[15] Donald R. Dickson, *The Fountain of Living Waters: the Typology of the Waters of Life in Herbert, Vaughan and Traherne* (Columbia: University of Missouri Press, 1987), p. 62. See also pp. 129–30, where Dickson explains the workings of this 'sacramental typology'.

[16] Herbert, *Works*, p. 26.

[17] Vaughan, *Works*, l. 8, p. 522. Subsequent quotations from Vaughan's poems will be taken from this edition, and will be identified by line numbers in the body of the text.

[18] For Hugh Kenner's influential discussion of this kind of rhyming in Pope, whose terms seem to underlie (though it is unacknowledged in) Hill's account, see 'Pope's Reasonable Rhymes', *English Literary History*, 41 (1974), 74–88.

destitution, deprivation . . ., darkness, blindness, deadness, silence are made the magnetic points of contact with the Divine Grace.'[19] He locates these poles in the rhyme words that end each line, and describes a dynamic of simultaneous attraction and repulsion between the concepts that are brought close in this way. 'One is impelled, or drawn', Hill writes, 'to enquire whether that metaphysical rapport felt to exist between certain English rhyme-pairings is the effect of a commonplace rumination or the cause of it.'[20] The pair that he has in mind is, of course, 'night' and 'light', which appears at the end of the first stanza:

> Wise *Nicodemus* saw such light
> As made him know his God by night.

Hill demonstrates that this is a very common rhyme indeed in Vaughan's poetry: he cites another twenty-five instances of its appearance in *Silex* alone – two in this poem. But the point is not just to suggest a lack of imagination when it came to line-endings, or even to remark on the relentlessness with which Vaughan exploits this fortuitous correspondence of sound and sense; Hill wants to work out how the fact that the words rhyme may have influenced his poetry at some other level. 'There is in God (some say) | A deep, but dazling darkness' (ll. 49–50): here, for example, at the start of the last stanza, the same rhyme of ideas appears submerged in an elegant and resonant paradox; Vaughan is aiming not for the gratifying shock of novelty, but for the profound assent of the long-familiar idea. The natural opposition between the states of light and darkness is somehow tempered, their relationship made more complex, by the bare fact of this rhyme; it establishes a connection of similarity, even dependence, that works alongside and against the more overt connection of conflict between two antithetical notions of dark and light. 'Darkness, to Vaughan, is not only the absence of light': it is, in addition, 'a necessary condition of light'.[21] When, time and again, one of this rhyming pair inexorably calls up its twin, this necessity seems verbal as well as conceptual.

　　Hill is interested in the way in which this commonplace rhyming works, and what it reveals about the structures of a poet's thought; of the night–light pair, he says: 'Such a rhyme embodies more than an opposition. It is a twinning: a separation which is simultaneously an at-one-ment . . . and a

---

[19]　Geoffrey Hill, 'A Pharisee to Pharisees: Reflections on Vaughan's "The Night"', *English: the Journal of the English Association*, 38 (1989), 97–113 (103).

[20]　Hill, 'A Pharisee to Pharisees', 103.

[21]　S. Sandbank, 'Henry Vaughan's Apology for Darkness', in *Essential Articles for the Study of Henry Vaughan*, ed. by Alan Rudrum (Hamden, CT: Archon Books, 1987), pp. 128–40 (p. 129).

conjunction which exacerbates the sense of divorce.'[22] There is another recurrent rhyme in Vaughan's poetry that does this, one he reaches for with almost the same frequency. This is the final stanza of 'Chearfulness', a characteristically Herbertian lyric from the first part of *Silex*:

> O that I were all Soul! that thou
> Wouldst make each part
> Of this poor, sinfull frame pure heart!
> then I would drown
> My single one,
> And to thy praise
> A Consort raise
> Of *Hallelujahs* here below.   (ll. 17–24)

As here, 'heart' is, more often than not, matched with 'part' – and 'part' mostly as noun rather than verb; the synecdochic emblem of the title page can be written into the poems that follow in other ways, perhaps, than Lewalski imagines. In this poem, the synecdoche is explicit. The heart, though it is often figured as unregenerate stone, is also the seat of grace because it is the site of conversion, the first to be quickened to flesh by the touch of God's word. Here, Vaughan asks that this part be taken for and turned into the whole; 'pure heart' is both 'unspotted heart' and 'completely heart': both 'holy' and 'wholly' heart.

There are other instances in the first section of *Silex* where the rhyme heralds such a familiar synecdochic connection; in 'Christs Nativity', for example, Vaughan ponders the mystery of the incarnation by imagining Christ housed in the poet's own flesh:

> I would I had in my best part
> Fit Roomes for thee! or that my heart
> Were so clean as
> Thy manger was!   (ll. 19–22)

The 'best part' *is* his 'heart', and its state of corruption (it is 'all filth, and obscene' (l. 23)) stands for the unfitness of the whole man to receive his saviour: an expression of the emptiness and deprivation of a world denied even the memorial of Christ's presence in the priestly re-enactment of this miracle of incarnation. It is an oblique reference to Parliament's decision to outlaw the celebration of communion, and the eucharistic allusion is strengthened by the

---

[22] Hill, 'A Pharisee to Pharisees', 104–5. For Hill's explication of the principle of 'At-one-ment', see 'Poetry as Menace and Atonement', in Hill, *The Lords of Limit: Essays on Literature and Ideas* (Oxford: Clarendon Press, 1984, pp. 1–18). Christopher Ricks provides a challenging assessment of the implications of this essay in 'Geoffrey Hill 2: At-one-ment', in Ricks, *The Force of Poetry* (Oxford: Clarendon Press, 1984), pp. 319–55.

rhyme that recalls the symbolism of the frontispiece. That this is indeed the direction of Vaughan's thought is made clear when the second section of the poem goes on specifically to denounce those other great Cromwellian outrages on the liturgy: the prohibition, in 1644, of celebrations of Christmas and Good Friday. 'Are we all stone, and Earth?' he asks, incredulous; 'Neither his bloudy passions mind, | Nor one day blesse his birth?' (ll. 14–16).[23] The notion of the heart as God's house is important to Vaughan's sense of an individual as opposed to a corporate communion. The churches, those 'reverend and sacred buildings', were to him in his time 'vilified and shut up'; that God should find alternative lodging in the breasts of the faithful was for Herbert a spiritual craving, and for Vaughan rather more of a practical necessity.[24]

The rhyme works as a sacramental surrogate, too, when it does not expressly trace the shape of the introductory emblem: when, that is, the 'part' that terminates the end of one line is not the 'heart' it calls up in the next. The emblem of the flashing flint functions at the level of sound as well as image: its associative rhyme, even when it has a different reference, serves by the simple fact of being there at all to reinforce the sacramental motif of the synecdochic heart in the ear and mind of the reader. When Vaughan writes, as he does in 'Repentance', of 'The Dust, of which I am a part, | The Stones much softer than my heart' (ll. 35–6), the rhyme works within and apart from its frame of imagery to suggest a connection with the salvific grace of the eucharist, the end to which the poem aspires but cannot experience. A few lines later, Vaughan makes the connection more explicit in asking for his sins to be cleansed with Christ's blood; 'give them in those streams a part', he pleads, 'Whose spring is in my Saviours heart' (ll. 55–6). Christ's heart, the wellspring of the mingled blood and water of the sacraments, is in some sense superimposed on the flinty heart of the believer that bleeds and weeps at God's touch; these linked themes recur throughout *Silex*, each facet of the image recalling the whole complex of associations.

SCRIPTURAL POETICS AND THE BOOK OF NATURE

Vaughan finds he can supply the absence at the centre of his work, that surprising lack of any real sense of an incarnated and sacrificial God, by a rhyming reference to the eucharistic motif that stands at its head. The price is immediacy. His is essentially a bookish approach, and it works by

---

[23] See also 'Rules and Lessons': 'Yet keep those cares without thee, let the heart | Be God's alone, and choose the better part' (ll. 35–6).

[24] Vaughan, *The Mount of Olives* (1652), in *Works*, p. 147.

substitution.[25] But the Bible and *The Temple* seem to distance as they mediate the divine Word; 'He does not', Martz asserts, 'memorialise the Passion as a present reality.'[26] Even when the image is explicitly drawn, as it is in this prayer from *The Mount of Olives*, Vaughan cannot convince: 'grant that I may suck salvation from thy heart, that spring of the blood of God, which flows into all believers. Thy flesh is meat indeed, and thy blood is drink Indeed.'[27] This has none of the shockingly visceral quality of, for example, Crashaw's verses on the subject, or the urgent appeal of Herbert's. For all that, it is difficult to decide exactly where and why this prayer of Vaughan's falls short: it is rather in an accumulation of minutiae than in any serious or obvious defect that it gives the impression of having been thought but not quite felt – of betraying something less than complete engagement with the sacramental ideal. Consider, for example, the implications of imagining the grace of the eucharist as a spring that flows freely on to 'all believers': for the liturgically dispossessed Vaughan, this is clearly an exercise in wish-fulfilment, but that there is no sense here of struggle or difficulty either internally experienced or externally imposed lends it, under the circumstances, a slight air of unreality. The paraphrase of St John ('my flesh is meat indeed, and my blood is drink indeed' (John 6:55)) points up Vaughan's powerlessness to effect the communion he craves: these are not the words of institution, and Vaughan's is no priestly voice. When Jonathan F. S. Post points out that 'The middle portion of *The Mount of Olives* is given over to recreating the structure and the experience of Holy Communion,' his choice of verb in commenting on the poet's self-positioning – 'Vaughan *plays* both minister and communicant' – is telling (my italics).[28]

Vaughan's bookishness is profound and complicated. 'Others might expound the letter,' Molly Mahood writes; 'Vaughan lived the text.' She goes on to make the argument that this scholarly absorption in Scripture is an index, perhaps surprisingly, of the *difference* between Vaughan and those of his forebears who did not, as he did, lack priestly agency: 'He surrendered his sensibility as a poet to the Authorised Version with a wholehearted abandonment which would have been impossible to such poet-priests as Donne and Herbert.'[29] Certainly it is true that Vaughan's work betrays constant and

---

[25] 'Vaughan is led to mystical experience more by book (one or the other) than by Eucharist' (Arthur L. Clements, *Poetry of Contemplation: John Donne, George Herbert, Henry Vaughan, and the Modern Period* (State University of New York Press, 1990), p. 151).

[26] Martz, *The Paradise Within*, p. 15.   [27] Vaughan, *Works*, p. 163.

[28] Post, *Henry Vaughan*, p. 126.

[29] Molly Mahood, *Poetry and Humanism*, 2nd edn (New York: Kennikat Press, 1967), p. 255.

inventive recourse to the Bible.[30] Mahood's judgement is not, however, sufficiently nuanced: what is effaced in such an observation is, first, the status of *The Temple* as a source text of almost equal importance for *Silex*, and, second, any sense that Vaughan might have had of the vulnerability of his model; the wish to believe in an all-containing, all-consuming Book – a text completely unified and inviolable – is underlain by a conviction that the 'book! life's guide!' (as he apostrophises it in 'To the Holy Bible' (l. 1)) from which the young Vaughan learnt to read, and later to write, is no such thing. Matthew Prineas presents an alternative view of the poet's engagement with Scripture, one that stresses these uncertainties: 'for Vaughan', he argues, 'the integrity of the Christian Bible is a fragile idea evoked largely in reaction to its contemporary "abuse".'[31] The typological connections Vaughan makes, his incessant interscripturality, seem to serve to shore up a sense of the Bible as a complete and cohesive entity that may actually be in some doubt.

'The Book', the pre-penultimate poem in the 1655 *Silex*, is a work much concerned with the idea of unity. It takes in turn the physical constituents of a particular copy of the Bible, and traces them to their origins in the natural world. Vaughan's intention is presumably to illustrate the interconnectedness of things: his poem wonders at the omnipotence of the divine will that moves objects to their ends, and the omniscience of the divine eye that knows and watches these movements.

> Thou knew'st this *papyr*, when it was
> Meer *seed*, and after that but *grass*;
> Before 'twas *drest* or *spun*, and when
> Made *linen*, who did *wear* it then:
> What were their lifes, their thoughts & deeds
> Whither good *corn*, or fruitless *weeds*.
>
> Thou knew'st this *Tree*, when a green *shade*
> Cover'd it, since a *Cover* made,
> And where it flourish'd, grew and spread,
> As if it never should be dead.
>
> Thou knew'st this harmless *beast*, when he
> Did live and feed by thy decree

---

[30] Philip West provides a convincing demonstration of the degree of Vaughan's imaginative dependence on both Old and New Testaments in *Henry Vaughan's 'Silex Scintillans': Scripture Uses* (Oxford: Clarendon Press, 2001).
[31] Prineas, 'The Dream of the Book', 355.

> On each green thing; then slept (well fed)
> Cloath'd with this *skin*, which now lies spred
> A *Covering* o're this aged book (ll. 5–19)

But to demonstrate the unity of the book, Vaughan has had to break it into fragments; he has unstitched the binding, and separated out the paper, wood and leather of its component parts. Each of these is followed back through its history to the time when it was a living thing: not just grass, but seed; a verdant tree; a slumbering bull. There is something inescapably melancholy in this genealogy; the scenes of pastoral contentment are interrupted by the knowledge of their imminent termination, as the grass is cut, the tree felled and the beast slain to become the materials that make up the sacred volume Vaughan holds. And although he starts off by contemplating the happy eventual outcome ('Thou knew'st this *papyr*') and moving back in time to its genesis, the poet's interest soon changes direction and comes instead to focus first on the living source of the 'aged book' he contemplates: 'Thou knew'st this *Tree*', begins the next section; and then 'Thou knew'st this harmless *beast*'. This subtle shift of emphasis, combined with a couple of casual, animating details – the beast is 'harmless', the tree thought it 'never should be dead' – sound again the unexpected note of pathos; despite their glorious afterlife as vehicles for the dissemination of the divine word, there is a sense of sadness at their passing.

It is designed to be momentary. Prineas describes a poem at the other end of *Silex*, 'Regeneration', as making an 'attempt to recollect the fragments of a unified book'.[32] If that is true, 'The Book' ironically performs precisely the opposite movement: it ends with a vision of a volume come apart and regenerated, its component elements once more their autonomous selves:

> when
> Thou shalt restore trees, beasts and men,
> When thou shalt make all new again (ll. 25–7)

This notion that the whole of the natural world, and not just humankind, might be resurrected on the day of judgement is mildly heretical: the corollary of this universalism is that creatures are sentient and capable of acts of worship, a view expressed also in the poem 'And do they so?'[33] What seems to be the emphasis here, however, is the idea of Scripture imprinted

---

[32] Prineas, 'The Dream of the Book', 354.
[33] See Alan Rudrum, 'Henry Vaughan, the Liberation of the Creatures, and Seventeenth-Century English Calvinism', *Seventeenth Century*, 4 (1989), 33–54. 'And do they so?' takes as its epigraph and its justification a verse from Romans 8 in the Latin translation of Beza: *Etenim res Creatæ exerto Capite observantes expectant revelationem Filiorum Dei* ('for the creatures, watching with lifted head, wait for

upon and within nature: if the trees and beasts whose mortal remains comprise Vaughan's Bible are to be restored to their previous animate state, that book must necessarily vanish. Or, rather, it must come to exist in a different form, its whole substance and essence represented by each disparate revivified part: the Word imagined, as it were, growing in forests and ruminating in meadows. In this poem, Vaughan overcomes his anxieties about incompleteness by embracing it and, to an extent, by redefining it: when he talks of things 'Now scatter'd thus' (l. 24), it is elements scattered *into* the form of a book that he is describing. The relationship between Scripture and nature is, here, structured quite clearly around the idea of synecdoche: each part of the book continues to stand for the whole, even when restored to its former shape. This connection works both ways; it reaches back as well as forward through the sequence of beast–book– beast, to argue for a vision of the unified Word incarnated in nature. Once again, the poet relies on this synecdochic sense to supply a perceived absence or incompleteness; the integrity of Scripture, that 'uneasy idol in need of repeated poetic rehearsals', is asserted through the implicit suggestion that God's 'works' (l. 29) can be completely understood from just a fragment.[34]

ANGLICAN RECUSANCY AND THE *BOOK OF COMMON PRAYER*

The Bible, though, for all its huge importance to the poet, is not in fact the religious text that causes him the most anxiety. At the beginning of this chapter, I suggested that the keenest of the absences felt by Vaughan, the lack for which his verse seeks most urgently to compensate with this strategy of synecdoche, is liturgical, and not scriptural: it is the *Book of Common Prayer*, whose use was denied him, that he attempts to recreate rhetorically, not the Bible that – however fragile his sense of its integrity – was his constant resource and inspiration. Cranmer's liturgy in its revised form of 1559 had been in constant use in English churches since Elizabeth's accession, and its prohibition by Parliament was greeted with widespread

---

the revelation of the sons of God'). This choice of text is worth remarking, given that 'an overwhelming majority of Vaughan's biblical citations are from the Authorised Version' (West, *Henry Vaughan's 'Silex Scintillans'*, p. 20; see also pp. 119–20). It differs from that translation in the activeness of the interest it ascribes to the animals (the Authorised Version has: 'For the earnest expectation of the creature waiteth for the manifestation of the sons of God' (Romans 8:19)), and this detail clearly pleased Vaughan. 'Can they their heads lift'? (l. 3) he asks, before deciding that they can: 'Some rise to seek thee ... with heads | Erect' (ll. 25–6).
[34] Prineas, 'The Dream of the Book', 334.

consternation, even distress.[35] John N. Wall's account of this response to a historical moment, in his important book *Transformations of the Word*, is perceptive and convincing. 'The relationship Vaughan wants his readers to have with his text', Wall argues, 'is one of finding in it a common meeting ground in a shared experience of loss.'[36] He tries, in other words, to make *Silex* stand in for, or at least stand for, the services that were forbidden to him and those of his faith; to create a community of like-minded readers which is also in some sense a congregation, though he is of course no priest. As Wall points out, however, George Herbert was: 'In the experience of reading *Silex Scintillans*, the context of *The Temple* functions in lieu of the absent Anglican services.'[37] A crucial poem for Wall's argument is 'The Match', Vaughan's response to a work of particular significance for him in *The Temple*: 'Obedience'. The earlier poem is dominated by a succession of legal terminology, which allows Herbert to imagine his writings as a deed of gift signing their author entirely over to God. This performative fantasy ends with a call for another to join with him in the enterprise, an appeal which emphasises the importance for Herbert of his power, both as poet and priest, to influence others (the ostensible impulse behind the preservation and publication of *The Temple*):

> How happie were my part,
> If some kinde man would thrust his heart
> Into these lines; till in heav'ns Court of Rolls
> They were by winged souls
> Entred for both, farre above their desert![38]

Vaughan answers this call with a verse whose punning title describes the complexities of his response. 'The Match' is at once a device that ignites (as Herbert's poems have caused the sparks of *Silex Scintillans* to fly), a contest between two sides (a submerged admission of the challenge inherent in Vaughan's poetic project), and a counterpart or parallel (as Vaughan hopes his own efforts will match, or match up to, those of his predecessor). The poem comes at the exact centre of the 1650 *Silex*, and Post remarks on the ceremonial significance of this positioning: 'The thirty-seventh of the

---

[35] For an account of the composition of the Prayer Book and its various revisions between 1549 and 1559, see the introduction, pp. 19–30 above. Vaughan evidently shared the conservative attitude of his countrymen noted by Maltby: 'Conformists from North Wales', she writes, 'described themselves as people "who cannot without trembling entertain the thought of change"' (*Prayer Book and People*, p. 131; she quotes Thomas Aston, *A Collection of Sundry Petitions* (London, 1642), p. 49).

[36] Wall, *Transformations of the Word*, p. 282.   [37] Wall, *Transformations of the Word*, p. 289.

[38] Herbert, 'Obedience' (ll. 41–5), in *Works*, ed. by Hutchinson, p. 105. Notice, too, the 'part'/'heart' rhyme, which might perhaps have had its own appeal for Vaughan.

seventy-three poems (not counting the "Dedication"),' he writes, ' "The Match" appears midway between the author's baptism in "Regeneration" and his transfiguration in "Ascension-Day".'[39] The poem is thus a poetic equivalent to the rite of ordination, Vaughan's attempt 'to join hands with Herbert in his priestly role as poet and to accept his "Duties" '.[40] This is the first section, the part addressed directly to the earlier poet, in full:

> Dear friend! whose holy, ever-living lines
>> Have done much good
>> To many, and have checkt my blood,
> My fierce, wild blood that still heaves, and inclines,
>> But is still tam'd
>> By those bright fires which thee inflam'd;
>
> Here I joyn hands, and thrust my stubborn heart
>> Into thy *Deed*,
>> There from no *Duties* to be freed,
> And if hereafter *youth*, or *folly* thwart
>> And claim their share,
>> Here I renounce the pois'nous ware.   (ll. 1–12)

Herbert asks that another may 'set his hand | And heart unto this Deed' (ll. 37–8), may 'thrust his heart | Into these lines' (ll. 42–3). Vaughan instead *joins* hands (as the hands of priests and bishops are jointly laid upon the head of the ordinand), and thrusts his heart not into the poet's lines, but into his '*Deed*', and here the word carries the sense of an action as well as the legal notion of contract primarily intended by Herbert. In his anxiety to supply the absent rites of the Anglican Church, Vaughan ordains himself by proxy, accepting Herbert's proffered hand as imposition and in brotherhood. Immediately before, in 'The Resolve', Vaughan confirms his vocation ('I have consider'd it' (l. 1)); immediately afterwards, in 'Rules *and* Lessons' (a direct imitation of Herbert's homiletic poem 'The Church Porch'), he delivers his first sermon.

   Those poems in *Silex* which formally celebrate the sacrament of the eucharist all come after this point: they follow, that is, both Vaughan's assumption of the 'priestly' mantle, and the address to his notional congregation – the correct

---

[39] Post, *Henry Vaughan*, p. 117. Post, too, sees the poem as a liturgical substitute, but not for the ordination of priests; he puts forward the view that 'the lyric recreates a surrogate for the Anglican rite of Confirmation', again a ceremony suppressed under the new regime. His account also stresses the importance of the 'laying on of hands' imagery, but is I think mistaken in the detail of the service to which he relates it (pp. 117–18).

[40] Wall, *Transformations of the Word*, p. 294.

order of service as it is set down in the *Book of Common Prayer*. But they do not, on the whole, represent a triumphant expression of a new agency in faith. The first is 'Dressing', a poem Martz criticises for being too obsessed with contemporary doctrinal struggles to conjure a proper sense of devotional imperative.[41] This is a fair judgement; 'Dressing' shows most spirit and warmth in its final lines, where Vaughan builds to a climactic fulmination against those who would refuse to adopt the proper posture for receiving communion (the Puritans preferred to sit, regarding kneeling as tantamount to idolatrous adoration of the Host). The rest of the poem fails to muster much emotional or intellectual engagement with its subject; Vaughan's desire for sacramental experience is genuine enough, but it is not something that he lives through his verse in the same way that Herbert does. R. V. Young's tireless quest for latent Catholicism leads him to misread 'Dressing' as a much more vital work than in fact it is: 'even in this poem', he asserts, though he cannot demonstrate it, 'there is a strong pull towards something more concrete and immediate than what is allowed by the Calvinist teaching that Christ's presence in the sacrament is wholly subjective.'[42] When Vaughan asks,

> Give to thy wretched one
> Thy mysticall *Communion*,
>   That, absent, he may see,
>   Live, die and rise with thee   (ll. 13–16)

it is the sense of absence, however, and not the longing for presence, that is most powerfully felt. A refusal to speculate on the mechanics of the eucharist, that position of trustful acquiescence familiar from Herbert's works and even, ultimately, from Crashaw's, in Vaughan somehow speaks of a kind of carelessness; it is as if there has been no struggle for understanding, no urgent need to reach an accommodation between seeing and believing: 'Whatever thou dost bid, let faith make good,' the poet directs, 'Bread for thy body, and Wine for thy blood' (ll. 23–4).[43] Part of the problem at a metrical level is the jaunty jog-trot of the sudden dactyls in the second half of the couplet, but the whole lyric suffers, too, from the marked absence of that wonder and curiosity that is so characteristic of Vaughan's verse at its most convincing; when he considers the mystery of death, for example, as he does in 'They are all gone into the world of light!'

---

[41] Martz, *The Paradise Within*, p. 15.   [42] Young, *Doctrine and Devotion*, p. 146.

[43] Compare Herbert, 'Divinitie': 'what he doth there designe, | Is all that saves, and not obscure.' (ll. 23–4; *Works*, p. 135); and Crashaw, 'The Hymn of Sainte Thomas in Adoration of the Blessed Sacrament': 'Faith is my force. Faith strength affords | To keep pace with those powrfull words' (ll. 13–14; Crashaw, *Poems*, p. 292).

(an attempt to see past another kind of veil), his lines have a fluidity and an intellectual energy that is entirely missing here.

Vaughan's surrogate priesthood, then, might seem to falter a little at this opportunity for sacramental enactment. His project is to ensure the endurance of a threatened liturgical tradition by the judicious preservation of certain parts of it; he seeks to enshrine in his verse an Anglican way of worship that is in danger of eradication by the depredations of the Puritan regime, and thus to ensure a kind of continuity with a literary and devotional past. The term coined by John Morrill to describe this impulse is 'Anglican survivalism'; Claude J. Summers defines its poetic expression as 'indignantly and defiantly anti-Puritan', and as 'embrac[ing] Anglican liturgical practices, particularly those found objectionable by the Puritans and especially those associated with the Eucharist'.[44] That the communion poems of *Silex* should seem so unsatisfactory is, perhaps, a little surprising given this emphasis, but it is capable of explanation if the poet's underlying strategies are understood. Vaughan chooses to pursue his survivalist policy by allying himself spiritually with Herbert, and in the absence of any possibility of actual ordination, by assuming the character of poet-priest with his mentor in the notional role of officiating bishop. This imaginative response to a historical emergency cannot, though, give him quite the command of sacramental language that the earlier poet enjoys; his holding back at times seems almost a kind of shyness. Wall's analysis of these motivations and aspirations is brilliantly insightful, but he is optimistic in celebrating their success: 'His taking on of Herbert's priest-poet role enables a recasting of the central acts of Anglican worship – Bible reading, preaching, prayer, and sacramental enactment – in new terms so that the old language survives even in the absence of the acts themselves.'[45] The old language survives, but thus divorced from its liturgical enactment, and in the mouth of one who does not speak with the authority of a living church, cannot have the same force and urgency. Vaughan's belief in the power of allusion suggests a way for him to overcome this deficiency: he tries to make present in his works those texts he considers most crucial to this endeavour (*The Temple*, the Bible) by a careful process of quotation, reference and active imitation. In a complex act of ventriloquy, he situates *Silex* as an

---

[44] '[T]he greatest challenge to the respectable Puritanism of the Parliamentarian majority came from the passive strength of Anglican survivalism' (Morrill, 'The Church in England, 1642–1649', p. 90). Summers, 'Herrick, Vaughan and the Poetry of Anglican Survivalism', in *New Perspectives on the Seventeenth-Century English Religious Lyric*, ed. by John R. Roberts (Columbia: University of Missouri Press, 1994), pp. 46–74 (p. 49).

[45] Wall, *Transformations of the Word*, p. 340.

alternative to the suppressed *Book of Common Prayer*, but as a liturgy that finds expression solely through language – which is, of course, only a part of its practice and purpose.[46]

If Vaughan's eucharistic poems lack immediacy, it is in some measure because they never try to represent or convey the whole experience of communion; in another example of synecdoche at a structural level, the poet adopts the strategy of concentrating his imaginative attention on one part of the sacrament as a way of gesturing at the complexities of the rest. 'Dressing' finds its focus in a contemporary dispute over ritual, while 'The Holy Communion' is chiefly concerned with one aspect of the eucharist's operation, the action of grace on the individual. The 'sweet, and sacred feast' (l. 1) that prompts these speculations is not referred to directly after the first line. 'The Sap' makes more of an effort to describe the inward experience, but again approaches its subject obliquely, through the metaphorical frame of a flower (the communicant) thirsting for dew, a favourite device of Vaughan's for signifying Christ's blood in the eucharist.[47] As so often, though, the experience is mediated through borrowed language: the poem's most directly sacramental moments are echoes of various lines of Herbert's, in this case from 'Peace', 'Grace' and 'The Sacrifice'. In some ways his most successful eucharistic poem, 'The Feast' is also absolutely typical in following this distinctive shape. It is among the last few poems of the 1655 *Silex*, and opens with lines taken almost verbatim from the beginning of Herbert's 'Dooms-day': the earlier poet's 'Come away | Make no delay' is augmented with an initial 'O'.[48] Despite its title, and its position at the climax of the volume, the poem's emphasis is still not actually on the eucharist itself as an immediate felt experience: it concentrates instead on the process of preparation, the necessity of 'Making dust and ashes ready' (l. 6) to receive; for all its joyful and confident expectation of eventual sacramental fulfilment, it celebrates, as always, that act in its absence.

> O drink and bread
> Which strikes death dead,
> The food of mans immortal being!

---

[46] 'The Prayer Book is more than a text: it provided a framework of words and actions to address a wide range of human needs and was intended to involve its participants fully' (Maltby, *Prayer Book and People*, p. 3).

[47] See, among other examples, 'The Morning-Watch': 'This Dew fell on my Breast; | O how it *Blouds*, | And *Spirits* all my Earth!' (ll. 7–9); 'Disorder *and* Frailty': 'Thy bloud | Too, is my Dew, and springing wel' (ll. 18–19).

[48] Herbert, 'Dooms-day', ll. 1–2, in *Works*, p. 186. The first two lines of 'The Feast' are: 'O come away | Make no delay'.

> Under veyls here
> Thou art my chear,
>   Present and sure without my seeing.   (ll. 37–42)

This is the language of substance and element, the expression of a belief that under the accidents of bread and wine are the body and blood of Christ; but that is not quite what is being affirmed in these lines. It is, at least grammatically, the 'drink and bread' of the eucharist which Vaughan needs to assert is 'Present and sure without my seeing': more pressing than any worry about the question of real presence is, at this moment, the anxiety over the absent Host.

'VITALL GOLD': COMMUNIONS OF LIGHT

Among all this unfulfilled longing, there is one moment at which the reality of God's presence is, after all, triumphantly asserted; this comes not under the accidents of the eucharist with which 'The feast' is chiefly concerned, however, but through a characteristic figure of incarnatory imagery that is related but ultimately quite distinct: 'I victory | Which from thine eye | Breaks as the day doth from the east' (ll. 19–21). These complex lines turn on the identification of Christ with the sun allowed by that most commonplace of devotional puns (on the homophones 'sun' and 'son'), which nonetheless possesses great imaginative energy in Vaughan's verse; it appears in 'The Night', too, when Nicodemus has managed 'what never more can be done': to speak 'at mid-night . . . with the Sun!' (ll. 11–12). The 'victory' here in 'The Feast', though, is the vanquishing of death achieved by Christ's sacrifice on the cross, the promise of eternal life for which the sacrament is seal and pledge; here God made manifest in the Host is associated with a more visible yet less tangible form of presence: God as the sun (his son) in the sky. The symbolism is extended so that the sun–son is identified not just with the visible, but with the source of vision itself; God is simultaneously a watchful eye and an eternal sun casting rays of penetrating and illuminating light into the minds of the faithful.[49] This pattern of imagery has huge significance for Vaughan, and it is where his verse finds its true sacramental focus. To imagine God as a great eye that is also the sun – the source of all light, seeing and making sight possible – is, for this poet, to imagine him absolutely real

---

[49] This he does, in a further layer of symbolism not explicitly developed here, through the words of the Bible. Consider 'The Agreement': 'O beamy book! . . . Thy lines are rays, the true Sun sheds' (ll. 13, 35); or 'To the Holy Bible': 'oft left open [thou] would'st convey | A sudden and most searching ray' (ll. 19–20), where the word 'searching' identifies the ray as one of vision as well as of light.

and present to the most important of the senses:[50] this is a sacramental synecdoche far more successful than that of the flashing, flinty heart which stands at the head of the 1650 *Silex*, and whose image ghosts both volumes.[51]

The idea that God's presence might be made manifest as light is not by any means an original one. As so much in *Silex*, it comes with scriptural authority and an interpretative tradition stretching back centuries: 'God is light, and in him is no darkness at all' (John 1:5); as Judith Anderson points out, 'Substance was a code word in eucharistic debate, . . . and analogies between the sun, its sunbeams, and Christ's substantial presence are recurrent in it as well.'[52] Vaughan, though, seizes on the notion with peculiar intensity and particularity as a way of combating what he saw as the spiritual darkness of his age; to be touched with this divine gaze of light is to experience the presence of God even in the absence of sanctioned church ritual:

> I am so warm'd now by this glance on me,
> That, midst all storms I feel a Ray of thee.
>
> ('Mount of Olives', ll. 15–16)

The lines play on this absolute equivalence between sun, son and eye, which is understood without being made explicit (neither 'sun' nor 'son' is mentioned, and the only eye that appears in the poem is the poet's – which, nonetheless, has its own significance in the economy of this imagery); Vaughan succeeds in imagining a tangible awareness of grace, something his specifically eucharistic poems have trouble with, and it comes, naturally enough, as warmth: he is 'warm'd now by this glance'. There is nothing quite comparable in Herbert. Ross's account recognises this distinctive preoccupation of the later poet: 'Certainly when Vaughan moves but one inch beyond his master', he writes with characteristically mordant affection, 'he enters a world of strange white light which would

---

[50] 'Sight is not merely the primary but almost the single exclusive sense-faculty of Vaughan's poetry' (Michael Bird, 'Nowhere but in the Dark: On the Poetry of Henry Vaughan', in *Essential Articles for the Study of Henry Vaughan*, ed. by Alan Rudrum (Handen, CT: Archon Books, 1987), pp. 278–97 (p. 289).

[51] My account of this eye–sun–son imagery in Vaughan is indebted to Raymond B. Waddington's explication of what he calls 'the synecdoche of God functioning as vision' in Milton's *Paradise Lost*. He stresses the importance of this synecdoche as a figure of Christ mediating between God and man, again a symbolic connection with the redemptive power of his presence in the eucharist. See 'Here Comes the Son: Providential Theme and Symbolic Pattern in *Paradise Lost*, Book 3', *Modern Philology*, 79 (1982), 256–66 (256).

[52] Anderson, *Translating Investments*, p. 57. Cranmer, for example, uses the analogy in his *Aunswere*: 'But if the substance of the Sonne be here corporally present with us upon earth, then I graunt that Christes body is so likewise. [But] Is the light of the candle the substance of the candle? or the light of the fire the substance of the fire? Or is the beames of the sonne any thing but the cleere light of the sonne?' (p. 93).

have set the eye of any sturdy Elizabethan to blinking.'[53] It is true that Vaughan's poetry is suffused at times with a startling general luminosity; he is, though, quite capable of concentrating this diffuseness into a single directed beam, and the idea of the spiritual power thus harnessed clearly holds some fascination: 'The Sun | With scatter'd locks | Scarce warms,' as he explains in 'The Resolve', the poem in which his proto-priestly vocation is confirmed, 'but by contraction | Can heat rocks' (ll. 13–16).

The synecdoche of God as eye, and its related complex of imagery, is the most convincing realisation of a sacramental imperative in the whole of *Silex*. It inhabits Vaughan's verse in the way that more familiar eucharistic tropes cannot, as an alternative and universal vehicle of grace in a liturgically destitute era. The pun that allows the identification of this eye–sun with Christ (as opposed to its more usual identification with God the father) operates at such a deep level that Vaughan's most startling extrapolation seems almost unconscious: the rays of the sun become Christ's blood streaming in the firmament, a confusion of red and gold, life-giving and light-giving.[54] The connection is made clear in the cluster of poems on the Passion that Post describes as the 'liturgical fulfilment' of *Silex*: 'Dressing', 'Easter-day', 'Easter Hymn' and 'The Holy Communion'.[55]

> Arise, arise,
> And with his healing bloud anoint thine Eys,
> Thy inward Eys; his bloud will cure thy mind,
> Whose spittle only could restore the blind.
>
> ('Easter-day', ll. 13–16)

In a poem shot through with images of divine light dispersing the darkness of sin, this final exhortation imagines that light – the thing that makes vision possible – as Christ's eucharistic blood, the whole a sort of healing salve to combat spiritual blindness. There is such a degree of association here that it is difficult fully to unravel the constituents and allusions of this composite image; even the miracle of the blind man restored to sight by Christ's saliva is prefaced, in the version given in the gospel of St John, by an affirmation of the sun–son pun that must have resonated deeply with Vaughan: 'As long as I am in the world, I am the light of the world' (John 9:5). It is an exemplary

---

[53] Ross, *Poetry and Dogma*, p. 153.

[54] For the traditional association between the two colours, see *OED*, 'red', *a.* and *n.*, senses 3a and 3b.

[55] Post, *Henry Vaughan*, p. 143. See also Dickson, *The Fountain of Living Waters*: 'at the center of *Silex* 1650 is a liturgical and typological sequence on Christ's Passion, beginning with "Dressing" and culminating with "The Holy Communion"' (p. 157).

instance of the poet's synecdochic reach: one brief reference to a story of Scripture recalls, contains and is amplified by its context.[56]

Vaughan's visual universe is overwhelmingly characterised by images of light and dark, by shafts of sunlight and patches of shadow, by day and night and dawn and dusk; the recurrent image of the clouded human eye granted sight by returning the gaze of the divine eye in the heavens, an eye which is also the sun and the son, is a related ocular trope that is also of great importance. It supersedes the flashing flint as the symbolic frame of *Silex* after that image disappears from the second edition of 1655; in the emblem's place is a prefatory verse that offers the volume as 'an eye-salve for the blinde'. This feature of Vaughan's poetics has been widely recognised, but not always convincingly interpreted, as Bird argues: 'Vaughan's visuality', he writes, 'is a thread of gold that his critics have always tried to anchor in a world of sense or, at spiritual remove, in cogent mysticism. So we inherit the Nature poet and the Mystic.'[57] This preoccupation, though, is much more straightforwardly devotional in impulse than is usually acknowledged; the rays of light that illuminate Vaughan's verse are, to a significant extent, sacramental surrogates, evidence of grace that is present to the senses even in a time of liturgical adversity. His nostalgia for the purity of a past state, whether the innocence of his own childhood or the spiritual contentment of the Old Testament patriarchs, is invariably wreathed around with this light, a radiance that both conveys and signifies grace. Vaughan looks back to a time when he 'Shin'd in my Angell-Infancy' ('The Retreate', l. 2), or when 'Man in those early days | Was not all Stone, and Earth, | He shin'd a little' ('Corruption', ll. 1–3); he contemplates Isaac's effortless sanctity as the redeemed sacrifice in similarly luminous terms:

> Religion was
> Ray'd into thee, like beams into a glasse,
> Where, as thou grewest, it multipli'd and shin'd
> The sacred Constellation of thy mind. (*'Isaacs* Marriage', ll. 7–10)[58]

Vaughan was, of historical necessity, the poet of real absence who so saddened Martz's meditative sensibility, but who tried nonetheless to stand on the 'firm common ground of English Protestant tradition' celebrated by Lewalski.[59] His

---

[56] The parity between Christ's blood and his luminescence is also reiterated more explicitly in the last of this liturgical section of poems, 'The Holy Communion': 'After thy blood | (Our sov'rain good,) | Had clear'd our eies, | And given us sight' (ll. 26–9).

[57] Bird, 'Nowhere but in the Dark', p. 284.

[58] Compare also the 'Admonitions for Morning-Prayer' in *The Mount of Olives*: 'shed into me thy most sacred light . . . . Ray thy selfe into my soule that I may see what an Exceeding weight of glory my Enemy would bereave me of for the meer shadowes and painting of this world' (*Works*, p. 144).

[59] Martz, *The Paradise Within*; Lewalski, *Protestant Poetics*, p. 332.

verse, as Wall demonstrates, lacks the intimate eucharistic and liturgical engagement of Herbert's, and tries, not always successfully, to compensate for this in a
number of ways; he is a poet of disappointment, in Seelig's terms, and of failure,
in Post's and Prineas's. But Vaughan is also a poet of faith and resource, and
what he doesn't have immediate poetic access to – the spiritual and sensory
experience of the Anglican communion service – he borrows or refigures; the
light that sparks and floods through *Silex Scintillans* is transformed, through the
rhetorical alchemy of an enabling synecdoche and a commonplace devotional
pun, into a specifically sacramental substance: the absence of blood is, here,
supplied by light. The direct authority for this association is Calvin's account of
how the grace of God can operate through the sacraments: 'For if we see that the
sun, by shining on the earth with its rays, in a sense casts its substance on it, to
generate, nurture, and give growth to her offspring', he writes, 'why should the
radiance of Christ's Spirit be any less able to impart to us the communion of his
body and blood?'[60] If the significance of this imagery in Vaughan is recognised,
there is no real case for claiming that he lacks a eucharistic imagination; while
those of his poems which ostensibly deal directly with the subject often seem
distanced or oblique, others achieve passing moments of quiet belief.

Consider, finally, the first poem in *Silex*, of which Martz claims, as I
remarked at the beginning of this chapter, that '[t]here is in "Regeneration"
not a single reference that could be called Eucharistic.'[61] With this pattern of
imagery in mind, that is not so. When the poet-pilgrim makes the arresting
observation that 'The unthrift Sunne shot vitall gold' (l. 41), the eucharistic
metaphor is clearly in operation. Both overt and subordinate meanings are
held in balance with exquisite economy and another pun: the rays are 'vitall' –
necessary for life – both in that they are life-giving (and indeed eternal life-
giving), and that they represent Christ's life-blood, shed for the salvation of
humankind. Vaughan's second analogy for the elect, after his pilgrim has
puzzled over the bright and dull pebbles in the fountain, plays on this notion:
his restless eye lights on 'Some fast asleepe, others broad-eyed | And taking in
the Ray' (ll. 67–8). Some will be saved, others not, but all have the opportunity
to experience grace, this sacrament of light, freely given. And here, unusually
among Vaughan's poems, is at last an incontrovertible divine presence; the
pilgrim's curious questioning ('I listning sought | My mind to ease | By
knowing, where 'twas, or where not') is finally answered by God. He speaks,
characteristically, in Herbert's voice: 'It whisper'd: *Where I please*' (ll. 77–80).

---

[60] Calvin, *Institutes*, trans. by Beveridge, IV. xvii. 12 (pt II, p. 565).
[61] Martz, *The Paradise Within*, p. 12.

CHAPTER 6

Milton and metaphor

If Vaughan's experience of the religious life of the Interregnum years was one of depredation and dispossession, the same cannot quite be said of the last writer this study will consider, John Milton. He was, broadly speaking, a republican in politics and a Puritan in religion, without any of the attachment to the established church and its liturgy that led the younger poet to mourn its eclipse with such elegiac dedication. Milton is commonly thought to have had little use for the rites and ceremonies whose absence Vaughan feels so keenly, either in his worship or at the more abstract and imaginative level of his writing.[1] His verse, though overwhelmingly theological in subject, is not read as straining for a divine presence in anything like the same way as that of the other devotional poets. It is frequently noted, for example, that Milton finds it impossible to write convincingly of the incarnate Christ; his one youthful poem on the subject, 'The Passion', is an acknowledged failure, painfully self-conscious and abandoned after fifty lines with a lame excuse: 'This Subject the Author finding to be above the yeers he had, when he wrote it, and nothing satisfi'd with what was begun, left it unfinisht.'[2] He did not return to the subject. Ross's conclusion on Milton's outlook has never been seriously challenged, or even really modified: 'It seems beyond doubt', he writes, 'that Milton was unable to imagine poetically the humanity of God. His symbolization of Christ was never incarnational.' Ross sees this inability as highly significant, not just for an understanding of Milton, but for the development of literature during the seventeenth and eighteenth centuries: 'It is not merely that Milton comes at the end of the great Christian tradition. In a real sense he ends that tradition.'[3] Forty years later, Richard Rambuss expresses his sense of this

---

[1] Though for an alternative view, see Gordon Campbell and Thomas N. Corns, *John Milton: Life, Work, and Thought* (Oxford University Press, 2008), which argues that Milton in his youth had been a 'contented Laudian both in his personal loyalties and his theology' (p. 95).
[2] *Poems of Mr John Milton* (London, 1645), p. 19. [3] Ross, *Poetry and Dogma*, pp. 188, 183.

lack of corporeal engagement in Milton's verse, and its implications, in rather similar terms: 'In Milton's devotional corpus Christ appears hardly to have a body at all. Coincident with that absence, Milton himself hardly seems like a devotional poet.'[4]

To characterise Milton's habits of belief is, however, no straightforward task, and a less rigid approach seems prudent; resisting the representation of the incarnate Christ is not necessarily a failure of imagination, nor does it automatically disqualify Milton from writing devotional poetry. 'As a theologian', Robert Entzminger cautiously, and quite correctly, points out, 'Milton was sufficiently idiosyncratic to make any attempt at categorizing him extraordinarily difficult,' and the same is true of Milton as a theological poet.[5] Such an attempt would have to take into account not just the views which are embodied in his verse, but the stances he adopts in the pamphlets through which he engaged in contemporary controversies, as well as the more systematic expression of his beliefs represented by *De Doctrina Christiana*.[6] This chapter will not essay any kind of comprehensive calibration of Milton's idiosyncratic, inconsistent theology: it will instead, through close and contextual reading in some passages of *Paradise Lost*, offer a significant reassessment of what has generally been perceived as Milton's decidedly anti-sacramental poetic practice. Book v, and particularly Raphael's lunch in the garden with Adam and Eve, is one focus of its attention; the reach and resonance of the forbidden fruit, the central symbol of *Paradise Lost*, the other.

Though there can be little question of Milton having an intellectual intimacy with eucharistic symbolism comparable to that of Herbert, for example, my contention is that the notions which have preoccupied this book – chiefly the urgent possibility of a rhetorical artistry that can express, even replicate, a eucharistic dynamic – are not so distant from Milton's

---

[4] Richard Rambuss, *Closet Devotions* (Durham, NC: Duke University Press, 1998), p. 134. An important exception to this trend is John C. Ulreich, Jr, whose views I shall discuss below.

[5] Robert Entzminger, *Divine Word: Milton and the Redemption of Language* (Pittsburgh: Duquesne University Press, 1985), p. 16.

[6] This last instance is particularly problematic: a manuscript treatise discovered in the late nineteenth century and long attributed to Milton, its authorship has recently been the subject of some debate. In what follows I shall accept the current scholarly consensus: that the treatise is at least substantially written by Milton, and can therefore be considered at least to some extent a reflection of the structures of his theological beliefs. William Hunter was the first to raise significant doubt about Milton's authorship, in an article entitled 'The Provenance of the *Christian Doctrine*', *Studies in English Literature*, 32 (1992), 129–42. A committee of scholars has since produced a cautious rebuttal of Hunter's claims: Gordon Campbell, Thomas N. Corns, John K. Hale, David I. Holmes and Fiona J. Tweedie, 'The Provenance of *De Doctrina Christiana*', *Milton Quarterly*, 31 (1997), 67–117; see also their book, *Milton and the Manuscript of 'De Doctrina Christiana'* (Oxford University Press, 2007).

poetic concerns as they might at first appear, and as critics have generally taken them to be. It may be right to think of the trajectory of Milton's thought as moving fundamentally 'away from the incarnate towards the ideate', but this movement is perpetual and aspirational rather than an achieved distancing.[7] An absence that is successfully supplied is very different in character from one perpetually felt, and the imaginative conditions under which Milton achieves this supreme rejection of Catholic ontology – an unfallen world at the dawn of creation – must not be overlooked.

METAPHOR AND CHRISTIANITY

In previous chapters, I have argued for connections between eucharistic understanding and rhetorical expression that are specific, precise and textually demonstrable at the level of line or trope. With Milton, the case is different. He was not in holy orders, as were Southwell, Donne, Herbert and Crashaw: the greatest devotional poet of the seventeenth century was, like Vaughan, a layman with an encyclopaedic knowledge of Scripture. Unlike Vaughan, however, he did not have an affectionate familiarity with the liturgy of the established church, and he did not see in its systems of worship a shape for poetic aspiration.[8] Guibbory notices the anti-clerical leanings of *Paradise Lost*: 'Milton's poem takes a self-consciously oppositional relation to the established English church that sets him apart from Herbert.'[9] In his contemptuous rejection of the Catholic ritual of the Mass, Milton rejects too the ardent, often half-articulated, Protestant longing for Christ's presence in the world: 'the Mass', he complains, 'brings down Christ's holy body from its supreme exaltation at the right hand of God. It drags it back to the earth.'[10] To such doctrinal impetus – ahistorical, numinous, incarnational – Milton was vehemently and sincerely opposed: he is no closet sacramentalist seeking to reiterate or to replace the performative actions of the priest by the power of his words. Quite the contrary: *Paradise Lost* attempts not to replace, but to reverse; the ideal movement it describes, from flesh to spirit, acts as a profound rethinking of the sacramental dynamic as it had been conventionally understood, both in

---

[7] J. B. Broadbent, 'The Nativity Ode', in *The Living Milton: Essays by Various Hands*, ed. by Frank Kermode (London: Routledge, 1960), pp. 12–31 (p. 23).

[8] For an alternative reading of *Paradise Lost* as inflected by the *Book of Common Prayer*, see Rosendale, *Liturgy and Literature*, pp. 178–92.

[9] Guibbory, *Ceremony and Community from Herbert to Milton*, p. 191.

[10] *De Doctrina Christiana*, trans. John Carey and ed. by Maurice Kelley, in *Complete Prose Works of John Milton*, gen. ed. Don M. Wolfe, 6 vols. (New Haven: Yale University Press, 1953–83), VI. 560.

traditional Catholic belief and in a less literal way by the reformed church. This chapter will advance two arguments, related but distinct: the first, that an acknowledgement of this reconceptualisation of eucharistic theology is central to a reading of *Paradise Lost*. The second is that this is, and indeed must be, effected through Milton's subtle exploitation of the possibilities of rhetoric: the kind of theological insight his poem describes is of necessity expressed metaphorically.

Metaphor is the most important of the rhetorical tropes: it is a figure of thought as well as of words, and it underwrites the creative imagination. Perhaps because of this pervasiveness, a satisfactory account of its operation is hard to come by. Metaphor is defined by Puttenham as 'the most commendable and most common' of the figures, by Richards as 'the omnipresent principle of language', and by a recent guide to literary terminology as the 'basic figure in poetry'; it is, in very simple terms, the device whereby a thing is described in terms of something it is not, 'a kinde of wresting of a single word from his own right signification to another not so naturall', Puttenham explains, 'but yet of some affinitie or conveniencie with it'.[11] He follows the ancient authorities (Aristotle in the *Poetics*, Quintilian in the *Institutes*) in describing more or less what happens, but not how, nor what the cognitive effect of the trope might be; Aristotle's definition ('a metaphor is the application of a word that belongs to another thing'[12]) seeks to explain, not to explore, and subsequent writers have tended to follow this example. Richards is an influential twentieth-century theorist of metaphor, and his *Philosophy of Rhetoric* goes further than traditional accounts into the mechanics of its operation. He distinguishes the two constituent parts of this foundational rhetorical manoeuvre: 'tenor', the underlying thought or subject, not necessarily itself explicitly present, and 'vehicle', the image or figure through which it is expressed.[13] It is clear that there is a disjunction between the two: they exist on different conceptual planes, and therefore demand different kinds of intellectual assent. Notionally, at least, the vehicle can be discarded or discounted once it has embodied the tenor; having yielded its sense through an apt or startling comparison, the vehicle is exhausted, and can have no claim to an independent truth. In reality, reading aright can be difficult, and an element of

---

[11] Puttenham, *The Arte of English Poesie*, pp. 150, 148; Richards, *The Philosophy of Rhetoric*, p. 92; *The Penguin Dictionary of Literary Terms and Literary Theory*, ed. by J. A. Cuddon (Harmondsworth: Penguin, 1999), p. 542.

[12] Aristotle, *Poetics*, trans. and ed. by Stephen Halliwell (Cambridge, MA: Harvard University Press, 1995; repr. 1999), 21 (p. 105).

[13] Richards, *The Philosophy of Rhetoric*, pp. 96–101.

cross-contamination is almost inevitable. It is this potential for meaning to become shrouded or confused that led some seventeenth-century thinkers to reject figurative, and specifically metaphorical, language altogether. One of these was Hobbes, writing just after the Civil War: in his estimation, to use words metaphorically is to use them 'in other sense than that they are ordained for; and thereby deceive others'. His belief is that such rhetorical practices obscure meaning, and interfere with the process of communication: 'Metaphors, and senseless and ambiguous words, are like *ignes fatui*; and reasoning upon them, is wandering amongst innumerable absurdities; and their end, contention, and sedition, or contempt.'[14]

The low regard in which Hobbes held metaphorical language comes from an imagined distinction between words which signify 'properly', and the parasitic or joking use of language in poetry and other related types of discourse.[15] This assumed dichotomy between literal meaning and metaphorical meaning implies a distinction between the kinds of significance such meanings have and, ultimately, the kinds of truth to which they can make claim. The corollary of this assumption is that metaphorical language is inferior, and to have any valid meaning, a word or phrase must be reducible, without loss, to literal terms. If this logic is accepted, there seems no reason not to prefer literal expression at all times, and certainly where the chief aim is to communicate or to convey information. Hobbes's own prose, however, complicates, if it does not confute, such a simplistic conclusion. He would have had to write a far more laborious sentence to express his objections to metaphorical speech had he not used the metaphor of meaning as light ('The light of humane minds is Perspicuous Words'), and the simile of the *ignis fatuus* for the treacherous deceptions of figurative language – always assuming, that is, he could have done so at all.[16] For if one subscribes instead to the view that metaphor participates in the act of creating meaning, it follows that some thoughts may only be expressible as metaphor, because only apparent once the conjunction of the two originary terms has been effected. This dynamic is explained by Richards: 'When we use a metaphor we have two thoughts of different things active together and supported by a single word, or phrase, whose meaning is a

[14] Thomas Hobbes, *Leviathan: Or, the Matter, Forme, & Power of a Common-Wealth Ecclesiasticall and Civill* (1651), ed. by Richard Tuck (Cambridge University Press, 1996), pp. 26, 36.
[15] J. L. Austin is an influential representative of this position, and it is from him that my terms are derived: 'Language in such circumstances [in a poem or play] is in special ways – intelligibly – used not seriously, but in ways *parasitic* upon its normal use – ways which fall under the doctrine of the *etiolations* of language' (*How to do Things with Words*, p. 22).
[16] Hobbes, *Leviathan*, p. 36.

resultant of their interaction.' He goes on to make clear the distinctive quality of this meaning, which can be produced in no other way: 'the co-presence of the vehicle and tenor results in a meaning (to be clearly distinguished from the tenor) which is not attainable without their interaction'.[17]

Hobbes's lapse points up something of a paradox, though his argument is not completely undermined by it: as well as creating, clarifying or refining a thought, figurative language can indeed, if not correctly interpreted, obfuscate meaning, and this problem becomes particularly acute when considering the writings of Scripture. It was widely accepted that the Bible was, to some degree, metaphorical – that its message was on occasion transmitted through parable or analogy, as when Jesus describes preacher as labourer, and the unreceptive heart as stony ground: 'The sower', he explains to his disciples, 'soweth the word' (Mark 4:14). The difficulties this raises are obvious and profound: just how much of Scripture, then, is supposed to be understood figuratively? And why could not the same message have been expressed in literal terms? Jesus' answer on this second point, that he speaks in parables so that his meaning remains unclear to some ('That seeing they may see, and not perceive; and hearing they may hear, and not understand' (Mark 4:12)), might have been of considerable polemical use in the fight over the Bible's strategies of meaning and what form its truth takes, though it is not an explanation commonly offered. Augustine describes the difficulty of interpretation as 'a healthy and helpful obscurity'.[18] Swynnerton, too, prefers to maintain that metaphorical language in the Bible has some special import or signification – that it means more, rather than just more obscurely: 'This translacion of vocabules, is not used of tholy goost withoute an urgent cause,' he writes in his chapter on 'Metaphora'. 'There is more pithe and bewty in these Metaphoricall phrasies, then is in playne speche beyng unfigure.'[19] From the beginning, Protestantism was faced with an awkward task: it needed to establish that the correct, that is, the natural, the commonsense, interpretation of some crucial passages was in fact metaphorical (most significantly for the purposes of this book, the import of Jesus' words at the Last Supper: 'Take, eat, this is my body'). In addition, though, it had to explain why the straightforwardly accessible, literal meaning of these passages was to be rejected so vehemently: not just as inadequate, but as wrong to the point

---

[17] Richards, *The Philosophy of Rhetoric*, pp. 93, 100.

[18] Augustine, *De Doctrina Christiana*, trans. and ed. by R. P. H. Green (Oxford: Clarendon Press, 1995), p. 223.

[19] Swynnerton, *A Reformation Rhetoric*, p. 117.

of blasphemy. Some inventive thinking was needed to account for the fact, or justify the belief, that Scripture did not mean what it said. This is not a challenge that starts in sixteenth-century Europe, though the Reformation does have the effect of widening its scope to embrace parts of the Bible that are not absolutely self-evidently in need of interpretation: the distinction turns on the difference in the *way* that the phrases 'I am the vine' and 'This is my body' might be true. Aquinas, for example, responded to the incontest-ably figurative nature of the parables by holding that the *literal* sense of Scripture is actually its *intended* sense. Soskice explains the subtleties of his position: 'Aquinas was able to argue that, despite its figurative nature, Scripture is "literally true" since, in his terms, "the metaphorical sense of a metaphor is then its literal sense, so also the parabolic sense of a story".'[20] A similar strategy of redefinition characterises the scriptural interpretations and liturgical innovations of the Protestant reformers: Luther, Calvin and Cranmer all exploit the possibilities offered by the potential fissure between word and referent to retain the traditional rhetoric of the sacraments, but with a realigned (now figurative) meaning – a point discussed at greater length in the introduction to this book.[21]

A thoroughly Protestant stance on scriptural interpretation has, then, far-reaching implications for literary language: it must valorise the figurative and the metaphorical as ideal modes of expression, a position quite contrary to that of Hobbes and his fellow advocates of plain speech. Milton was one of the boldest interpreters of Scripture of his age: licensed by the notion that the elect were invested with an 'internal scripture' to supply the fissures, obscurities and inconsistencies of the imperfectly transmitted Word of God, he subjected biblical texts to a vigorously polemical rereading, as for example in the *Doctrine and Discipline of Divorce*. 'What thing more instituted to the solace and delight of man then marriage,' Milton asks; 'and yet the mis-interpreting of some Scripture ... hath chang'd the blessing of matrimony not seldome into a familiar and co-inhabiting mischiefe; at least into a drooping and disconsolate houshold captivitie, without refuge or redemption.'[22] Moments in the Bible which make sexual incapacity or infidelity the only grounds for divorce are understood metaphorically. 'It is better to marry than to burn': St Paul does not mean burning with sexual desire, Milton argues, but burning for intellec-tual companionship; emotional incompatibility is a far more rational reason for separation than those base carnal imperatives usually cited, 'a mind to all

---

[20] Soskice, *Metaphor and Religious Language*, p. 86.   [21] See pp. 14–30 above.
[22] John Milton, *The Doctrine and Discipline of Divorce ... Wherein also Many Places of Scripture have Recover'd their Long-Lost Meaning* (London, 1643), p. 2.

other due conversation inaccessible' a greater misery for a husband than 'a body impenetrable'.[23] The physical is consistently reinterpreted as the spiritual, in a pattern that will be repeated throughout his writings in both poetry and prose. As Hobbes and Milton are opposed rhetorically, so they are opposed ideologically: Milton's interpretative liberty is set against Hobbes's linguistic conservatism, and both men recognise the political implications of their stances: 'From the reading, I say, of such books,' Hobbes writes, diversifying his wariness of figuration, 'men have undertaken to kill their kings.'[24] Anything that allows, as rhetoric does, a gap to open up between sign and what it signifies, can only end in the chaos of proliferated meaning, which leads directly to rebellion. 'For they say not Regicide, that is, killing of a King, but Tyrannicide, that is, killing of a Tyrant is lawfull': republican rhetoric separates the man from his office, breaks the sacrament of royal unction and unkings the king.[25]

Milton's understanding of sacramental operation, as expounded in *De Doctrina Christiana*, is (as might be expected) firmly Protestant, indeed Puritan: his conception of the eucharist is as an entirely memorial act, shorn of independent efficacy, or any sense of longing for such a thing. 'The Sacraments cannot impart salvation or grace of themselves. They are merely seals or symbols of salvation and grace for believers.' He attributes the Catholic notion of transubstantiation, which he considers 'utterly alien to reason, common sense and human behavior', to a misreading, a refusal correctly to apprehend scriptural rhetoric: 'In the so-called sacrament, as in most matters where the question of analogy arises, it is to be noted that a certain trope or figure of speech was frequently employed,' he writes. 'Failure to recognise this figure of speech in the sacraments, where the relationship between the symbol and the thing symbolized is very close, has been a widespread source of error, and still is today.'[26] As far as his formal expository writings are concerned, Milton's beliefs are quite clear; this situation is, however, complicated by his poetic practice in a number of respects. Having posited a correlation between Protestantism and metaphorical language, one of them is at first quite surprising: 'It seems true that Milton's style is not very metaphorical,' Ricks decides, 'and that this is in some ways a pity.'[27] He is referring here to the local verbal texture of *Paradise Lost*, which he characterises as rich in patterns of epic simile and complex wordplay, but lacking in the kind of inventive metaphor that ornaments the individual line or verse paragraph. In another sense, however,

---

[23] Milton, *Doctrine and Discipline*, p. 8.   [24] Hobbes, *Leviathan*, p. 226.
[25] Hobbes, *Leviathan*, p. 226.   [26] Milton, *Works*, vol. VI, ed. by Kelley, pp. 556, 554, 555.
[27] Christopher Ricks, *Milton's Grand Style* (Oxford: Clarendon Press, 1963), p. 47.

Paradise Lost is profoundly metaphorical: a poem largely ventriloquised by angels, and accommodated to the understanding of humankind through a series of structural substitutions. As a public writer, in arguing for what he characterises as the 'three species of liberty without which it is scarcely possible to pass any life with comfort – ecclesiastical, domestic or private, and civil', Milton was committed to the emancipating power of metaphor; poet and polemicist, in this respect at least, are not so very far apart.[28]

THE EUCHARIST IN PARADISE

A discussion of Milton's poetic response to contemporary eucharistic controversy must begin with the moment in *Paradise Lost* when he addresses the issues most directly (though not, even then, all that explicitly): Raphael's meal with Adam and Eve in Book v.[29] There is no direct scriptural precedent for this encounter, so that without a received authority to negotiate, Milton's position on the theological matters he finds occasion to touch on can be made to carry considerable weight.[30] The episode begins when Adam, resting in his 'coole Bowre' at lunchtime, catches sight of the 'glorious shape' of the brightly winged Raphael, which 'seems another Morn | Ris'n on mid-noon'.[31] As Raphael approaches, Adam starts to became flustered about what he might offer by way of hospitality to this angelic visitor; Eve replies tartly to his conjectures on domestic economy, and sets about with some considerable speed preparing a lavish, varied and carefully composed menu from the abundant resources of the garden:

> So saying, with dispatchful looks in haste
> She turns, on hospitable thoughts intent

[28] *Defensio Secunda* (*Second Defence of the English People*), 1654; in *Areopagitica and Other Political Writings of John Milton* (Indianapolis: Liberty Fund, 1999), p. 365; W. R. Parker's view (in *Milton's Contemporary Reputation: an Essay* (New York: Haskell, 1940), p. 48) of Milton as having 'emerged from the chrysalis of controversy' to write *Paradise Lost* has been challenged by later accounts, which instead find continuities of interest across the oeuvre.

[29] 'It would be difficult to overestimate the amount of critical energy that has been expended on these lines', Denise Gigante remarks, 'or to overemphasize their importance' ('Milton's Aesthetics of Eating', *Diacritics*, 30 (2000), 88–112 (96)).

[30] Though there is no corresponding event in Genesis 2–3, Milton is not writing entirely without precedent: John E. Parish and Jack Goldman demonstrate his reliance on other biblical stories of angels dining with men (including the visit of the three angels to Abraham and Sarah in Genesis 18), and on rabbinical commentaries. See Parish, 'Milton and the Well-Fed Angel', *English Miscellany*, 18 (1967), 87–109, and Goldman, 'Perspectives of Raphael's Meal in *Paradise Lost*, Book v', *Milton Quarterly*, 11 (1977), 31–7.

[31] John Milton, *Paradise Lost. A Poem in Twelve Books*, 2nd edn (London, 1674), v. 300, 309, 310–11. Future references will be to this edition, and will be given in the form of book and line numbers in parentheses in the text.

What choice to chuse for delicacie best,
What order, so contriv'd as not to mix
Tastes, not well joynd, inelegant, but bring
Taste after taste upheld with kindliest change,
Bestirs her then, . . .
                              fruit of all kindes, in coate,
Rough, or smooth rin'd, or bearded husk, or shell
She gathers, Tribute large, and on the board
Heaps with unsparing hand; for drink the Grape
She crushes, inoffensive moust, and meathes
From many a berrie, and from sweet kernels prest
She tempers dulcet creams, nor these to hold
Wants her fit vessels pure, then strews the ground
With Rose and Odours from the shrub unfum'd.   (v. 331–7, 41–9)

There has been a great deal of critical debate about the intricacies and implications of this passage. Some commentators have judged it to be a poetic failure; Shirley, in Charlotte Brontë's novel of the same name, is rather scathing about what she regards as the cosy domesticity of the scene. 'Milton tried to see the first woman', she tells her friend, 'but, Cary, he saw her not.' She goes on: 'It was his cook that he saw; or it was Mrs Gill, as I have seen her, making custards, in the heat of summer, in the cool dairy, with rose-trees and nasturtiums about the latticed window, preparing a cold collation for the Rectors.'[32]

The question of precisely what kind of food Eve serves has also attracted considerable interest, with those who hold that it is an entirely abstemious and vegetarian repast (the majority) in contention with others who believe that both meat and wine were involved: specific reference to 'inoffensive moust' (the juice of grapes before fermentation), and the emphasis throughout on Nature's unstinting and unworked-for bounty, strongly suggest that this latter interpretation is mistaken, however.[33]

---

[32] Charlotte Brontë, *Shirley*, ed. by Herbert Rosengarten and Margaret Smith (Oxford: Clarendon Press, 1979), p. 359. C. S. Lewis wasn't impressed either; he finds these and the succeeding lines 'poetically grotesque', though this may stem rather from the same kind of squeamishness over alimentary concerns that for so many years dogged Crashaw's critical reputation (*A Preface to Paradise Lost* (Oxford University Press, 1942), p. 106). This judgement is made almost in passing: 'the whole passage becomes intelligible', he writes, 'and much less poetically grotesque, when we realise that Milton put it there chiefly because he thought it true'.

[33] Anthony Low agrees with Parish in asserting that 'only uncooked fruits of the earth are served' ('Angels and Food in *Paradise Lost*', *Milton Studies*, 1 (1969), 135–45 (136); see also Parish, 'Milton and the Well-Fed Angel'). So does Nuttall, calling it an 'unalcoholic, uncooked meal' (*Overheard by God*, p. 88). Goldman, however, rejects this interpretation, though on no very good grounds: 'There are several references to the juice of the grape which could easily be construed as wine' ('Perspectives of Raphael's Meal', 33).

If the local detail of the episode is controversial, then its resonance and symbolism is even more so: why, with no explicit licence in his source, did Milton choose to bring angel and man together in this act of ceremonial eating at all? The obvious answer – that it gives occasion for Adam to offer, and Raphael to accept, some prelapsarian hospitality – itself raises a number of important questions. The shared meal is clearly an index of the intimacy that existed between the different orders of creation before the Fall; the chronicle of that disastrous occurrence, Book IX, begins with some ominous lines which calibrate the distance in refectory terms: there is now to be

> No more of talk where God or Angel Guest
> With Man, as with his Friend, familiar us'd
> To sit indulgent, and with him partake
> Rural repast   (IX. 1–4)

And the next time an angel visits, when Michael arrives to dispossess Adam and Eve of the garden, the lack of any like exchange of courtesies is pointed: though 'Adam bowd low, hee Kingly from his State | Inclin'd not' (XI. 249–50). But that is not the only event this scene prefigures. Because it represents man's closeness to Heaven before the breach caused by transgressive eating, it can be seen as 'a type or foreshadowing of the Last Supper, celebrated by the first Adam and anticipating the second'.[34] If such a reading is accepted (and there is much to support it), the corollary is that this lunch in the garden has a further range of reference: it offers Milton an opportunity to engage with contemporary disputes over the administration of the sacrament, the reiteration or remembrance of the historical event that is here prefigured.[35] Milton's strategy is to align the behaviour of Adam and Eve with Protestant (and specifically Puritan) practice, and then to draw a number of implicit comparisons between their actions and the rituals of the Catholic Mass. There may be in this passage, for example, a comment on what was seen as one of the chief abuses of the traditional rite, the withholding of communion wine from the laity. The small and highly decorated chalices used in celebration of the Mass were drunk from by the priests alone, on the grounds that, according to the doctrine of concomitance, all the components meet in each element of the eucharist, rendering participation in both kinds unnecessary. The large plain cups of the Puritan service were, in contrast, offered to all communicants. Though she serves no wine, the 'fit vessels pure' (v. 348) which Eve finds to hold the various juices

---

[34] Low, 'Angels and Food', 143.
[35] 'Eucharistic parody in *Paradise Lost* is deeply engaged with contemporary religion and politics' (John N. King, 'Miltonic Transubstantiation', *Milton Studies*, 36 (1998), 41–58 (41)).

she has pressed work to recall this disparity, just as her liberality contrasts with Catholic restriction: '*Eve* ... thir flowing cups | With pleasant liquors crownd' (v. 443–5). The fresh flowers with which she strews the ground might also have a polemical force: they are 'unfum'd' (v. 349), a word that appears to have been coined by Milton. Elsewhere he uses 'fumed' to mean 'perfumed with incense', and seems here to intend a favourable comparison between the scent of Eve's flowers and the aromatic smoke which suffused Catholic services.[36] King also sees the attitudes and costume of the diners as comments on the period's religious controversies; 'the seated position of Adam and Raphael hints at one of two postures acceptable to Puritans for receiving Communion', he notes, before going on to suggest that Eve's nakedness as she administers lunch cocks a snook at the elaborately vested clergy to whom the Puritans objected so vehemently.[37]

Though King's accretion of correspondent detail argues persuasively for a satirical impulse behind the details of this episode's prefiguration of the eucharist, his account overlooks the issues raised by a more fundamental objection to the idea put forward by an earlier critic. 'This particular meal has been called "sacramental",' John R. Knott writes, 'but the word suggests a kind of self-consciousness (in the celebration of a holy mystery or the attempt to achieve communion with God) that Adam and Eve do not have.'[38] That the participants might be unaware of the significance of their experience is not in itself a reason to discount its symbolic resonance: Milton throughout *Paradise Lost* exploits degrees of irony in the knowledge his readers might have that is necessarily unavailable to the prelapsarian couple. Knott's point is rather that, as far as the internal dynamic of the poem is concerned, no savour of the sacramental can attach to this event, presumably (although he does not say so) because Adam and Eve in their unfallen state have as yet no need of a specific conduit of God's grace, which animates unsought the world around them. Also at work here is Milton's strong sense of the incarnation and Passion of Christ as isolated historical events, which happened once and are not iterable. The fruit and fruit juices which take the place of bread and wine at this rustic board appear leached of all symbolism: Christ's sacrifice has not yet been occasioned by their trespass, and the food Adam and Eve share with Raphael is innocent even of the memory of his body and blood.

---

[36] See *OED*, 'unfumed', *ppl. a.* and 'fume', *v.*, sense 1b.

[37] King, 'Miltonic Transubstantiation', 44.

[38] John R. Knott, Jr, 'The Visit of Raphael: *Paradise Lost*, Book v', *Philological Quarterly*, 47 (1968), 36–42 (36). Knott is quoting J. B. Broadbent, *Some Graver Subject* (London: Chatto and Windus, 1960), p. 207.

To allow an objection to the description of this episode as in some sense 'sacramental', however, is to seek to confine the reader's understanding of its resonance within the limits of that which could notionally be understood by the poem's protagonists. This seems an unsatisfactory and unnecessarily restrictive interpretative policy, particularly given the wider epistemological concerns of *Paradise Lost*: the complex negotiation between fallen and unfallen states of knowledge played out in this moment is no isolated instance, but a marked feature of Milton's method in his poem. That Milton was aware of the particular difficulties he faced in conveying a prelapsarian world from a postlapsarian standpoint is clear, and much has been written about the linguistic strategies he evolves to signify a distance he cannot measure. One such is to allow fallen words into Eden, but forcibly shorn by context of their fallen meanings: 'wanton' as a description of Eve's hair at III. 306 (in its original sense of 'undisciplined' or 'unrestrained', without taint of the negative connotation of lasciviousness that it will acquire after the Fall) is a frequently cited example.[39] Milton also employs the opposite strategy, much subtler in effect: he deliberately avoids using terms to which an unwanted sense necessarily attaches, however nice the etymological (or theological) point. John Leonard observes that the word 'Christ' never appears in *Paradise Lost*: '"Messiah" and "Christ" both mean "anointed",' he explains, 'but Milton prefers the Hebrew word. As a Greek word belonging to the New Testament, Christ is more appropriate to the incarnate Son than to the Son's anointing as King of the angels.'[40] The absence of a corporeally imagined divinity, it seems, extends even to the implications of a name: Milton's careful exclusion of all but the very beginnings of human history from his epic prevents the apprehension (as anything other than a prophecy) of the incarnation that will expiate for the Fall. As Michael unfolds the future of his race to a crestfallen Adam in Book XII, even the nails that fix Christ's flesh to the cross stay literal only for a line; 'naild to the Cross', the angel reveals, 'But to the Cross he nailes thy Enemies' (XII. 413, 415). It does not therefore follow, however, that what is absent from the poem is not important to it: just as the success of the blameless 'wanton' depends on fallen knowledge and its attempted suppression, so the dynamic of the whole of *Paradise Lost* depends on a sometimes suspended awareness of the economy of sin and salvation of which its

---

[39] See, for example, Ricks, *Milton's Grand Style*, p. 112, and Stanley Fish, *Surprised by Sin: the Reader in 'Paradise Lost'*, 2nd edn (Cambridge, MA: Harvard University Press, 1997), pp. 92–4.

[40] John Leonard, *Naming in Paradise: Milton and the Language of Adam and Eve* (Oxford: Clarendon Press, 1990), p. 104.

action forms a part. If it is not of itself sacramental, the meal in the garden nonetheless takes its place in a pattern of symbolism that reaches forward through the Old Testament meetings of men with angels, to the occasion of the Last Supper, and to its liturgical afterlife as the sacrament of the eucharist. The tension between innocence and blame, between event and iteration, is held delicately in balance.

  The invented episode of the last lunch in paradise, then, acts as a kind of prefiguration of the Last Supper, but also is itself prefigured by another last supper. As he eats with them, Raphael tells Adam and Eve of the feast held in Heaven on the evening of the rebel angels' defection. Just as in Eden, inconceivable abundance falls a tiny but perfect distance short of excess:

> They eate, they drink, and in communion sweet
> Quaff immortalitie and joy, secure
> Of surfet where full measure onely bounds
> Excess, before th' all bounteous King, who showrd
> With copious hand, rejoycing in thir joy.   (v. 637–41)

These lines were added to the 1674 edition of *Paradise Lost*; the first edition reads simply: 'They eat, they drink, and with refection sweet | Are filled, before the all bounteous king, who showered | With copious hand . . .' The most significant revision is the movement from 'refection' to 'communion' to describe the process of angelic eating: the word appears only twice in the poem, and its inclusion here conforms with the pattern of allusion to contemporary liturgical debate begun with Eve's culinary preparations.[41] In this context, it is another of Milton's unloaded words: its inevitable resonance compels a curious juxtaposition between this instance of fallen knowledge and the absolute ignorance (in innocence) of the angels. Stanley Fish describes Milton's knowing play with words as a spiritual diagnostic: 'Fall, wanton, light, dark, dishevelled, loose are like litmus paper. They test acidity (sin) by taking on the hue of the consciousness that appropriates them.'[42] The response to a word like 'communion' is, however, complicated by its lack of the kind of simple moral valency that most of Fish's examples possess: the excluded – that is, postlapsarian – meanings of his words might shame a consciousness to an acid red by their intrusion on the purer senses

---

[41] King detects in the substitution a direct response to the contemporary scandal of the Duke of York's conversion to Catholicism, which was announced in 1669 and gave rise to the Test Act of 1673. See King, 'Miltonic Transubstantiation', 45. The other time the word 'communion' occurs in *Paradise Lost* is again in conversation with Raphael, as Adam remembers his appeal to God for a companion (a desire for the other sacrament, marriage). Unlike God, Adam explains, he cannot raise the creatures around him to 'Union or Communion', and therefore needs a fit mate (VIII. 431).

[42] Fish, *Surprised by Sin*, p. 103.

Milton's lines primarily intend, but the same is not quite true of a word whose semantic disjunction is historical rather than moral.

TRANSUBSTANTIATING TRANSUBSTANTIATION II

A much more vexed example of this dynamic, and one that has a central significance for this argument, is the word that Milton chooses to describe the process of angelic digestion. When Raphael eats with Adam and Eve, it is made absolutely clear that he is not, for example, miming, or ingesting his lunch only spiritually:

> So down they sat,
> And to thir viands fell, nor seemingly
> The Angel, nor in mist, the common gloss
> Of Theologians, but with keen dispatch
> Of real hunger, and concoctive heate
> To transubstantiate . . .   (v. 433–8)

Raphael, we are told, has a hearty appetite, and he transubstantiates his food. Unlike 'communion', which has strong associations of fellowship, commonality and union which fit it to its context even without the sacramental overtones, 'transubstantiate' really has only one primary meaning: in the Catholic understanding of the eucharist, it denotes the conversion of the whole substance of the bread and wine into the whole substance of the body and blood of Christ. It is a technical term, a term of medieval scholastic theology current in this sense since the mid-twelfth century:[43] in the garden of Eden, it stands out like a talking snake. It is used here to signify a kind of assimilation and transformation of matter, the process whereby an angel can 'convert . . . To proper substance' (v. 492–3) the food that Eve puts before him; this is precisely the opposite of its usual meaning.[44] The explanation Raphael gives of this digestive phenomenon, to which I shall return below, sets it in a universal system of conversion and reciprocity, where elements are refined from substance to spirit and move naturally and inexorably from the earthly to the divine: 'body up to spirit work, in bounds | Proportiond to each kind' (v. 478–9). It is a vision of prelapsarian harmony, in which all created matter inclines instinctively and effectively towards God.

---

[43] See *The Oxford Dictionary of the Christian Church*, 3rd edn, ed. by F. L. Cross and E. A. Livingstone (Oxford University Press, 1997), p. 1637.

[44] As Gigante points out: 'here it means turning the corporeal into the incorporeal' ('Milton's Aesthetics of Eating', 98).

Milton's decision to employ 'transubstantiate' figuratively – metaphorically, in fact – to describe such an arrangement ('wresting' the word, in Puttenham's formulation, 'from his own right signification to another not so naturall') continues to provoke speculation in commentators: how is this surprising appropriation to be interpreted? It may be useful to bear in mind here a precedent: Donne's appropriation of the same word to express a notion of epiphanic repentance dear to his reformed sensibility (the 'true Transubstantiation' of Saul into Christ).[45] Just as Donne does in his sermons, Milton demonstrates an absolute and implacable objection to the idea of transubstantiation in its conventional sense in his polemical writings, particularly *De Doctrina Christiana*:

Finally the Mass brings down Christ's holy body from its extreme exaltation at the right hand of God. It drags it back to earth, though it has suffered every pain and hardship already, to a state of humiliation even more wretched and degrading than before: to be broken once more and crushed and ground, even by the fangs of brutes. Then, when it has been driven through all the stomach's filthy channels, it shoots it out – one shudders even to mention it – into the latrine.[46]

Unafraid to pursue the implications of the doctrine to their logical end, Milton's powerfully scatological image denies absolutely the possibility of an accommodating continuity that would allow matter to be transformed into spirit: if Christ is taken in as matter, then it is as matter that he will be digested and excreted. Stephen M. Fallon interprets the passage in *Paradise Lost* in the light of this position: 'For Milton, "transubstantiate" can mean only such a refinement of substance as is outlined in Raphael's plant metaphor.' This, he explains, is because '[i]n the *Christian Doctrine*, Milton heaps scorn on the Catholic notion of eucharistic transubstantiation, with its claim that a substance can be transformed ritually into a substance of another kind.'[47] Such a conclusion obviously risks oversimplification: to impose a reading on the grounds that it is consistent with an opinion expressed elsewhere may prove insensitive not just to the poetry, but to the possibility of a significant disparity between polemical theory and poetic practice. Regina Schwartz misapprehends the passage in a different way; she recognises the inconsistency, but makes it too glaring in failing to acknowledge that 'transubstantiate' here operates metaphorically. 'In his prose', she writes, 'Milton may have found transubstantiation to be a

45 Donne, *Sermons* (VI, 209). See Chapter 2, pp. 95–7, above.
46 Milton, *Works*, vol. VI, ed. by Kelley, p. 560.
47 Stephen M. Fallon, *Milton among the Philosophers: Poetry and Materialism in Seventeenth-Century England* (Ithaca: Cornell University Press, 1991), p. 144.

cannibalistic doctrine, but in *Paradise Lost*, he has delineated an entire vision of a transubstantiating universe.'[48] Neither reading is sufficiently subtle to account satisfactorily for Milton's choice of this particular word at this particular moment; both start with assumptions that the text is then made to justify – in Fallon's case, that Milton's poetry can be explained by his prose treatise, and in Schwartz's, that it cannot.

Interrogating the word as it stands in the text offers the possibility of an alternative approach. To ask, as Leonard might, how Milton imagined 'transubstantiate' sounding in an unfallen ear, or, as Fish might, what the implications are of its inevitable resonance in a fallen one, is to encounter a different set of interpretative difficulties; the response of a reader, antici-pated or actual, is unlikely to be straightforward. Milton's decision to use a technical theological term in this less precise context naturally leaches some of its particular significance, and it is in this semantic diffusion that King, among others, locates the anti-Catholic satire: 'The text draws a distinction between "true" spiritual transubstantiation and the alleged confusion of Catholic theology,' he claims; 'Raphael's body thus transmits a satirical message without being implicated in or tainted by it.'[49] The distinction, properly speaking, is drawn by King, and his exculpation of Raphael's metabolism may be over-optimistic. While the deliberately indiscriminate use of a dangerous word acts to some extent to diffuse it, the process cannot help but be, however faintly, reciprocal: some of the original association creeps back along the connection to infect the lines. By elevating the physical process of digestion into a transubstantiation, Milton diminishes the term's sacramental significance, but at the same time he borrows from that significance for his vision of a universe in perfect harmony with itself and with God. There can be no question that the word bears the full weight of the poet's scorn for Catholic doctrine; it also, however, expresses an interest in some of its mechanisms that complicates the polemicist's literal-minded absolutism.[50] A reader catches in Raphael's 'real hunger' an echo of a 'real presence' (v. 358); the passage is predicated on a model of sacramental interchange which is imaginatively necessary to Milton's vision of commu-nion in paradise.

[48] Regina M. Schwartz, 'Real Hunger: Milton's Version of the Eucharist', *Religion and Literature*, 31 (1999), 1–17 (9).
[49] John N. King, *Milton and Religious Controversy: Satire and Polemic in 'Paradise Lost'* (Cambridge University Press, 2000), p. 141.
[50] As John C. Ulreich, Jr, points out: 'Milton's use of the technical term suggests that . . . he embraces certain of its philosophical and imaginative implications – chiefly the idea of participation' ('Milton on the Eucharist: Some Second Thoughts about Sacramentalism', in *Milton and the Middle Ages*, ed. by John Mulryan (Lewisburg, PA: Bucknell University Press, 1982), pp. 32–56 (p. 44)).

COVENANT AND SACRAMENT

In paradise: what Raphael's account makes clear is that this state of affairs persists only so long as perfect love is met with perfect obedience. 'O *Adam*,' the angel explains, 'one Almightie is, from whom | All things proceed, and up to him return,' but with this caveat: 'If not deprav'd from good' (v. 469–71). Once Eve tastes the forbidden fruit, the universe moves out of joint ('Earth felt the wound' (IX. 782)), and the prospect of the eventual refinement of base earthly substance to something divine is forfeit: matter and spirit, which before had been contiguous, 'Differing but in degree, of kind the same' (v. 490), are irrevocably sundered. The transactions between corporeal and incorporeal which had been a commonplace of prelapsarian life become impossible, unthinkable: the transubstantiation of matter is, following the Fall, an absurdity and a blasphemy. 'Consubstantiation and particularly transubstantiation and papal *anthrophagy* or cannibalism are utterly alien to reason, common sense and human behavior,' Milton writes in *De Doctrina Christiana*. 'What is more, they are irreconcilable with sacred doctrine, with the nature and the fruit of a sacrament, with the analogy of baptism' – and, of course, 'with the normal use of words.'[51] There is under the circumstances something a little disingenuous in this last comment, but the utter rejection of the Catholic doctrine of the eucharist here is not inconsistent with the clear interest in it reflected in Book v of *Paradise Lost*. Marshall Grossman, in his subtle examination of how transubstantiation works in this passage, posits a metaphorical connection between eating and knowledge that turns on the Latin *sapere* and contrasts a Protestant way of understanding God (the conversation over lunch in the garden) with the Catholic one, represented by Eve's tasting of the fruit. '[T]his distinction', he notices, 'is one of the orientation of metaphor, of the relation of analogous perceptions as referents and signs.'[52] Grossman's argument is suggestive: unrestricted either by a need to interpret *Paradise Lost* as either narrowly Protestant (and therefore completely anti-sacramental) or unwittingly Catholic in its deployment of eucharistic rhetoric, he gestures instead towards a reading that identifies the thematic structure of the poem with deeply held sacramental concerns. Eve mistakes the fruit, whose proper interpretation is as a visible sign or token of her relationship to God, for something efficacious in and of itself – a vessel, not a symbol. Her idolatrous

---

[51] Milton, *Works*, vol. VI, ed. by Kelley, p. 554.
[52] Marshall Grossman, 'Milton's "Transubstantiate": Interpreting the Sacrament in *Paradise Lost*', *Milton Quarterly*, 16 (1982), 42–7 (44).

adoration of the tree ('O sovran, vertuous, precious of all Trees' (IX. 795)), to which she bows as she leaves to find Adam, indicates the extent of her delusion. The problem is quite clearly one of a false understanding of sacramental operation; the prospect Raphael holds out of ideal participation through which humankind might contrive to eat themselves nearer to God, 'when men | With Angels may participate, and find | No inconvenient Diet, nor too light fare' (v. 493–5), is fatally distorted by Satan. 'And what are Gods', the insinuating serpent asks, 'that Man may not become | As they, participating God-like food?' (IX. 716–17). The momentary ambiguity of his 'God-like' points up the transubstantiatory subtext: the Host, after all, seems 'God-like' food to Catholic eyes.

Ulreich couches his discussion in more ambitious terms than does Grossman, though the conclusions he comes to are tentative. He puts forward at least as a possibility the idea that *Paradise Lost* may in fact be regarded as sacramental at a primary level, that of its metaphoric structure: 'The architectonic coherence of Milton's epic argues the presence of a common metaphoric substrate underlying the varieties of Neoplatonic, typological, and other symbolic structures. Whether that substrate can properly be called "sacramental" is of course another question.'[53] Common to both arguments is a sense that Milton's engagement with eucharistic theology is more complex than is usually recognised, particularly by those critics who rely on *De Doctrina Christiana* as an interpretative tool, and that this engagement is played out in the thematic and rhetorical frameworks of his epic poem – for Grossman, 'the orientation of metaphor', and for Ulreich, 'a common metaphoric substrate'. *De Doctrina Christiana* presents a problem chiefly because of its insistence on an absolute distinction between figurative meaning and literal meaning, an insistence that is conceptually related to, for example, Hobbes's reductive position on metaphor: 'a thing which in any way illustrates or signifies another thing', Milton claims, 'is mentioned not so much for what it really is as for what it illustrates or signifies.'[54] This seems to disallow the potential of figurative language, and in particular of metaphor, to generate distinct meaning through the interaction of its terms, and by implication to deny what Milton elsewhere asserts: that there is a way of understanding theological truths that is necessarily and inescapably metaphorical. Another way of thinking about it is as a kind of accommodation: Scripture bends down to our fallen capacities; its language has itself a special representational potency, and this is what Milton claims for his poem, and why it is so important for him to ask for divine inspiration

---

[53] Ulreich, 'Milton on the Eucharist', 40. [54] Milton, *Works*, vol. VI, ed. by Kelley, p. 555.

at the start. Accommodation is predicated on there being layers of meaning, literal and figurative, but it is a mode of description that is neither literal nor figurative: the reader must engage in active reading, must exercise a significant imaginative freedom.[55] When Raphael describes 'th'invisible exploits' of the battling angels to Adam in Book v, his account is explicitly accommodated: 'what surmounts the reach | Of human sense' he describes 'By lik'ning spiritual to corporal forms' (v. 565, 571–3). His relation is not only metaphorical in that it seeks to express a spiritual conflict in material terms; it also acts as a parable, a sadly unheeded warning to the listening Adam – at this point still ignorant of any intimation of sin, let alone its actual experience – against insurrection and disobedience. This moment is crucial for the poem's interpretation: difficult to envisage as the war in Heaven is, it is still only a translation, an accommodation to human understanding; what really happened is beyond expression. What Raphael does here, 'measuring things in Heav'n by things on Earth' (vi. 893), Milton does too: certainly the long stretch of the middle books is told by angels and must be interpreted in metaphorical terms.[56]

This rather sidesteps than confronts the problems raised by *De Doctrina Christiana*'s rooted objections to what might perhaps be termed sacramental meaning – the implacable literal-mindedness that insists that Christ's body is 'crushed and ground, even by the fangs of brutes', destined to end up, if one subscribes to a Catholic theology of the eucharist, in the 'latrine'.[57] No mystical accommodation between matter and spirit here. *Paradise Lost* must, though, in some important sense be considered both metaphorical and sacramental, because it is ultimately concerned with the central metaphor of Christianity, the incarnation. Despite Milton's apparent rejection of this mode of figurative operation in prose, his poem is predicated on a series of substitutions, culminating in Christ's standing in for humankind in the economy of divine justice, that can properly be regarded as metaphorical. Whether *De Doctrina Christiana* is read as a problematic contradiction of such a configuration (the legitimate, if awkward, divergence of theological theory from poetic practice), or as somehow surprisingly consistent with it, is almost immaterial: *Paradise Lost* is at an overarching level a

---

[55] 'Accommodation found literal truths in figurative interpretations, but it also claimed to complicate the distinction by offering a mode of description that was neither literal nor figurative' (Joad Raymond, *Milton's Angels: the Early Modern Imagination* (Oxford University Press, 2010), p. 164).

[56] Entzminger's analysis of the angel's narration finds in it a resonance that goes beyond this rhetorical plane: 'The relationship between matter and spirit in the early part of Raphael's account is thus genuinely sacramental: physical warfare is not simply a metaphor to accommodate, but a potentiation of, the spiritual discord that gives it rise' (*Divine Word*, p. 51).

[57] Milton, *Works*, vol. vi, ed. by Kelley, p. 560.

metaphorical construct, and this is dictated by the necessary mode of conveyance of its subject matter. '[T]he task of saying the unsayable', Soskice points out in her discussion of metaphor in a religious context, 'is aligned to that of knowing the unknowable.'[58] A consequence of this is that the poem cannot be regarded as anti-sacramental in any straightforward sense. If it avoids the imagination of a convincingly corporeal Christ, that is because Milton's interest tends in the opposite direction, from flesh to spirit: a reverse transubstantiation can still claim a stake in sacramentalism.

EVE'S MISREADINGS: OF SACRAMENTAL SYMBOLS AND THE FRUIT

The final section of this chapter turns to consider once more the central symbol of *Paradise Lost*, the fruit of the tree of knowledge of good and evil. I argued above that at the moment of the Fall it acts as a kind of fatally misconstrued sacrament; I want now to explore some of the ways in which this comes to be true, and its implications for the poem's thematic structure and for Milton's sacramental theology more generally. It is, unquestionably, a significant object. It makes its first appearance as the emphatic final syllable of the opening line of *Paradise Lost*, where it is identified as the subject of the poet's song. Even here, though, for the space between the end of one line and the beginning of the next, its status is unclear; it hovers briefly as the fruit (figurative) of man's disobedience, before settling as the fruit (literal) of the tree of knowledge. This momentary ambiguity resolves itself easily enough, but the pun it points up is not one likely to be long resisted by Milton; nor is it, and the word retains a consequent indeterminacy throughout the poem. Cause or consequence: the first lines are resolutely undecided.

> Of Mans First Disobedience, and the Fruit
> Of that Forbidden Tree, whose mortal tast
> Brought Death into the World, and all our woe, . . .
> Sing Heav'nly Muse (1. 1–3, 6)

This phrase, 'whose mortal tast', can mean one of two things: either that the savour of the fruit is of itself fatal or, as a more elliptical construction, that it

---

[58] Soskice, *Metaphor and Religious Language*, p. 63. Jackson I. Cope makes the connection more explicit in his account of *Paradise Lost* : 'The perennial tropes of Christianity, of religion itself are metaphors precisely because they reflect models of thinking which defy the normal processes of linear syntax, because they are paradoxes' (*The Metaphoric Structure of Paradise Lost* (Baltimore: The Johns Hopkins University Press, 1962), p. 124). See also Noam Reisner, *Milton and the Ineffable* (Oxford University Press, 2009).

is man's action in eating it – the taste of a mortal – that makes it so. The interpretation of these lines clearly has a significant bearing on the question of whether the fruit is to be regarded as efficacious (in this negative sense) or not: whether, in other words, it is analogous to a sacrament in the Catholic or in the Protestant understanding of the term. Both readings are possible, and, if anything, it is the former that is the more obvious. But no easy conclusion can be drawn; even were one to decide that the 'mortal tast' belongs properly to the fruit and that the alternative is hopelessly strained, this is a poem and not a theological disquisition. In these portentous opening lines, it would be natural to reach for a *hypallage* to stress the fatefulness of the object, however innocent, that is to occasion the Fall: as Homer's Achilles, at least in Pope's translation, makes to draw a 'deadly Sword' against Agamemnon.[59] Grammatically, the mortal taste might be the fruit's, but that is not to say it is not being made to bear the weight of others' guilt.

From the beginning, then, there is uncertainty about precisely how the reader is to understand the fruit, whether as tangible entity, dangerous in itself, or as the symbol of a covenant which cannot be transgressed. As the narrative unfolds, however, it becomes obvious that it must in fact be both: it comprehensively resists the notion to which *De Doctrina Christiana* firmly subscribes, that a thing must be understood *either* literally *or* figuratively. It is at once entirely literal, a fruit that can be smelled, touched and eaten, 'Fair to the Eye, inviting to the Taste', and entirely symbolic: 'The pledge of thy Obedience and thy Faith' (IX. 777, VIII. 325). A commonplace now, perhaps, but a useful one, to point out that the thing is consistently referred to by everyone apart from Satan as a 'fruit'.[60] Milton's overwhelming preference for the generic term allows him, first, a certain play of meaning: the almost-pun on fruit as 'consequence' in the first line of the epic is succeeded by a host of actual puns, some more knowing than others. Before the Fall, for example, God watches his creatures at work in the garden, 'Reaping immortal fruits of joy and love' (III. 67); afterwards, there is no possibility of such happy industry, and the bitter pun makes stark the contrast: 'they in mutual accusation spent | The fruitless hours' (IX. 1187–8). But there

---

[59] Alexander Pope, *The Iliad of Homer* (1715), ed. by Maynard Mack, with Norman Callan, Robert Fagles, William Frost and Douglas M. Knight, 2 vols. (London: Methuen, 1967), I. 255, (vol. I, p. 98). The epithet is so firmly transferred here it barely feels out of place; a more obvious example of the figure, from Milton, is the line from *L'Allegro* where he refers to 'Jonson's learned Sock' (l. 132): it is presumably the poet, and not his footwear, that Milton intends to compliment on erudition (*Complete Shorter Poems*, ed. by John Carey, 2nd edn (Harlow: Longman, 2007), p. 143).

[60] 'Satan alone speaks of "apples" in *Paradise Lost*' (Leonard, *Naming in Paradise*, p. 90).

is another reason for favouring the broader term, one that becomes obvious in those instances when it is *not* used. Satan describes the fruit as an 'apple' twice in *Paradise Lost*, and both times, but for somewhat different reasons, his intention is to diminish its symbolic significance. The first time he uses the word is as part of his complex and contradictory persuasion of Eve; the main thrust of his attack is to convince her that the fruit is absolutely desirable and miraculously potent, but there is a subsidiary argument that runs counter to this one – something along the lines of: 'This is only an apple. How much trouble can it get you into?' (IX. 585). The second occasion is equally significant: back in Hell after slinking off from an intently sinning Eve, Satan relates his triumph over man to the other devils. 'Him by fraud I have seduc'd | From his Creator, and the more to increase | Your wonder,' he scoffs, 'with an Apple' (X. 485–7). The implication of these words is clear: the fruit has no 'intrinsic magic', so the divine prohibition is arbitrary, and Satan's feat of guile in tempting Eve to transgress for something never worth having so much the greater.[61]

It may be that Satan believes this, or that he is simply confused about what in fact the inherent qualities of the fruit are, and it happens to be in his interest at each juncture to downplay its importance. Whatever the explanation, Milton marks Satan's dangerous dismissiveness with the reductive term 'apple': the warning note the word sounds is another caution against too narrow an interpretation of the fruit's symbolism and resonance. If Satan is confused, however, he is not alone. The difficulty over the precise role played by the apple in the drama of the Fall, and how this is to be expressed, is one Milton inherits from his patristic sources and never conclusively resolves. Augustine, to take an influential example, involves himself in some impressive logical contortions when attempting to demonstrate the correct sequence of events. The main challenge, it seems, is to establish that the Fall proceeds from the act of transgression, and not the object which is the occasion of that transgression: 'this failure does not consist in defection to things which are evil in themselves; it is the defection in itself that is evil'.[62] This implies that evil must, however briefly, pre-date the tasting of the apple, or such a thing could never have happened; Augustine embraces this reasoning, and posits a second, or rather a first, Fall – a Fall of the will, which happens earlier, and in secret. Though this exonerates the apple, it presents a number of other difficulties, neatly

[61] Lewis, *Preface*, p. 68. Alastair Fowler quotes Lewis in the notes to his edition (*Paradise Lost*, 2nd rev. edn (Harlow: Longman, 2007), p. 566).

[62] Augustine of Hippo, *City of God*, trans. by Henry Betterton (London: Penguin, 2003), 12. 8 (p. 480).

summarised by William Poole: 'it is hard to see why from God's omniscient point of view the second of these falls is any more significant than the first', he points out. 'If God had to decide on one, surely the fall of the will would be a better choice than the apple-taking?'[63] In order to detract from the awkward implications of his bifurcated Fall, Augustine resorts to some sleight-of-hand concerning the apple; he draws on the same conceptual pun Milton turns to such account, and suggests that it might be understood metaphorically as itself the consequence (or 'fruit') of the first Fall: 'the will itself was, as it were, the evil tree which bore evil fruit, in the shape of those evil deeds'.[64] For Augustine, then, the apple is simultaneously entirely symbolic, the mere outward sign of a transgression that has already happened inwardly, and the concrete embodiment of evil: the occasion of the act, and a metaphor for the act. As Poole makes clear, though, this solution raises an insuperable narrative obstacle: 'Augustine's attempt to equate the will with its object by means of visual metaphor evasively freezes the causality of paradise into a tableau of incompletion.'[65]

In *Paradise Lost*, there can be no such impasse: 'she pluck'd, she eat' (IX. 781). Whatever its other associations, Milton's apple has an important role as a simple tangible object, 'that fair enticing Fruit' (IX. 996), and cannot be made to vanish into an iterated symbol of the act of taking itself, as Augustine's does. Instead, Milton confronts these difficulties of interpretation by edging the fruit towards a sacramental status: Eve fails to understand the fruit properly, because she does not give it the dual signification it requires. 'Eve, when she falls, misses the word and invests the sign with magic powers: she takes the sign literally.'[66] Too literally, and in another sense not literally enough: despite Satan's hint, she does not realise that it is, though such a thing is rather difficult to express, *also* only an apple. The terrible efficacy that the fruit possesses is not intrinsic, as Eve believes, but due to the absolute performativity of the divine voice which has uttered the prohibition; her mistake is a misreading.

It is clearly associated with a Catholic understanding of the eucharist. When Satan presents the fruit to her imagination, it is unlike that of other trees in the garden in a very particular way: it is 'of fairest colours

---

[63] William Poole, *Milton and the Idea of the Fall* (Cambridge University Press, 2005), p. 27. Though Milton does not explicitly draw on the idea of the two Falls in *Paradise Lost*, it may be that there is a suggestion of something of the sort at IX. 523. Milton's implicit comparison of Eve to the sorceress Circe is an ominous foreshadowing of future events: it is clear from a phrase a few lines later that she is at this point still unfallen ('To whom thus Eve yet sinless' (IX. 559)), despite the sinister allusion.

[64] Augustine, *City of God*, 14. 11 (p. 568).   [65] Poole, *Milton and the Idea of the Fall*, p. 28.

[66] Grossman, 'Milton's "Transubstantiate" ', 45.

mixt | Ruddie and Gold' (IX. 577–8). Its aureate aspect is nothing unusual; vegetation like precious metal, or like gemstones, abounds in Eden, where the trees flaunt fruit and flowers 'of golden hue', 'with gay enameld colours mixt' (IV. 148–9), and blossoms are 'gemmed' rather than being put forth (VII. 325). There is fruit 'burnisht with Golden Rinde' (IV. 249), and, hanging from the branches of the tree of life, 'blooming Ambrosial Fruit | Of vegetable Gold' (VII. 219–20). The tree that stands next to this one, however, yields fruit that is 'Ruddie and Gold'; at least to the eye of the serpent, these apples, as well as having the characteristic Hesperian glint, look a little like flesh. For a fleeting moment, Eve's transgressive act is made to seem an even more sinister contrast to the vegetarian repast she prepares for Raphael.

At the heart of *Paradise Lost*, then, is an ideal of sacramental participation which is violated. The great central symbol, Eve's 'apple', acts as a metaphor for the eucharistic Host (among its many other significations); it is the misunderstanding of the mode of its operation, an error which is given contemporary satirical force, that causes Eve to fall. The reverse transubstantiation outlined by Raphael, where matter is gradually refined to spirit as the natural world moves inexorably closer to God, is thereby forfeit: the Edenic unity of substance which allows Milton to imagine spirit and matter in terms of one another, as two kinds of the same thing, lost forever through this trespass. Eve's fatal misreading is equated with a Catholic understanding of the operation of the sacrament, and her punishment fits her crime; just as the unworthy communicant eats his own damnation by participating in the Host, so Eve's literal-minded belief in the efficacy of the ingested sign proves her undoing: 'For he that eateth and drinketh unworthily, eateth and drinketh damnation to himself, not discerning the Lord's body' (1 Corinthians 11:29); 'Greedily she ingorg'd without restraint | And knew not eating Death' (IX. 791–2).[67] *Paradise Lost*'s engagement with eucharistic theology is profound and pervasive, and more complex than one might expect from the straightforward polemical stance of the prose writings: Milton uses Raphael's meal in the garden and Eve's act of transgressive eating to pillory Catholic misapprehension, and to outline a vanished state of perfect communion with God. In doing so, Milton rewrites 'transubstantiation' with such vigour, urgency and conviction that God's

---

[67] The warning is included in the priest's exhortation to the congregation before administering the sacrament: 'so is the danger great, if we receyve the same unworthely. For then we be gilty of the body and blud of Christ our saviour. We eate and drincke our owne dampnation, not considering the lordes bodye' (Cranmer, *Book of Common Prayer* (1559), ed. Cummings, pp. 132–3.)

absence is barely felt: his presence, in fact, becomes an obscenity.[68] That the poem is so often regarded as decidedly anti-sacramental, despite the evident importance of these concerns, is because all is expressed metaphorically. The body of Christ does not bleed in *Paradise Lost*; its flesh has no substance, its wounds are unsearched. It is presented as something less tangible even than Vaughan's rays of light, subsumed in a vision of a vast respiring universe that is bent on turning 'corporeal to incorporeal' (v. 413). The church can have no place in such an economy of grace, no more can the mediating actions of a priest. In paradise, the relation between worshipper and divinity is direct and aspirational: man seeks to lose his flesh, not to clothe his God in it. The metaphorical structure of *Paradise Lost* allows Milton to express this by insisting on the similarity between the potentially disparate terms of matter and spirit. He imagines an easy commerce between them that is not anti-sacramental so much as ultimately anti-incarnational, and which is, with the Fall of man, irrevocably lost.

---

[68] Janel M. Mueller writes: 'Milton's employment of transubstantiation, redefined as the unique vital process of unfallen creation, is the most successful Protestant compensation for denial of the Catholic ontology of presence' ('Pain, Persecution and the Construction of Selfhood in Foxe's *Acts and Monuments* ', in Claire McEachern and Debora Shuger (eds.), *Religion and Culture in Renaissance England* (Cambridge University Press, 1997), pp. 161–87 (p. 184).

Epilogue

As the seventeenth century progressed, it became increasingly difficult to preserve an instinctual or uncomplicated assent to the various transformative dynamics of the eucharist. The more alchemical aspects of the doctrine could not survive the harsh light of the dawning age of reason, and communion became commemoration: still central to the life of the church, but no longer a miraculous conjuring of God into the very mouths of the faithful. For a while, though, it was possible for a eucharistic understanding, in all its subtleties and gradations, to represent a primary intellectual foundation for poetic practice. The gaps that the Reformation opened between words and their meanings allowed the latter a brief afterlife in a kind of conceptual limbo: a horrified shrinking from the magic and mummery of the Catholic rite did not, at least for some, preclude an imaginative participation in its twin promises of divine presence and the performative power of the creative word. The writing that has been the subject of this book owes much of its richness to this conjunction of historical circumstance. The poetry of Southwell, Donne, Herbert, Crashaw, Vaughan and Milton is animated by a sacramentalism that is in some cases precarious but in all deeply held: to read their work in the light of this insight is to recover a sense of its particular force and reach.

Milton comes at the end of my list, and of this century and a half of possibility. Writers that follow his radical rethinking of sacramental belief can still, of course, feel an engagement with eucharistic theology and strive to express this in the cadence of their prose, or the figures and turns of their verse, but the intuitive faith in words and worship as analogous and efficacious is gone. The balance shifts from the spiritual to the intellectual – or rather, in the achieved interaction of rhetoric and religion, the word takes precedence over the Word. Jonathan Swift, born in the year that *Paradise Lost* was published, measures the distance a few generations has wrought: what these poets attempt in earnest, Swift rehearses as parody. 'I have deduced', the Dean writes in *A Tale of a Tub*, 'a Histori-theo-physi-logical

Account of *Zeal,* shewing how it first proceeded from a *Notion* into a *Word,* and from thence in a hot Summer, ripned into a *tangible Substance.*[1] David Nokes has described the attitude towards language exemplified here as incarnatory: 'Swift transubstantiates words into "things" to prove there's no trick in his argument.'[2] If he does so, though, it is from a very different impulse than the one that inspires the poets of the previous century; Swift, an embattled Anglican in a nation of Catholics and Dissenters, exploits the trope to demonstrate precisely that words *cannot* become things, as Nokes's shrewd quotation marks perhaps acknowledge. His whimsical conjurings offer an analogy, but it is a negative one: just as all the power of Swift's imagining cannot really make his words solidify, or accomplish the transformation of one substance into another, so the doctrine of transubstantiation must be mere empty assertion. When Peter, who figures the Catholic Church, tries to persuade his Protestant brothers that the bread he gives them is in fact meat, his bombast cannot convince and his words fail to perform. 'Look ye, Gentlemen, *cries* Peter *in a Rage,* to convince you, what a couple of blind, positive, ignorant, wilful Puppies you are, I will use this Plain Argument; By G——, it is true, good, natural Mutton as any in *Leaden-Hall* Market; and G—— confound you both eternally, if you offer to believe otherwise.'[3]

Though some of Swift's literary predecessors would not have disapproved the end of his satire, its means might have given them pause. The rejection of the sacramental possibilities of language evident in Swift represents an impoverishment of the resources of meaning that continues to be felt, and indeed to demand creative compensation, in succeeding centuries; as Catherine Pickstock remarks, the eucharistic sign 'is able to outwit the distinction between both presence and absence, death and life', and poetry did not suddenly stop being interested in such matters when systems of belief were modified.[4] The late sixteenth and early seventeenth century saw a particularly close and productive exchange between eucharistic theology and poetic practice; subsequent generations, attracted by the idea that a word might be so rich in meaning as to share in the status of an act, strove to reformulate this connection. Faith in its authenticity proved rather hard to

---

[1] Jonathan Swift, *A Tale of a Tub* (1704), in *The Prose Works of Jonathan Swift,* ed. by Herbert Davis, 14 vols. (Oxford: Blackwell, 1939–68), I. 86.

[2] David Nokes, '"Hack at Tom Poley's": Swift's Use of Puns', in *The Art of Jonathan Swift,* ed. by Clive T. Probyn (London: Vision Press, 1978), pp. 43–57 (p. 46).

[3] *Prose Works of Swift,* ed. by Davis, I. 73; italics reversed.

[4] Catherine Pickstock, *After Writing: On the Liturgical Consummation of Philosophy* (Oxford: Blackwell, 1998), p. 253.

retrieve, however. Even for John Keble, a leading light in the Oxford Movement that tried to 'reclaim the long-lost Catholic heritage of the Church of England', the emphasis is oddly secular: 'Poetry lends religion her wealth of symbols and similes: Religion restores these again to Poetry, clothed with so splendid a radiance that they appear to be no longer symbols, but to partake (I might almost say) of the nature of sacraments.'[5] Religion here is primarily a facilitator of beauty in poetry: their relation is detached (symbols are 'lent' between them, reappear not transformed in their essence, but merely differently dressed), and there is no sense of the intimate and urgent interconnection that so vivified the poetry of two hundred years before. In some ways, Keble is further from the position of a Herbert or a Crashaw even than Swift is: Swift secretly, at least, takes the notions he lampoons quite seriously. Keble's cautious parenthesis ('(I might almost say)') admits that he doesn't really believe in the terms of his own comparison: the suggestion that poetry is sacramental has become, in the end, just a figure of speech.

---

[5] Clark, *Eucharistic Sacrifice*, p. 6; Keble, *Lectures on Poetry* (1844), 2 vols., trans. by E. K. Francis (Oxford: Clarendon Press, 1912), II. 480, cited in Stephen Prickett, *Words and 'The Word': Language, Poetics and Biblical Interpretation* (Cambridge University Press, 1986), p. 48.

Select bibliography

PRIMARY

Andrewes, Lancelot, *Scala Coeli. Nineteene Sermons Concerning Prayer* (London, 1611).

XCVI Sermons by the Right Honorable and Reverend Father in God, Lancelot Andrewes, Late Lord Bishop of Winchester (London, 1629).

Aquinas, Thomas, *Summa Theologiae* (London: Blackfriars, 1964–80).

Aristotle, *Poetics*, trans. and ed. by Stephen Halliwell (Cambridge, MA: Harvard University Press, 1995; repr. 1999).

Augustine, *City of God*, trans. by Henry Betterton (London: Penguin, 2003).

De Doctrina Christiana, trans. and ed. by R. P. H. Green (Oxford: Clarendon Press, 1995).

Calvin, Jean, *Institutes of the Christian Religion (1559)*, trans. by Henry Beveridge (Grand Rapids, MI: Eerdmans, 1989).

Cranmer, Thomas, *An Aunswere by the Reverend Father in God Thomas Archbyshop of Canterbury ... Unto a Craftie and Sophisticall Cavillation, Devised by Stephen Gardiner ... Agaynst the True and Godly Doctrine of the most Holy Sacrament* (London, 1551), p. 37.

A Defence of the True and Catholike Doctrine of the Sacrament (London, 1550).

The Book of Common Prayer: the Texts of 1549, 1559, and 1662, ed. by Brian Cummings (Oxford University Press, 2011).

The First and Second Prayer Books of Edward VI, ed. by E. C. Ratcliff (London: Everyman, 1910; repr. 1999).

Crashaw, Richard, *The Poems, English, Latin and Greek, of Richard Crashaw*, ed. by L. C. Martin (Oxford: Clarendon Press, 1927).

A Directory for Publique Worship of God thoughout the Three Kingdoms of England, Scotland, and Ireland (London, 1645).

Donne, John, *The Divine Poems*, ed. by Helen Gardner (Oxford: Clarendon Press, 1952).

The Elegies and the Songs and Sonnets, ed. by Helen Gardner (Oxford: Clarendon Press, 1965).

Letters to Severall Persons of Honour (London, 1651).

Selected Prose, ed. by Helen Gardner and Timothy Healy (Oxford: Clarendon Press, 1967).

The Sermons of John Donne, ed. by George R. Potter and Evelyn Simpson, 10 vols. (Berkeley: University of California Press, 1953–62).

Evelyn, John, *The Diary of John Evelyn*, ed. by E. S. de Beer, 6 vols. (Oxford: Clarendon Press, 1955).

Fenner, Dudley, *The Artes of Logike and Rethorike ..., for the ... Resolution or Opening of Certayne Partes of Scripture* (Middleburg, 1584).

Harvey, Christopher, *The Synagogue*, 2nd edn (London, 1647).

Herbert, George, *The English Poems of George Herbert*, ed. by C. A. Patrides (London: Dent, 1974).

   The English Poems of George Herbert, ed. by Helen Wilcox (Cambridge University Press, 2007).

   Works, ed. by F. E. Hutchinson (Oxford: Clarendon Press, 1941).

His Majesties Proclamation, Concerning the Book of Common-prayer, and the Directory for Publike Worship ... With some Observations Thereupon (Oxford [London], 1645).

Hobbes, Thomas, *Leviathan: Or, the Matter, Forme, & Power of a Common-Wealth Ecclesiasticall and Civill (1651)*, ed. by Richard Tuck (Cambridge University Press, 1996).

Hooker, Richard, *Of the Lawes of Ecclesiasticall Politie: the Fift Booke* (London, 1597).

   Of the Laws of Ecclesiastical Polity, ed. by Arthur Stephen McGrade (Cambridge University Press, 1989).

Milton, John, *Complete Prose Works of John Milton*, gen. ed. Don M. Wolfe, 6 vols. (New Haven: Yale University Press, 1953–83).

   Complete Shorter Poems, ed. by John Carey, 2nd rev. edn (Harlow: Longman, 2007).

   The Doctrine and Discipline of Divorce [. . .] Wherein also Many Places of Scripture have Recover'd their Long-Lost Meaning (London, 1643).

   Eikonoklastes, 2nd edn (London, 1650).

   Paradise Lost, ed. by Alastair Fowler, 2nd rev. edn (Harlow: Longman, 2007).

   Paradise Lost. A Poem in Twelve Books, 2nd edn (London, 1674).

   Poems of Mr John Milton (London, 1645).

   The Reason of Church-Government (London, 1641).

Peacham, Henry, *The Garden of Eloquence* (London, 1577; 2nd edn, 1593).

Prideaux, John, *Sacred Eloquence: Or, the Art of Rhetorick, as it is Layd Down in Scripture* (London, 1659).

Radford, John, *A Directorie Teaching the Way to the Truth in a Brief and Plaine Discourse Against the Heresies of this Time* ([England], 1605).

Sidney, Sir Philip, *Sidney's 'Defence of Poesy' and Selected Renaissance Literary Criticism*, ed. by Gavin Alexander (London: Penguin, 2004).

Southwell, Robert, *Collected Poems*, ed. by Peter Davidson and Anne Sweeney (Manchester: Carcanet, 2007).

   An epistle of comfort to the reverend priestes, & to the honorable, worshipful, & other of the laye sort restrayned in durance for the Catholicke fayth (London, 1587).

   'Letter to Sir Robert Cecil' (1593), in *Two Letters and Short Rules of a Good Life*, ed. by Nancy Pollard Brown (Charlottesville, VA: Folger Shakespeare Library, 1973).

   Mary Magdalens Funerall Teares (London, 1591).

St Peters complainte. Wth other workes of the author R:S (London, 1620).

Spiritual Exercises and Devotions, trans. by P. E. Hallett and ed. by J.-M. de Buck (London: Sheed and Ward, 1931).

The triumphs over death: or, A consolatorie epistle, for afflicted mindes, in the affects of dying friends (London, 1595).

Swift, Jonathan, *The Prose Works of Jonathan Swift*, ed. by Herbert Davis, 14 vols. (Oxford: Blackwell, 1939–68).

Swynnerton, Thomas, *A Reformation Rhetoric: Thomas Swynnerton's The Tropes and Figures of Scripture*, ed. by Richard Rex (Cambridge: Renaissance Texts from Manuscript, 1999).

Tyndale, William, *The Obedience of a Christian Man*, ed. by David Daniell (London: Penguin, 2000).

Vaughan, Henry, *The Works of Henry Vaughan*, ed. by L. C. Martin, 2nd edn (Oxford: Clarendon Press, 1957).

Walton, Izaak, *The Lives of Dr John Donne, Sir Henry Wotton, Mr Richard Hooker, Mr George Herbert* (London, 1670).

Wilson, Thomas, *The Arte of Rhetorique* (London, 1553).

SECONDARY

Abbas, Sadia, 'Polemic and Paradox in Robert Southwell's Lyric Poems', *Criticism: a Quarterly for Literature and the Arts*, 45 (2003), 453–82.

Adams, Robert Martin, 'Taste and Bad Taste in Metaphysical Poetry: Richard Crashaw and Dylan Thomas', *The Hudson Review*, 8 (1955), 61–77.

Ahl, Frederick, 'Ars Est Caelare Artem (Art in Puns and Anagrams Engraved)', in *On Puns: the Foundation of Letters*, ed. by Jonathan Culler (Oxford: Blackwell, 1988), pp. 17–43.

Anderson, Judith H., 'Donne's (Im)possible Punning', *John Donne Journal*, 23 (2004), 59–68.

Translating Investments: Metaphor and the Dynamic of Cultural Change in Tudor–Stuart England (New York: Fordham University Press, 2005).

Asals, Heather A. R., 'Crashaw's Participles and the "Chiaroscuro" of Ontological Language', in *Essays on Richard Crashaw*, ed. by Robert M. Cooper (Salzburg: Institut für Anglistik und Amerikanistik, 1979), pp. 35–49.

Equivocal Predication: George Herbert's Way to God (University of Toronto Press, 1981).

Austin, J. L., *How to Do Things with Words*, 2nd edn (Oxford: Clarendon Press, 1975; repr. 1980).

Barker, Francis, *The Tremulous Private Body: Essays on Subjection* (London: Methuen, 1984).

Bates, Catherine, 'The Point of Puns', *Modern Philology*, 96 (1999), 421–38.

Baumlin, James S., *John Donne and the Rhetorics of Renaissance Discourse* (Columbia: University of Missouri Press, 1991).

Beckwith, Sarah, 'Stephen Greenblatt's *Hamlet* and the Forms of Oblivion', *Journal of Medieval and Early Modern Studies*, 33 (2003), 261–80.

Beddow, Robert, 'The English Verse of Robert Southwell: a Critical Study of Southwell's English Lyrics within their Recusant Context', unpublished doctoral dissertation (Cambridge, 1987).

Benet, Diana Treviño, 'Crashaw, Teresa and the Word', in *New Perspectives on the Life and Art of Richard Crashaw*, ed. by John R. Roberts (Columbia: University of Missouri, Press, 1990), pp. 140–56.

Bird, Michael, 'Nowhere but in the Dark: On the Poetry of Henry Vaughan', in *Essential Articles for the Study of Henry Vaughan*, ed. by Alan Rudrum (Hamden, CT: Archon Books, 1987), pp. 278–97.

Bonnell, William, '*Amnesis*: the Power of Memory in Herbert's Sacramental Vision', *George Herbert Journal*, 15 (1991), 33–48.

Brightman, F. E., *The English Rite: Being a Synopsis of the Sources and Revisions of the Book of Common Prayer*, 2 vols. (London: Rivingtons, 1915).

Broadbent, J. B., 'The Nativity Ode', in *The Living Milton: Essays by Various Hands*, ed. by Frank Kermode (London: Routledge, 1960), pp. 12–31.

Brooks, Peter Newman, *Thomas Cranmer's Doctrine of the Eucharist: an Essay in Historical Development*, 2nd edn (London: Macmillan, 1992).

Brownlow, F. W., *Robert Southwell* (New York: Twayne, 1996).

Burke, Kenneth, 'Four Master Tropes', in Burke, *The Grammar of Motives* (New York: Prentice-Hall, 1945), pp 503–17.

Campbell, Gordon and Thomas N. Corns, *John Milton: Life, Work, and Thought* (Oxford University Press, 2008).

Campbell, Gordon, Thomas N. Corns, John K. Hale, David I. Holmes and Fiona J. Tweedie, *Milton and the Manuscript of 'De Doctrina Christiana'* (Oxford University Press, 2007).

'The Provenance of *De Doctrina Christiana*', *Milton Quarterly*, 31 (1997), 67–117.

Carballo, Robert, 'The Incarnation as Paradox and Conceit in Robert Southwell's Poetry', *American Benedictine Review*, 43 (1992), 223–32.

Carey, John, *John Donne: Life, Mind and Art* (London: Faber, 1990).

Cave, Terence, *The Cornucopian Text: Problems of Writing in the French Renaissance* (Oxford: Clarendon Press, 1979).

Chambers, A. B., *Transfigured Rites in Seventeenth-Century English Poetry* (Columbia: University of Missouri Press, 1992).

Clark, Francis, *Eucharistic Sacrifice and the Reformation*, 2nd edn (Oxford: Blackwell, 1967).

Clarke, Elizabeth, *Theory and Theology in George Herbert's Poetry: 'Divinitie, and Poesie, Met'* (Oxford: Clarendon Press, 1997).

Clements, Arthur L., *Poetry of Contemplation: John Donne, George Herbert, Henry Vaughan, and the Modern Period* (State University of New York Press, 1990).

Collinson, Patrick, *The Reformation* (London: Weidenfeld and Nicolson, 2003).

Conley, Thomas M., *Rhetoric in the European Tradition* (University of Chicago Press, 1990).

Cope, Jackson I., *The Metaphoric Structure of Paradise Lost* (Baltimore: The Johns Hopkins University Press, 1962).

Corthell, Ronald J., ' "Friendship's Sacraments": John Donne's Familiar Letters', *Studies in Philology*, 78 (1981), 409–25.

'"The Secrecy of Man": Recusant Discourse and the Elizabethan Subject', *English Literary Renaissance*, 19 (1989), 272–90.

Cruickshank, Frances, *Verse and Poetics in George Herbert and John Donne* (Farnham: Ashgate, 2010).

Cuming, G. J., *A History of Anglican Liturgy*, 2nd edn (Basingstoke: Macmillan, 1982).

Cummings, Brian, *The Literary Culture of the Reformation: Grammar and Grace* (Oxford University Press, 2002).

Cunnar, Eugene R., 'Crashaw's "Sancta Maria Dolorum": Controversy and Coherence', in *New Perspectives on the Life and Art of Richard Crashaw*, ed. by John R. Roberts (Columbia: University of Missouri Press, 1990), pp. 99–126.

Davidson, Clifford, 'Robert Southwell: Lyric Poetry, the Restoration of Images, and Martyrdom', *Ben Jonson Journal*, 7 (2000), 157–86.

Davies, Stevie, *Henry Vaughan* (Bridgend: Poetry Wales Press, 1995).

Davis, Walter R., 'The Meditative Hymnody of Richard Crashaw', *English Literary History*, 50 (1983), 107–29.

Dickson, Donald R., 'Between Transubstantiation and Memorialism: Herbert's Eucharistic Celebration', *George Herbert Journal*, 11 (1987), 1–14.

The Fountain of Living Waters: the Typology of the Waters of Life in Herbert, Vaughan and Traherne (Columbia: University of Missouri Press, 1987).

Dillon, Anne, *The Construction of Martyrdom in the English Catholic Community, 1535–1603* (Aldershot: Ashgate, 2002).

DiPasquale, Theresa M., *Literature and Sacrament: the Sacred and the Secular in John Donne* (Pittsburgh: Duquesne University Press, 1999).

'Receiving a Sexual Sacrament: "The Flea" as Profane Eucharist', in *John Donne's Religious Imagination: Essays in Honour of John T. Shawcross*, ed. by Raymond-Jean Frontain and Frances M. Malpezzi (Conway: University of Central Arkansas Press, 1995), pp. 81–95.

Dix, Dom Gregory, *The Shape of the Liturgy* (London: A. and C. Black, 1945; repr. 1993).

Duffy, Eamon, *The Stripping of the Altars: Traditional Religion in England, c.1400–c.1580* (New Haven: Yale University Press, 1992).

Elsky, Martin, 'The Sacramental Frame of George Herbert's "The Church" and the Shape of Spiritual Autobiography', *Journal of English and Germanic Philology*, 83 (1984), 313–29.

Empson, William, *Seven Types of Ambiguity* (London: Chatto and Windus, 1930; repr. London: Penguin, 1995).

Entzminger, Robert, *Divine Word: Milton and the Redemption of Language* (Pittsburgh: Duquesne University Press, 1985).

Fallon, Stephen M., *Milton among the Philosophers: Poetry and Materialism in Seventeenth-Century England* (Ithaca: Cornell University Press, 1991).

Fish, Stanley, 'Catechizing the Reader: Herbert's Socratean Rhetoric', in *The Rhetoric of Renaissance Poetry from Wyatt to Milton*, ed. by Thomas O. Sloan and Raymond B. Waddington (Berkeley: University of California Press, 1974), pp. 174–88.

Surprised by Sin: the Reader in 'Paradise Lost', 2nd edn (Cambridge, MA: Harvard University Press, 1997).

Fletcher, Angus, *Allegory: the Theory of a Symbolic Mode* (Ithaca: Cornell University Press, 1964).

Gallagher, Catherine and Stephen Greenblatt, *Practicing New Historicism*, 2nd edn (University of Chicago Press, 2001).

Gerrish, B. A., *Grace and Gratitude: the Eucharistic Theology of John Calvin* (Edinburgh: T. and T. Clark, 1993).

Gigante, Denise, 'Milton's Aesthetics of Eating', *Diacritics*, 30 (2000), 88–112.

Goldman, Jack, 'Perspectives of Raphael's Meal in *Paradise Lost*, Book V', *Milton Quarterly*, 11 (1977), 31–7.

Grossman, Marshall, 'Milton's "Transubstantiate": Interpreting the Sacrament in *Paradise Lost*', *Milton Quarterly*, 16 (1982), 42–7.

Guibbory, Achsah, *Ceremony and Community from Herbert to Milton: Literature, Religion and Conflict in Seventeenth-Century England* (Cambridge University Press, 1998).

Hammond, Gerald, ' "Poor Dust Should Lie Still Low": George Herbert and Henry Vaughan', *English: the Journal of the English Association*, 35 (1986), 1–22.

Harland, Paul W., ' "A True Transubstantiation": Donne, Self-Love, and the Passion', in *John Donne's Religious Imagination*, ed. by Raymond-Jean Frontain and Frances M. Malpezzi (Conway: University of Central Arkansas, 1995), pp. 162–80.

Hester, M. Thomas, ' "This Cannot be Said": a Preface to the Reader of Donne's Lyrics', *Christianity and Literature*, 39 (1990), 365–85.

Hill, Geoffrey 'The Absolute Reasonableness of Robert Southwell', in Hill, *The Lords of Limit: Essays on Literature and Ideas* (Oxford: Clarendon Press, 1984), pp. 19–37.

'A Pharisee to Pharisees: Reflections on Vaughan's "The Night" ', *English: the Journal of the English Association*, 38 (1989), 97–113.

'Poetry as Menace and Atonement', in Hill, *The Lords of Limit: Essays on Literature and Ideas* (Oxford: Clarendon Press, 1984), pp. 1–18.

Hunt, Arnold, 'The Lord's Supper in Early Modern England', *Past and Present*, 161 (1998), 39–83.

Hunter, Jeanne Clayton, ' "With Winges of Faith": George Herbert's Communion Poems', *Journal of Religion*, 62 (1982), 57–71.

Hunter, William, 'The Provenance of the *Christian Doctrine*', *Studies in English Literature*, 32 (1992), 129–42.

Hutchinson, F. E., *Henry Vaughan: a Life and Interpretation* (Oxford: Clarendon Press, 1947).

Jakobson, Roman, 'Two Aspects of Language and Two Types of Aphasic Disturbances', in Jakobson and Morris Halle, *Fundamentals of Language* ('S-Gravenhage: Mouton, 1956); reprinted (partially) in *Modern Theory and Criticism: a Reader*, ed. by David Lodge (London: Longman, 1988), pp. 57–61.

Janelle, Pierre, *Robert Southwell, the Writer: a Study in Religious Inspiration* (London: Sheed and Ward, 1935).

Johnson, Jeffrey, '"Til We Mix Wounds": Liturgical Paradox and Crashaw's Classicism', in *Sacred and Profane: Secular and Devotional Interplay in Early Modern British Literature*, ed. by Helen Wilcox, Richard Todd and Alasdair MacDonald (Amsterdam: VU University Press, 1996), pp. 251–8.

Keach, William, 'Reflexive Imagery in Shelley', *Keats–Shelley Journal*, 24 (1975), 49–69; repr. in Keach, *Shelley's Style* (London: Methuen, 1984), pp. 79–117.

Kenner, Hugh, 'Pope's Reasonable Rhymes', *English Literary History*, 41 (1974), 74–88.

King, John N., *Milton and Religious Controversy: Satire and Polemic in 'Paradise Lost'* (Cambridge University Press, 2000).

'Miltonic Transubstantiation', *Milton Studies*, 36 (1998), 41–58.

Knott, John R., Jr, 'The Visit of Raphael: *Paradise Lost*, Book V', *Philological Quarterly*, 47 (1968), 36–42.

Kolb, Jocelyne, *The Ambiguity of Taste: Freedom and Food in European Romanticism* (Ann Arbor: University of Michigan Press, 1995).

Kuchar, Gary, *Divine Subjection: the Rhetoric of Sacramental Devotion in Early Modern England* (Pittsburgh: Duquesne University Press, 2005).

The Poetry of Religious Sorrow in Early Modern England (Cambridge University Press, 2008).

Lake, Peter, *Anglicans and Puritans? Presbyterianism and English Conformist Thought from Whitgift to Hooker* (London: Allen and Unwin, 1988).

'Anti-popery: the Structure of a Prejudice', in *Conflict in Early Stuart England: Studies in Religion and Politics 1603–1642*, ed. by Richard Cust and Ann Hughes (Harlow: Longman, 1989), pp. 72–106.

'The Rise of Arminianism Reconsidered', *Past and Present*, 101 (1983), 34–54.

Lanham, Richard A., *The Motives of Eloquence: Literary Rhetoric in the Renaissance* (New Haven: Yale University Press, 1976).

Leonard, John, *Naming in Paradise: Milton and the Language of Adam and Eve* (Oxford: Clarendon Press, 1990).

Lewalski, Barbara, *Protestant Poetics and the Seventeenth-Century Religious Lyric* (Princeton University Press, 1979).

Lewis, C. S., *A Preface to Paradise Lost* (Oxford University Press, 1942).

Lodge, David, *The Modes of Modern Writing: Metaphor, Metonymy, and the Typology of Modern Literature* (London: Edward Arnold, 1977).

Low, Anthony, 'Angels and Food in *Paradise Lost*', *Milton Studies*, 1 (1969), 135–45.

Lyne, Raphael, *Shakespeare, Rhetoric and Cognition* (Cambridge University Press, 2011).

McCanles, Michael, 'The Rhetoric of the Sublime in Crashaw's Poetry', in *The Rhetoric of Renaissance Poetry*, ed. by Thomas O. Sloan and Raymond B. Waddington (Berkeley: University of California Press, 1974), pp. 189–211.

MacCulloch, Diarmaid, *Reformation: Europe's House Divided, 1490–1700* (London: Penguin, 2003).

Thomas Cranmer (New Haven: Yale University Press, 1996).

McDonald, Russ, *Shakespeare and the Arts of Language* (Oxford University Press, 2001).

McDuffie, Felecia Wright, *To Our Bodies Turn We Then: Body as Word and Sacrament in the Works of John Donne* (New York: Continuum, 2005).

McGrath, Alister E., *Iustitia Dei: a History of the Christian Doctrine of Justification*, 2 vols. (Cambridge University Press, 1986).

Mack, Peter, *Elizabethan Rhetoric: Theory and Practice* (Cambridge University Press, 2002).

McNees, Eleanor, 'John Donne and the Anglican Doctrine of the Eucharist', *Texas Studies in Literature and Language*, 29 (1987), 94–114.

Mahood, Molly, *Poetry and Humanism*, 2nd edn (New York: Kennikat Press, 1967).

Malpezzi, Frances M., 'Dead Men and Living Words: Herbert and Revenant in Vaughan's "The Garland"', *George Herbert Journal*, 15 (1992), 70–8.

Maltby, Judith, *Prayer Book and People in Elizabethan and Early Stuart England* (Oxford: Clarendon Press, 1998).

Marotti, Arthur, 'Donne and "The Extasie"', in *The Rhetoric of Renaissance Poetry from Wyatt to Milton*, ed. by Thomas O. Sloan and Raymond B. Waddington (Berkeley: University of California Press, 1974), pp. 140–73.

John Donne: Coterie Poet (Madison: University of Wisconsin Press, 1986).

Martz, Louis, *The Paradise Within: Studies in Vaughan, Traherne and Milton* (New Haven: Yale University Press, 1964).

The Poetry of Meditation: a Study in English Religious Literature of the Seventeenth Century, 2nd edn (New Haven: Yale University Press, 1962).

Matthews, Gareth B., 'Sensation and Synecdoche', *Canadian Journal of Philosophy*, 2 (1972), 105–16.

Monta, Susannah Brietz, *Martyrdom and Literature in Early Modern England* (Cambridge University Press, 2005).

Morrill, John, 'The Church in England, 1642–1649', in *Reactions to the English Civil War, 1642–1649*, ed. by Morrill (Basingstoke: Macmillan, 1982), pp. 89–114.

Morris, Harry, 'John Donne's Terrifying Pun', *Papers on Language and Literature*, 9 (1973), 128–37.

Mueller, Janel M., 'Pain, Persecution and the Construction of Selfhood in Foxe's *Acts and Monuments*', in Claire McEachern and Debora Shuger (eds.), *Religion and Culture in Renaissance England* (Cambridge University Press, 1997), pp. 161–87.

Netzley, Ryan, 'Oral Devotion: Eucharistic Theology and Richard Crashaw's Religious Lyrics', *Texas Studies in Language and Literature*, 44 (2002), 247–72.

Nokes, David, '"Hack at Tom Poley's": Swift's Use of Puns', in *The Art of Jonathan Swift*, ed. by Clive T. Probyn (London: Vision Press, 1978), pp. 43–57.

Novarr, David, '*Amor Vincit Omnia*: Donne and the Limits of Ambiguity', *Modern Language Review*, 82 (1987), 286–92.

Nuttall, A. D., *Overheard by God: Fiction and Prayer in Herbert, Milton, Dante and St John* (London: Methuen, 1980).

O'Grady, Kathleen, 'The Pun or the Eucharist?: Eco and Kristeva on the Consummate Model for the Metaphoric Process', *Literature and Theology*, 11 (1997), 93–115.

Oliver, P. M., *Donne's Religious Writing: a Discourse of Feigned Devotion* (London: Longman, 1997).

Oxley, Brian, 'The Relation between Robert Southwell's Neo-Latin and English Poetry', *Recusant History*, 17 (1985), 201–7.

Parish, John E., 'Milton and the Well-Fed Angel', *English Miscellany*, 18 (1967), 87–109.

Pebworth, Ted-Larry and Claude J. Summers, '"Thus Friends Absent Speake": the Exchange of Verse Letters between John Donne and Henry Wotton', *Modern Philology*, 81 (1984), 361–77.

Petersson, Robert T., *The Art of Ecstasy in Teresa, Bernini, and Crashaw* (London: Routledge and Kegan Paul, 1970).

Pettavel, John, *Metanoia: Essays in the Interpretation of Certain Passages in the Gospels* (Haslemere: Phene Press, 1983).

Pettet, E. C., *Of Paradise and Light: a Study of Vaughan's 'Silex Scintillans'* (Cambridge University Press, 1960).

Pickstock, Catherine, *After Writing: On the Liturgical Consummation of Philosophy* (Oxford: Blackwell, 1998).

Pilarz, Scott, *Robert Southwell and the Mission of Literature, 1561–1595: Writing Reconciliation* (Aldershot: Ashgate, 2003).

Poole, William, *Milton and the Idea of the Fall* (Cambridge University Press, 2005).

Post, Jonathan F. S., *Henry Vaughan: the Unfolding Vision* (Princeton University Press, 1982).

Prickett, Stephen, *Words and 'The Word': Language, Poetics and Biblical Interpretation* (Cambridge University Press, 1986).

Prineas, Matthew, 'The Dream of the Book and the Poetry of Failure in Henry Vaughan's *Silex Scintillans*', *English Literary Renaissance*, 26 (1996), 333–55.

Rambuss, Richard, *Closet Devotions* (Durham, NC: Duke University Press, 1998).

Raymond, Joad, *Milton's Angels: the Early Modern Imagination* (Oxford University Press, 2010).

Read, Sophie, 'Lancelot Andrewes's Sacramental Wordplay', *Cambridge Quarterly*, 36 (2007), 11–31.

'Puns: Serious Wordplay', in *Renaissance Figures of Speech*, ed. by Gavin Alexander and Katrin Ettenhuber (Cambridge University Press, 2007), pp. 81–94.

Redfern, Walter, *Puns* (Oxford: Blackwell, 1984).

Reid, David, 'Crashaw's Gallantries', *John Donne Journal*, 20 (2001), 229–42.

'The Reflexive Turn in Early Seventeenth-Century Poetry', *English Literary Renaissance*, 32 (2002), 408–25.

Reisner, Noam, *Milton and the Ineffable* (Oxford University Press, 2009).

Rhodes, Neil, *The Power of Eloquence and English Renaissance Literature* (London: Harvester Wheatsheaf, 1992).

Richards, I. A., *The Philosophy of Rhetoric* (Oxford University Press, 1936; repr. 1965).

Ricks, Christopher, 'Andrew Marvell: "Its Own Resemblance"', in Ricks, *The Force of Poetry* (Oxford: Clarendon Press, 1984), pp. 34–59.

Milton's Grand Style (Oxford: Clarendon Press, 1963).

Roberts, John R. (ed.), *New Perspectives on the Life and Art of Richard Crashaw* (Columbia: University of Missouri Press, 1990).

Roberts, Lorraine, 'Crashaw's Epiphany Hymn: Faith out of Darkness', in *'Bright Shootes of Everlastingnesse': the Seventeenth-Century Religious Lyric*, ed. by Claude J. Summers and Ted-Larry Pebworth (Columbia: University of Missouri Press, 1987), pp. 134–44.

Rosendale, Timothy, *Liturgy and Literature in the Making of Protestant England* (Cambridge University Press, 2007).

Ross, Malcolm McKenzie, *Poetry and Dogma: the Transfiguration of Eucharistic Symbols in Seventeenth Century English Poetry* (Rutgers University Press, 1954; repr. New York: Octagon, 1969).

Rubin, Miri, *Corpus Christi: the Eucharist in Late Medieval Culture* (Cambridge University Press, 1991).

Rudrum, Alan, *Henry Vaughan* (Cardiff: University of Wales Press, 1981).

'Henry Vaughan, the Liberation of the Creatures, and Seventeenth-Century English Calvinism', *Seventeenth Century*, 4 (1989), 33–54.

Sandbank, S., 'Henry Vaughan's Apology for Darkness', in *Essential Articles for the Study of Henry Vaughan*, ed. by Alan Rudrum (Hamden, CT: Archon Books, 1987), pp. 128–40.

Schwartz, Regina M., 'Real Hunger: Milton's Version of the Eucharist', *Religion and Literature*, 31 (1999), 1–17.

Sacramental Poetics at the Dawn of Secularism: When God Left the World (Stanford University Press, 2008).

Seelig, Sharon Cadman, *The Shadow of Eternity: Belief and Structure in Herbert, Vaughan and Traherne* (Lexington: University Press of Kentucky, 1981).

Shami, Jeanne, 'Troping Religious Identity: Circumcision and Transubstantiation in Donne's Sermons', in *Renaissance Tropologies: the Cultural Imagination of Early Modern England*, ed. by Jeanne Shami (Pittsburgh: Duquesne University Press, 2008), pp. 89–117.

Shaw, Robert B., 'George Herbert: the Word of God and the Words of Man', in *Ineffability: Naming the Unnamable from Dante to Beckett*, ed. by Peter S. Hawkins and Anne Howland Schotter (New York: AMS, 1984), pp. 81–93.

Shell, Alison, *Catholicism, Controversy and the English Literary Imagination, 1558–1660* (Cambridge University Press, 1999).

Shen, Yeshayahu, 'Cognitive Constraints on Verbal Creativity: the Use of Figurative Language in Poetic Discourse', in Elena Semino and Jonathan Culpeper (eds.), *Cognitive Stylistics: Language and Cognition in Text Analysis* (Amsterdam: John Benjamins, 2002), pp. 211–30.

Shuger, Debora, *Sacred Rhetoric: the Christian Grand Style in the English Renaissance* (Princeton University Press, 1988).

Shulman, Ahouva, 'The Function of the "Jussive" and "Indicative" Imperfect Forms in Biblical Hebrew Prose', *Zeitschrift für Althebraistik*, 13 (2000), 168–80.

Simmonds, James D., *Masques of God: Form and Theme in the Poetry of Henry Vaughan* (University of Pittsburgh Press, 1972).

Simpson, Evelyn M., *A Study of the Prose Works of John Donne*, 2nd edn (Oxford: Clarendon Press, 1948).

Sloane, Thomas O., *Donne, Milton, and the End of Humanist Rhetoric* (Berkeley: University of California Press, 1985).

Sonnino, Lee A., *A Handbook to Sixteenth-Century Rhetoric* (London: Routledge and Kegan Paul, 1968).

Soskice, Janet Martin, *Metaphor and Religious Language* (Oxford: Clarendon Press, 1985).

Spinks, Bryan D., *From the Lord and 'The Best Reformed Churches': a Study of the Eucharistic Liturgy in the English Puritan and Separatist Traditions, 1550–1633* (Oregon: Wipf and Stock, 1984).

  Sacraments, Ceremonies and the Stuart Divines: Sacramental Theology and Liturgy in England and Scotland, 1603–1662 (Aldershot: Ashgate, 2002).

Stanwood, Paul G., 'Time and Liturgy in Donne, Crashaw, and T. S. Eliot', *Mosaic*, 12 (1979), 91–105.

Stone, Darwell, *A History of the Doctrine of the Holy Eucharist*, 2 vols. (London: Longmans, 1909).

Strier, Richard, *Love Known: Theology and Experience in George Herbert's Poetry* (University of Chicago Press, 1983).

Stubbs, John, *Donne: the Reformed Soul* (London: Penguin, 2006).

Summers, Claude J., 'Herrick, Vaughan and the Poetry of Anglican Survivalism', in *New Perspectives on the Seventeenth-Century English Religious Lyric*, ed. by John R. Roberts (Columbia: University of Missouri Press, 1994), pp. 46–74.

Sweeney, Anne, *Robert Southwell: Snow in Arcadia: Redrawing the English Lyric Landscape, 1586–1595* (Manchester University Press, 2006).

Targoff, Ramie, *Common Prayer: the Language of Devotion in Early Modern England* (University of Chicago Press, 2001).

  John Donne: Body and Soul (University of Chicago Press, 2008).

Thomas, Keith, *Religion and the Decline of Magic* (London: Weidenfeld and Nicolson, 1971; repr. Harmondsworth: Penguin, 1991).

Tuve, Rosamund, *A Reading of George Herbert* (London: Faber, 1952).

Tyacke, Nicholas, *Anti-Calvinists: the Rise of English Arminianism, c.1590–1640* (Oxford: Clarendon Press, 1987).

Ulreich, John C., Jr, 'Milton on the Eucharist: Some Second Thoughts about Sacramentalism', in *Milton and the Middle Ages*, ed. by John Mulryan (Lewisburg, PA: Bucknell University Press, 1982), pp. 32–56.

Vendler, Helen, *The Poetry of George Herbert* (Cambridge, MA: Harvard University Press, 1975).

Vickers, Brian, *In Defence of Rhetoric* (Oxford: Clarendon Press, 1988).

Waddington, Raymond B., 'Here Comes the Son: Providential Theme and Symbolic Pattern in *Paradise Lost*, Book 3', *Modern Philology*, 79 (1982), 256–66.

Wall, John N., *Transformations of the Word: Spenser, Herbert, Vaughan* (Athens, GA: University of Georgia Press, 1988).

Watson, Graeme J., '*The Temple* in "The Night": Henry Vaughan and the Collapse of the Established Church', *Modern Philology*, 84 (1986), 144–61.

Weatherford, Kathleen J., 'Sacred Measures: Herbert's Divine Wordplay', *George Herbert Journal*, 15 (1991), 22–32.

Weber, Max, *The Sociology of Religion*, trans. by Ephraim Fischoff (London: Methuen, 1965).

West, Philip, *Henry Vaughan's 'Silex Scintillans': Scripture Uses* (Oxford: Clarendon Press, 2001).

Whalen, Robert, '"How Shall I Measure out thy Bloud?," or, "Weening is Not Measure": *TACT*, Herbert, and Sacramental Devotion in the Electronic *Temple*', *Early Modern Literary Studies*, 5 (2000), 1–37.

  The Poetry of Immanence: Sacrament in Donne and Herbert (University of Toronto Press, 2002).

Wilson, Derek, *Out of the Storm: the Life and Legacy of Martin Luther* (London: Hutchinson, 2007).

Young, R. V., *Doctrine and Devotion in Seventeenth-Century Poetry: Studies in Donne, Herbert, Crashaw and Vaughan* (Cambridge: D. S. Brewer, 2000).

Index

IDEAS IN CONTEXT

Edited by David Armitage, Richard Bourke, Jennifer Pitts and John Robertson